LIFE OF THE VENERABLE ANNE OF JESUS

Companion of

ST. TERESA OF AVILA

By
A SISTER OF
NOTRE DAME DE NAMUR
With a Preface by
Father Benedict Zimmerman, O.D.C.

Republished by
𝔐𝔢𝔡𝔦𝔞𝔱𝔯𝔦𝔵 𝔓𝔯𝔢𝔰𝔰
www.mediatrixpress.com

MMXV

NIHIL OBSTAT:

       INNOCENTIUS APAP S.Th.M., O.P
         CENSOR DEPUTATUS

IMPRIMATUR:

      ✠ EDM. CAN. SURMONT VIC. GEN.
WESTMONASTERII DIE 23° NOVEMBRIS 1931

ISBN-13: 978-0692436042

©Mediatrix Press 2015
This work may not be reproduced for Commercial Purposes

NOTE

To His Eminence Cardinal Bourne respectful thanks are offered for his kind interest in this Life, and for attaching a Pardon to the recitation of a prayer in honour of Venerable Anne of Jesus.

The author also wishes to thank the many friends through whose help the writing of the book was made possible. Space will not permit the mention of every name, but special thanks are due to the Rev. Benedict Zimmerman, O.D.C., not only for information ungrudgingly given, but also for reading and correcting the whole book when in manuscript, and writing the Foreword.

Many interesting details are due to the kindness of Dom Placid Corballis, O.S.B., Dom Bede Coulthard, C.R.L., the Rev. John Macmillan, D.D., Ph.D., Dom Stephen Marron, O.S.B., and Dom Hugh Connolly, O.S.B. Also to the Rev. P. Fr. Bruno, O.D.C., for permission to quote from his Vie de St. Jean de la Croix, and reproduce some of its illustrations, with the consent of the publishers of the English translation, Messrs. Sheed and Ward.

The Rev. Mother-Prioresses of Chichester, Lanherne, and Darlington lent valuable books, manuscripts and prints, as did also the Rev. Mother-Prioress of the Convent of the Incarnation, Clamart (formerly at the rue d'Enfer, Paris). The nuns at Chichester read the Life in MS. and gave much helpful advice, besides providing a first sketch for the cover, afterwards elaborated by J.T.H.

To these, and to the many others who helped in various ways, the author again offers cordial thanks.

Feast of St. Gertrude,
15th November 1930.

Table of Contents

FOREWORD.. 1

CHAPTER I
    EARLY YEARS............................... 7

CHAPTER II
    A SOUL IN TRAINING....................... 17

CHAPTER III
    ANNE DE LOBERA BECOMES ANNE OF JESUS
    29

CHAPTER IV
    MOTHER AND DAUGHTER. 37

CHAPTER V

    FROM SALAMANCA TO VEAS............... 47

CHAPTER VI
    FIRST TRIENNIUM AT VEAS................ 61

CHAPTER VII
    LIFE AT VEAS BEHIND THE GRATE......... 75

CHAPTER VIII
    WORK FOR THE ORDER AT VEAS........... 87

CHAPTER IX
    THE FOUNDATION AT GRANADA.......... 101

CHAPTER X
    LIFE AT GRANADA........................ 117

CHAPTER XI
    THE FOUNDATION AT MADRID........... 141

CHAPTER XII
    TROUBLES CONCERNING THE CONSTITUTIONS
    155

CHAPTER XIII
    ST. TERESA'S DAUGHTERS ARE ASKED FOR IN FRANCE.................................. 167

CHAPTER XIV
    SALAMANCA ONCE AGAIN................ 185

CHAPTER XV
    THE JOURNEY TO PARIS................... 193

CHAPTER XVI
    THE CARMEL OF THE INCARNATION, PARIS
    209

CHAPTER XVII
    FOUNDATIONS AT PONTOISE AND DIJON... 217

CHAPTER XVIII
    FROM FRANCE TO FLANDERS.............. 235

CHAPTER XIX
    FOUNDATIONS AT LOUVAIN AND MONS... 247

CHAPTER XX
    DISCALCED FRIARS COME TO FLANDERS. THE OPENING OF THE ROYAL CONVENT........ 265

CHAPTER XXI
    LIFE IN THE ROYAL CONVENT............. 279

CHAPTER XXII
    SOME CHARACTERISTICS OF ANNE OF JESUS
    293

CHAPTER XXIII
    LAST WORKS AND FINAL PURIFICATION... 309

CHAPTER XXIV
    "THE HUMBLE SHALL BE EXALTED"........ 325

PRAYER IN HONOUR OF VENERABLE ANNE OF JESUS
    347

FOREWORD

THE name of Venerable Anne of Jesus is probably familiar to all those who are well acquainted with the life, the work of foundation and the correspondence of St. Teresa of Avila; it also occupies a not unimportant place in the life-story of St. John of the Cross; she, moreover, took the most prominent part in the establishment of the Teresian nuns in France and afterwards in the Low countries. It is, therefore, not too much to say that none of these subjects can be properly and fully understood unless one has a more than cursory knowledge of her own life and aims. Above all this she was endowed with talents not even second (according to the opinion of St. John of the Cross who was a good judge) to those of St. Teresa, and she reached a wonderful degree of sanctity even for a period which saw some of the greatest Saints of the Catholic church.

It was, then, a happy thought that one who in religion had received the same name should have spent many years in collecting all the facts of the life, and all the surviving writings, of her heavenly patroness. The present writer who was able to watch the inception and gradual growth of the biography can bear testimony to the scrupulous accuracy with which the biographer has fulfilled her task.

There is one point which requires a little explanation. Human life, according to the prophet, is a warfare, and Venerable Anne was in the thick of quarrels which to herself and her contemporaries appeared to be of paramount importance. Times have changed, and at present, when vital questions are at issue the quarrels of the late sixteenth and early seventeenth centuries are of secondary importance only. A full-dress rehearsal of those events would only be tedious, if not positively painful, to the twentieth century reader. This portion of the Life has therefore been reduced to the most indispensable indications. While the quarrels went on, excellent people were found among the champions on either side. The biographer has formed her own opinion, as was her right, which may or may not be shared by her readers; but she has endeavoured to keep it as much as possible in the background.

It is now about half a century since the heroicity of the virtues of Venerable Anne was established by the Sacred Congregation of Rites. Nothing is now wanting for her beatification but the approbation of some miracles. These are, indeed, not wanting, but up to the present the Carmelite nuns of Brussels have not seen their way to present any of them for approbation, and thus the cause of beatification is held up. We can only hope that the matter will in course of time be brought to the long wished for termination.

Carmelite Priory, Kensington,
28 August, 1931. BENEDICT ZIMMERMAN, O.D.C.

LIFE OF THE
VENERABLE ANNE OF JESUS

PORTRAIT OF VENERABLE ANNE OF JESUS.
(Artist Unknown)
Fronticepiece

CHAPTER I

EARLY YEARS

1545—1562

"As the saintly foundress of the Reform of Carmel, Teresa of Jesus was born in the very town of Avila where she was, later on, to lay the first foundations of her reform, so Anne of Jesus, called by God to be her coadjutrix, and to propagate St. Teresa's work in foreign lands, could only, so it seems, come into this world at Medina del Campo, the town where the second foundation of the Reform was made." So writes Father Peter of St. Andrew, one of the historians of the Discalced Carmelite Friars. Anne's parents came from widely differing regions of Spain, but before her birth they had settled at Medina del Campo, which, in the latter half of the sixteenth century was famous for its cloth. The austere beauty of Old Castile hardly commends itself to the majority of travellers. Districts of great fertility, devoid of trees, and devoted solely to the raising of cereals, alternate with regions abounding with stony hillocks, on some of which cluster unpicturesque mud-coloured villages, while others rise gradually into rugged and mountainous lands. This severe landscape no doubt influences the inhabitants, and little Anne, who for the first seven years of her life was a deaf mute, drank in her earliest impressions solely through her eyes.

Her father was Diego de Lobera, a native of Plasencia in Estramadura, a picturesque country where vast pasture-lands stretch southwards to the foot of the Sierra Morena. The grey-walled city stands on a hill, girt about with the river Jerte, as Toledo is with the Tagus. Famous in Roman times, it still yields occasional Roman remains, though its monuments were destroyed by the Moors. Plasencia boasts of two cathedrals, one dating from the fourteenth century, the other, still unfinished, was begun in 1498. In the former can still be seen the Lobera chantry where Diego's brothers were buried, and the shrine of Our Lady del Puerto, a mile or two outside the city, was built by the family, and still shows three escutcheons bearing the de Lobera coat-of-arms.[1] The family, though not rich, was connected with some of the noblest of the neighbourhood,[2] and there was fighting-blood in the veins of the humble Carmelite which, perhaps, helped her to sustain a prolonged and often-renewed conflict in her life-work—the maintenance of the primitive Rule of St. Teresa's Reform.

On the other hand, Anne inherited a strain of poetry and romance through her mother, Francesca de Torres, whose family, noble in its origin, belonged originally to Vizcaya, or Biscay. Its hills are clad with magnificent forests, and in its well-watered valleys nestle white-walled homesteads surrounded by fragrant orchards. The women of Biscay are remarkable for their purity of type—broad high forehead, straight nose, and finely-shaped mouth, chin and hands.

In Anne de Lobera these varying characteristics were

---

[1] The origin of the de Lobera family is lost in antiquity. Ancient writers connect it with the more or less mythical Queen Loba, who is said to have received the body of St. James, miraculously transported from Palestine to the shores of Galicia. Others connect it with the heroes who fought at Clavijo, in which battle, so runs the legend, St. James (Sant Iago) was seen mounted on a white charger and dealing destruction to the Moors.

[2] The famous Don Rodriguez Calderon married Doña Inez de Vergas, blood relation to Anne de Lobera, who wrote, 1620: "The Marquis de Siete Iglesias [a title bestowed on Don Calderon in recognition of his service in the Netherlands] is not related to me, except through his wife, who is from Plasencia and is connected with my family. . ."

united. Castilian dignity and reserve blended in her with Celtic qualities of quick, sensitive feelings and great imaginative power. Her intellect was of a high order; so much so that, in later years, Father Batiez said of her that "she was equal to St. Teresa in spiritual gifts, and surpassed her in those of the natural order." However this may be, it does not appear that Anne de Lobera had the affectionate vivaciousness and charm which made Teresa of Avila so lovable a saint. Her work for God was different, and God distributes His gifts to His children according to the particular work He requires from each.

On the feast of St. Catherine of Alexandria, 25th November, 1545, Anne de Lobera was born, a deaf mute. Her father died while she was still an infant, leaving the care of his two children to their mother, who devoted her whole time to their well-being. Christopher, the elder of the two, was old enough to understand his sister's affliction, and to join his prayers to those of his mother to obtain her cure. Seven years went by, and little Anne, though she won all hearts by her beauty, could neither hear nor speak. Quite unexpectedly she one day said aloud the "Ave Maria," and from that moment her speech and hearing became normal, so that the occurrence was regarded by all as a miracle. Her happy mother thought there could be no better way of showing gratitude to God for this favour than by dedicating her daughter anew to Him by the Sacrament of Confirmation. Anne was accordingly instructed, and chose for her patron St. Francis of Assisi. She even wanted to be called Frances in his honour, but her prudent mother counselled her not to change her name, but to keep that of Our Lady's mother, so that she might thereby have a greater claim on Mary's care. Possibly the pious Francesca had already a premonition of her own death, for two years later God called her to Himself.

Christopher and Anne had to leave their own home and go to that of their maternal grandmother, who also lived at Medina del Campo. There they received every kindness and were educated in a manner befitting their station of life, but the inner sanctities of home were never the same, and both children turned instinctively to Heaven for help.

Anne, with a wisdom and determination rare in one so young, begged Our Lady to be her Mother and Protectress in a very special way, promising in return to perform some definite practices of devotion in her honour. These were the daily recitation of the fifteen mysteries of the Rosary, and of the Little Office of the Blessed Virgin, to be said kneeling. Christopher seems to have shared in these devotions, for he reproached his sister with saying the office in Spanish, instead of in Latin. Anne said nothing, but quietly learnt enough Latin to be able to recite Our Lady's Office in the language of the Church. The third promise was harder still for a growing girl such as Anne was at the time. She undertook, as often as she woke in the night, to kneel up in bed in order to salute her heavenly Mother by reciting a Hail Mary. This resolution was faithfully kept until she entered Carmel. Towards the end of her life the Servant of God confessed to her infirmiarian that whereas, before she made this promise to Our Lady she slept soundly, as a healthy child should, after making it she used often to awake, and as each time she faithfully knelt up and said her Ave, she concluded that God and Our Lady must have been pleased to be so remembered, since the occasion of giving them this homage was so often sent to her.

When she was only ten years old grace had so far taken possession of Anne's soul that she consecrated herself to God by a vow of chastity. Her grandmother, however, had very different views, and Anne often had to sit and listen to the old lady, who told her of the handsome dowry awaiting her, of the family jewels and heirlooms, and of all the advantages of her position. After a few months the question of marriage was broached, and the claims of possible suitors discussed. Silence was no longer honourable, and Anne respectfully informed her grandmother of her vow. The anger of Doña de Torres was unbounded, the claims of the King of Heaven being utterly disregarded. What right had a slip of a girl to interfere with what was arranged for her good by those who loved her and were caring for her education? In hot haste learned canonists and others were consulted. The verdict was unanimous. A vow made by a minor could be annulled by her lawful guardian.

Accordingly, Anne was summoned to her grandmother's presence. She obeyed at once. God had already made known to her what she had to say, and she stood before her triumphant grandmother in respectful silence, but without a tremor—erect, graceful and perfectly self-possessed.

With all the solemnity of Spanish etiquette, the decision of the canonists was repeated for Anne's benefit, and she was informed that her resolve not to marry was null and void in the eyes of the Church. No one was prepared for her reply. Quite respectfully, but with unmistakable determination, she answered without a moment's hesitation: "I shall renew my vow every day until I am of age to make it irrevocably."

A complete deadlock ensued. The grandmother would not acknowledge herself beaten, and Anne was equally determined to have no spouse but Jesus Christ. For a time things went on as before. Anne, who grew more attractive every day as her beauty developed, was the centre of a circle of admiring relations and friends. More than one approached her grandmother in the hope of winning her ward as a bride. Doña de Torres kept open house for all Anne's admirers, hoping thereby to break down her resolution, and reflecting astutely that where many came others were sure to follow, so that finally one might take Anne's fancy and persuade her to cancel her vow. At any rate, the old lady argued, so much coming and going, and the forced attendance of her granddaughter at so many pleasure parties, would distract her mind from her pious intention, or win her by flattery or pride of power to change her purpose.

But God was watching over His chosen servant, and Anne passed through all these gaieties unshaken and untouched. She even endeavoured, by frequently washing her face and exposing it to the rays of the sun, to spoil her beauty, but her complexion remained a delicate pink and white. Nor did the manifest distaste with which she met all advances discourage her suitors.

At last Anne took her brother Christopher into her confidence, and begged him to write to their father's mother at Plasencia, asking her to receive them into her home. Doña de Lobera had already been anxious to take care of her orphaned grandchildren, so, notwithstanding the reluctance of Doña de Torres to let them go, the transfer was finally arranged. An uncle came from Plasencia to fetch the brother and sister, and so well did he negotiate matters that their grandmother let them go with a good grace, entirely ignorant, as she was, of Anne's leading part in the affair. This was in 1560, Anne being then fifteen. But change of residence did not remove the temptation, for Doña de Lobera's many visitors soon came to admire her grandchild and to seek her in marriage. One in particular, whose family connections gave him right of entry to the Lobera home, aroused Anne's interest, until God warned her of the instability of human happiness by striking down suddenly a young girl with whom she had formed an intimate friendship.

Inconsolable at first, Anne's spirit of prayer came to her

EARLY YEARS   13

rescue, and on her knees before God she accused herself of carelessness in His service and of want of mortification, for at Plasencia they were just as anxious as at Medina del Campo that she should make a brilliant match, and her life was one round of social pleasures and entertainments. In answer to her prayer God inspired her what to do.

On 6th December, 1560, the de Lobera family and their numerous friends assisted at the ordination to the priesthood of one of Anne's cousins. Her grandmother prepared a magnificent dinner for the occasion, at which she was bidden to appear. When the meal was served, however, Anne's place remained empty. Twice Doña de Lobera sent for her, while the guests were kept waiting. "She is taking a last look in her mirror," said one, for no one dreamed of what was really delaying her.

Anne was, indeed, dressing for the banquet, but before coming downstairs she knelt down in her room to renew, once again, her vow of chastity. At last the door opened and Anne went in to greet her grandmother's guests. Sudden and complete silence fell upon them as they gazed upon her. She was dressed in a coarse black garment, her wealth of hair clipped close and her forehead covered with a "toque" or cap of unbleached linen.[3] Her delay was at once explained, and so great was the esteem in which she was held that no one present doubted the sincerity of her purpose.

From that day Doña de Lobera and her other relations no longer opposed Anne's desire to give herself wholly to God; the young kinsman who had hoped to marry her reconciling himself to his loss by the reflection that it was for no earthly lover that he was set aside. Anne was now left free to dispose of her time as she liked. Her first act was to make

---

[3] This costume, or one similar to it, was customary in Spain for girls who had taken a vow of virginity and who were not, as yet, religious.

her vow of chastity in perpetuity, adding to it a solemn promise to become a religious in the strictest and most perfect Order in the Church. What Order this might be she had no idea, but she was content to pray that God would make it known to her in His own good time. Another resolution taken by this girl of sixteen was that of never completely satisfying herself in any respect whatsoever, were it only in taking a drink of water, and she persevered faithfully in this heroic resolution even to the end of her life.[4] To help her to climb the steep heights of perfection God provided for her a saintly guide, Father Peter Rodriguez, S. J., who was at that time stationed at the Jesuit College in Plasencia. In 1562 Anne put herself under his spiritual direction, asking him to "pull up ruthlessly all the weeds in the garden of her soul and to plant in their stead all sorts of virtues," at the same time promising him implicit obedience. This was on the Feast of the Finding of the Child Jesus in the Temple, a mystery to which Anne had great devotion, and from the contemplation of which she derived much strength.

In the de Lobera household her life went on much as before. She was no kill-joy, and it was at this very time that she earned the nickname, "Queen of Women." Though not of the world, she mingled freely in it. Unseemly jests were hushed at her approach, but her growing sanctity did not make her any the less charming, and she was still the centre of attraction.

As a rule, the early part of the morning was devoted to prayer. She attended Mass daily in the cathedral, and always remained for the recitation of the Little Hours. The

---

[4] In her deposition for the cause of beatification (1635) Sister Margaret of the Mother of God says: "I have heard her [Anne of Jesus] say that never once in her life had she satisfied herself completely in anything whatsoever—not even in drinking water."

afternoon saw her visiting the hospitals or carrying relief to the poor in their own homes. Though not yet of age to be bound by the laws of the Church, Anne observed rigorously every fast and took no food at all from Holy Thursday till Easter Sunday.

A great sacrifice was asked of her about this time. Her only brother was one of the first to enter the Society of Jesus at Plasencia, and when he told Anne of his intention she was, at first, overwhelmed with grief. In her room, alone with God, the struggle was fought out. Then, coming down to her grandmother, Anne hid her sacrifice with a bright smile. "I am not going to cry any more about Christopher," she said; "on the contrary, I am delighted that he is giving himself to God in religion, and I have made up my mind to follow his example."[5]

---

[5] Christopher de Lobera distinguished himself in the Society of Jesus by his great modesty, recollection and silence, and by a quite extraordinary love of the Blessed Sacrament. He developed a special gift for preaching, but weak health obliged him to resign the pulpit for the writer's desk. Among other works, he wrote two volumes of sermons, one for every Sunday in the year. Towards the end of his life Father de Lobera suffered from a complication of painful maladies, which he bore with unalterable peace and serenity. On 22nd December 1616 he gave up his pure soul to God, and at the same moment his holy sister, then prioress of the Brussels' Carmel, saw it going up to heaven.

Another of Anne's relatives whose name has come down to us was Luis de Lobera of Avila, who had been head physician to the Emperor Charles V. He wrote a famous treatise on Surgery, a copy of which his daughter, Juana, presented to St. Teresa in 1569, the year before Anne of Jesus went to Avila to become a Carmelite.

CHAPTER II

A SOUL IN TRAINING

1562—1570

FROM her seventeenth year to her twenty-fifth Anne de Lobera followed the direction of Father Rodriguez faithfully and minutely. During those seven years she was closely associated with two of her cousins, Maria de Lobera and Maria de Cabreras, both of whom became religious. The latter also chose Father Rodriguez for her confessor, and as she shared Anne's room and lived in intimate converse with her, the holy Jesuit made use of her to help Anne to reach a high degree of perfection. His first care was to draw up for her a Rule of Life and to regulate her mode of dress. Instead of the garments fashionable at the time Anne wore a plain dress of dark, inexpensive material over a tunic of sackcloth, beneath which was a hair-cloth inter-woven with iron points. On legs and arms she wore sharp steel bracelets, which cut into her flesh so deeply that the scars were visible till the end of her life. She slept habitually on a board and had made of unplaned wood, studded with nails, a cross which fitted her back and shoulders and which she wore both day and night.

Maria de Cabreras writes:[6]

> "When I lived in my grandmother's house I used to sleep with her [Anne de Lobera]. She used to draw the

---

[6] Maria de Cabreras became a Franciscan nun, and in 1622 she was Abbess of her convent. The MS. from which these details are taken is dated 12th September 1622; that is, it was written six months after the death of her cousin, Anne of Jesus.

plank to her side of the bed, and left me the mattress, but even this was very thin and hard, and in the morning I used to ache all over after sleeping on it. I often asked my mother only to send me to my grandmother's for the day, and not to oblige me to spend the night there. One day I was alone in the room, and thought I would make the bed. Hidden in it were all kinds of instruments of penance, the use of which I knew nothing about at the time. I never dared tell her what I had seen for fear she would turn me out of her room."

As for lodging, so for food. Though Anne constantly fasted, she never allowed any special dish to be prepared for her. At table she served herself to what was least appetising, and often poured water into her plate, alleging as an excuse that the sauce was too thick or too pungent. At one time she forced herself to abstain from beverages of any sort—even water. The ill-effects of this imprudent penance remained with her for the rest of her life.

Fixed hours were allotted to prayer and silence. Ordinarily Anne prayed from nine p.m. till eleven p.m. and then rose at three a.m. to pursue the same exercise till seven o'clock. Maria de Cabreras says that when she herself fell asleep Anne was on her knees, motionless, and absorbed in prayer, and that when she awoke in the morning her cousin was in exactly the same position, as though she had been praying all night.

Both girls had certain household tasks to perform, but when these were done they spent the rest of the day as they liked. Anne devoted herself to visiting the sick poor, and many a time her natural daintiness and delicacy revolted at the tasks she had to perform. But the love of Christ urged her to overcome herself, and after a time all repugnance left her. One Lent she nursed Maria de Cabreras through a passing attack of leprosy.[7] No servant was allowed to set foot inside their room, and Maria afterwards declared that it was Anne's devotedness which saved her life.

In the evenings the three cousins used to make altar linen or embroider vestments for poor churches. So great was Anne's love for the poor, that her grandmother used to entrust her with large sums for their relief. Nevertheless, it sometimes happened that a poor person called when Anne had nothing to give. After speaking kindly to the disappointed beggar Anne would go back to her cousins, and say: "Since we have nothing to give away, let us, at least, say two Hail Marys that somebody else may be inspired to help these poor people."

In all her dealings with the poor Anne acted with great tact and delicacy of feeling. Sometimes she left her gift on their doorstep, and as often as she could she prevented the recipients of her bounty from knowing whence her gifts came. At home Anne ever showed herself kind and approachable. Towards Maria de Lobera, who was older than herself, she showed great deference and respect. Maria de Cabreras was younger, with a happy and sunny disposition, ardently devoted to games and amusements of all sorts. To her Anne would give friendly counsel, especially with regard to self-indulgence at table. It is to the credit of both that the advice was invariably taken in good part and acted upon without delay.

In the sixteenth century it was considered extraordinarily devout for the laity to approach the Sacraments once a week. Anne obtained permission to receive Holy Communion much more often. Her confessor left it on record that, though she confessed her sins with

---

[7] At that date many skin-diseases besides leprosy itself were included under this name.

many sighs and tears, he never found her guilty of any deliberate venial sin, and this during the whole seven years she was his penitent. Nevertheless he enjoined severe exterior penances upon her which she fulfilled to the letter. To mortify her fastidiousness he ordered her to put on the cloak of one of her grandmother's slaves,[8] and taking a basket, to go and fetch the meat for dinner. Another day, when friends were expected, he insisted that she should meet them at the door and water their horses. Father Rodriguez must have been a frequent visitor to the de Lobera home, for when Anne started out in slave's garb, as he had prescribed, he stopped her, and satisfied with her obedience, would not allow her to proceed any farther. He allowed her to water the horses, however, and devised many other ingenious tests for her virtue. He even put her under obedience to Maria de Lobera, whom he privately instructed to mortify her as often as she could. Much that followed was probably put down by Anne to Maria's quick temper, but both girls faithfully obeyed their confessor's injunction. One day during some service in the cathedral Maria said loud enough for those around to hear: "Sister [the usual form of address for cousins], how can you be so distracted? Do you think I cannot read your thoughts, and see how little attention you are giving to the words you are saying." In an instant Anne was on her knees before Maria, asking pardon, after which she stooped to kiss her cousin's feet. At the same moment Our Lord showed Himself to her. He touched her lips and, blessing her, disappeared. "Never could I describe," Anne used to say in later years, "the joy and sweetness of that moment."

---

[8] At that date the more menial household offices were fulfilled in Spain by slaves. In spite of their low status, however, they were always regarded as forming part of the family household.

So far as is known this is the first time Anne had a vision of Our Lord in Person. It was the prelude to many favours to come, but from this date onwards, the devil began to molest her in visible form. As a rule these visitations took place on the eve of her Communion days. After a night spent in conflict with the evil one, Anne would get up early, and go to call Maria de Lobera, alleging that it was time to go to Church, but in reality to get rid of the Tormentor, who had no permission from God to trouble her except when she was alone.

One day when she was with Father Rodriguez, a messenger came to summon him, post haste, to hear the confession of a man about to be hanged. The priest hurried off, while Anne moved with compassion, set about obtaining a reprieve for the criminal.

So great was the esteem in which she was held in Plasencia, that she actually obtained a commutation of the death-sentence into ten years' penal servitude in the galleys. During the following night, however, this act of clemency caused her much anxiety. The criminal was in excellent dispositions. Had she saved his life merely to be instrumental in the death of his soul? How could she tell what temptations might overwhelm him during his hard term as a galley-slave? But God was watching over Anne and her protégé; that same night saw the birth of Isabella-Clara-Eugenia, daughter of Philip II, in thanksgiving for which several prisoners were liberated the next day. Anne saw to it that her criminal was among the number. In after years the Spanish princess conceived a great friendship for Anne of Jesus. "Her Serene Highness did me a favour at her birth," the Servant of God used to say, "and she has gone on granting them to me ever since."

Anne's courage was equal to her compassion, for on hearing that one of her uncles was about to fight a duel she sent an urgent message to the governor, giving notice of the intended combat, which was contrary to law. The result was that Don de Lobera was stopped at the city gate and obliged to return home. His anger at first was very terrible. He declared that the whole affair was entirely secret and that Anne's knowledge of it must have come from the devil. In many other ways God was pleased to manifest the sanctity of His future spouse; but one more well authenticated example must suffice.

In 1568 or 1569 a great tournament and bull-fight was announced at Plasencia. Ordinarily Anne took no interest in such events, but this time she inquired about every particular, and noted carefully the dates for each amusement, while she kept saying to her cousins that she wished something would happen to prevent the festivities from taking place. So uneasy was she, that at last she wrote to the bishop, begging him to intervene by an exercise of his spiritual authority. Her letter impressed his lordship so deeply that he actually issued an edict forbidding any of his flock to attend the tourney under pain of excommunication. This censure fell like a thunderbolt on the town, for everything was ready, even to the cooking of the banquet to be served after the jousting. Nevertheless, the bishop's command was obeyed, though it excited much comment and not a little discontent, at what seemed a quite unreasonable curtailment of expected pleasure. The event justified the precaution, for on the day on which the tournament was to have taken place it was found that the arena and houses where it was to have been held had been mined, and that barrels of gunpowder with time-fuses attached to them had been placed in readiness to blow up jousters and spectators while the merriment was at its height. The treachery was put down to the Moors, who revolted at Granada between 1568 and 1570, but the affair was hushed up, probably for political reasons. From that day Anne de Lobera was regarded with greater veneration than ever. To escape the dangers which beset her she longed more and more for the peaceful life of the cloister, and often made pilgrimages barefoot to Our Lady del Puerto, in order to learn her vocation. One thing seemed wanting to her, she thought. So far God had not sent her any physical suffering. One day, after meditating on Our Lord's Passion, she started for the cathedral, but not without taking a glance at herself in her mirror. She smiled at her own rosy complexion, "A nice face for a would-be sufferer," she thought, and went off to her devotions. Before the Holy Sacrifice was over, however, God laid His hand upon her, and she was carried home in what appeared to her friends a dying condition.

Doctors were hastily summoned, but nothing they prescribed brought relief. To make matters worse, a great spiritual darkness fell upon Anne's soul. Was this sickness God's answer to her unspoken prayer for suffering? Or was it a punishment sent to bring home to her His displeasure at her delay in becoming a religious? It happened that Father Rodriguez had been sent to Toledo, and there was no one at Plasencia to whom Anne could open her heart. For three months she lay between life and death. Twenty-two times was she bled, besides being subjected to other violent remedies, until at last she was reduced to utter prostration. It was resolved, as a last resource, to try a remedy so dangerous that it was known as "the Spanish Dispatch." If the patient did not recover, death was inevitable. Anne's consent being given, the experiment was tried. To the delight of her grandmother an improvement set in, though it was many a long week before the patient could leave her bed.

Meanwhile, at Toledo, Father Rodriguez met Father Paul Hernandez, S. J., at that time confessor to St. Teresa. The latter spoke to Anne's friend of the saintly Mother and of her Reform, and, after giving him an outline of her Rule and of the manner of life of the Discalced Carmelites, finally introduced him to St. Teresa, who was just then at Toledo.

Father Rodriguez felt at once that here was what Anne de Lobera had been seeking for so long, and one morning her sick-bed was cheered by a letter from her former confessor, containing the following lines:

"... I have found here a holy woman, who, in virtue of apostolic authority, is founding convents wherein God is served in the manner for which you are seeking. She is a native of Avila, and is called Teresa de Ahumada. Her rule and constitutions are as follows." Here Father Rodriguez gives a brief summary of the chief points of the Rule for Discalced Carmelites as observed in the six convents already founded,[9] and then continues: "Ask God to deign to enlighten you, my daughter, as to whether this is the Order to which He is calling you. For myself, I think it is. Let me know, in case you would like me to speak to the Mother Foundress about you."[10]

No sooner had Anne mastered the contents of this letter than she felt God speaking to her heart. She wrote back at once, saying that the life described suited her exactly, and begging Father Rodriguez to make all arrangements for her with St. Teresa. "Tell her why I have delayed so long," she wrote, "and let me know if she will receive me, and when and how, for I dare not write myself." This was about March 1570, and in April St. Teresa's answer arrived, written by her own hand, for God had revealed to the blessed Mother what a treasure He had prepared for her comfort and help in

---

[9] Avila, Medina del Campo, Valladolid, Malaga, Pastrana, Toledo.

[10] In 1597 Anne countersigned Father Rodriguez's letter as testimony in the process of St. Teresa's canonisation.

Anne de Lobera.

"April 2nd, 1570.

"It is with the greatest pleasure, my dear daughter, that I receive you among my religious. From this moment, I accept you, not as novice and subject, but as my own companion and coadjutrix." The letter goes on to name the six convents already founded, leaving to Anne the choice of which she would enter, though recommending Avila to her special notice, as Teresa herself was prioress there. The saint ended on an affectionate note: "Do not bring any dowry, but divide your inheritance between your two cousins. Only make haste and get well, and as soon as you are able, come without delay."

Had St. Teresa any inkling of the marvel her words were to effect? They reached Anne de Lobera when she was lying in bed, weak and listless, but, rendering instant obedience to her chosen mother and guide, she rose as soon as she had read the letter, and from that moment all trace of illness left her. She wrote at once to tell St. Teresa she would enter the Carmel of Avila, and gave abundant alms for masses to be said in thanksgiving for her cure. Events now moved quickly. God had already taken to Himself her maternal grandmother at Medina del Campo, and on Whit Sunday, 14th May 1570, Doña de Lobera was called to her reward, so that Anne was free to dispose of herself as she pleased. Only one thing troubled her. St. Teresa had said in her letter that the new postulant should "assist in the business connected with new foundations." The more Anne thought about this, the more disturbed she felt. After consulting Father Rodriguez, who assured her that her vocation to Carmel was from God, Anne wrote again to St. Teresa, thanking her for her trust, but exposing what she felt was her unfitness for any post of importance. The holy foundress, delighted with Anne's humble opinion of herself, wrote a second time, telling her to lay aside all doubts. "All you have to do," she wrote, "is to enter, like any other novice, simply to obey." This was what Anne wanted. Three months had already slipped by whilst these letters were being exchanged. Now, at last, all seemed clear, and the date for her entry into the Convent of the Reform at Avila was fixed for 26th July, 1570, the feast of her own patron the great Saint Anne.

THE TREE OF CARMEL

CHAPTER III

ANNE DE LOBERA BECOMES ANNE OF JESUS

1570. July to November

GOD sent Anne de Lobera to Saint Teresa just at the time when the Foundress most needed support and help.

When Father Rodriguez spoke to St. Teresa of his holy penitent in Plasencia Our Lord reassured the saint with these words: "You must receive Anne de Lobera, because she will be of great help to your foundations." Anne's response to the blessed Mother's invitation has already been related. It was arranged that the journey to Avila should be made by night, on account of the great heat of the summer season in Estremadura and Castile. The uncle who had conducted Anne and her brother from Medina del Campo had promised to travel with her to Avila and see her safe into the convent. Anne disposed of all her little possessions, arranged for her inheritance to be divided among her cousins, and packed her few personal effects, together with some linen for use in the Carmel infirmary, which was the only thing St. Teresa had asked for.

Before her departure Maria de Lobera and Anne arranged to sit up one night to copy some letters from Blessed John of Avila, containing useful spiritual advice. They provided themselves with four large sheets of paper and a candle long enough to burn till midnight. Anne dictated while Maria took down the notes in a large round hand. The work proceeded slowly, and dawn began to creep over the sky as the cousins finished their self-imposed task. What was their surprise to find the four original sheets still blank and lying on the table, while five others were covered with Maria's laborious writing. Turning to extinguish the candle, they found it no shorter than it was when it was first lit, while the ink remained undiminished.[11]

On the Feast of St. Anne good-byes had to be said. This took up the whole of the afternoon, for all at Plasencia were anxious for a last word from one whom they held in such high esteem. About six o'clock in the evening Anne retired to her room to get ready for her long ride. Her heart was torn between grief at leaving those she loved, desire of giving herself wholly to God, and fear lest what she was about to do was not according to His Will. Casting herself upon her knees, she earnestly begged Our Lord to be Himself her Guide. An hour passed. Her uncle, with his escort, and other friends were already on horseback, for several wished to accompany their "Queen of Women" during the first stages of her journey. The jingling of the harness rang out clearly on the still warm air, yet Anne did not appear. The two Marias, with several other cousins, including the two little daughters of another uncle, Alphonso de Lobera, went together to her room. There they stopped short, for from beneath the door came a bright steady light, unlike any illumination from candles. Exclamations of astonishment broke from their lips, and this recalled Anne to herself—for she had been rapt in God and wholly oblivious of the lapse of time. She came downstairs at once, and then went round saying a last good-bye to each.

When it came to Maria de Lobera's turn Anne drew her a little aside. "Do not grieve, Sister mine," she said, "but give thanks to God, for soon I shall have you with me." Then

---

[11] Manriquez in his "Life" says he had in his possession Maria de Lobera's written statement of this prodigy. "She who did the writing testifies that this was so. I have her testimony, signed with her name." Maria at that date (c.1623) was still living.

turning towards the two little girls who were weeping bitterly, she said: "As to these little maidens, console them as well as you can, for God will not fail to take care of them both."

Last of all came Maria de Cabreras, with whom she had shared so many of her secrets.

"Little Sister, should you be weeping like this, when God is showering on me so many graces? Know, then, that I have just been asking Him that, if this journey is according to His good pleasure, He would deign to bless me and to be Himself my Guide. And His Divine Majesty, in His great mercy, told me He would be my Guide and that it is His Will that I should make this journey." God amply fulfilled this promise.

It was about nine p.m. when the little party rode out of the gates of Plasencia, for by dint of earnest persuasion, in view of the lateness of the hour, Anne had prevailed upon her friends not to accompany her any farther. She stopped for a few minutes at the shrine of Our Lady built by her ancestors to offer herself once more to God through the hands of His Immaculate Mother. Then she was in the saddle again, and the cavalcade proceeded on its way.

Avila is distant from Plasencia some seventy or eighty English miles as the crow flies, but the route crossed two ranges of mountains so precipitous that horses had to be exchanged for more sure-footed mules. The Sierra de Gredos are the third highest mountains in Spain, and the Sierra de Avila were infested at that time with brigands, the roads, besides, being very bad. But Our Lord's promise to Anne held sure. Hardly had the shrine of Our Lady del Puerto been left behind, than a young man came up, and of his own accord acted as their guide. He seemed about thirty years of age, and had an indefinable air of distinction, though his garments were tattered, his legs and arms being bare. One arm was covered with painful-looking wounds right up to the shoulder, while a large shred of torn flesh hung from his elbow. The *arrieros* (muleteers) and the de Lobera servants resented the company of this young man, who uttered no word, but looked at them beseechingly, with large dark eyes full of gentleness. Soon ungracious words gave place to cruel acts, and more than one stinging blow fell upon the stranger's body. But in spite of this he continued in the company, till at last Anne, roused by the discordant voices, sharply reprimanded her servants, who fell into their places, while the young man gave her a look of deep gratitude. Almost at the same moment a venerable old man in shepherd's garb came up. "How dare you lay hands on that young man," he said, "and ill-treat him like this? Do you take him for a vagabond?" Before his hearers recovered from their astonishment the old man had disappeared. Anne bade them bring the young man to her, but neither he nor the old shepherd could be found, and the party at last gave up the search. For the next five nights the journey continued, the daytime being spent in resting. The young man again walked beside Anne, but she found that he was invisible to her servants. She herself, though she spoke to him more than once, received no answer, so that she wondered whether she was under a delusion. However, on the fifth morning the travellers reached Avila, and at a turn in the road the same young man presented himself, this time visible to all, and offered to show them the way to St. Joseph's Convent. At the same time he gave Anne a look of such penetrating sweetness that forty years later she could say to her religious daughters: "I can still see his eyes as I saw them that day. Their memory is printed deep in my soul." That look revealed to Anne that the young man who had so mysteriously accompanied her had indeed been sent by God, and she resolved more firmly than ever to suffer and work for Him alone. Silently turning over these thoughts,

ANNE DE LOBERA BECOMES ANNE OF JESUS

she reached the convent.

As St. Teresa was away the sub-prioress, Mother Mary of St. Jerome,[12] welcomed her to St. Joseph's, and after Anne had rested she was taken to see the house. Perhaps under some secret inspiration, Anne asked to be taken first of all to the little hermitages in the garden, where she knew the Foundress liked her daughters to retire for private prayer. On entering the one dedicated to St. Joseph, what was her surprise to see hanging on the wall a painting of the Scourging at the pillar, in which Our Lord resembled in every particular the young man who had guided her from Plasencia: stature, features, expression, all were exactly the same, even to the shred of wounded flesh hanging from the elbow. Anne fell on her knees. Now she knew without a doubt that Our Lord had indeed fulfilled His promise to be her guide, and that it was He who had accompanied her under the guise of a poor man. From that moment all hesitation about her vocation to Carmel left her, and with a full heart she consecrated herself anew to Jesus Christ. As for the old man who had rebuked her servants and then disappeared so mysteriously, Anne felt sure that he must have been St. Joseph, and ever afterwards she cherished a tender devotion to the foster-father of Our Lord.

Avila to-day is much the same as it was in St. Teresa's time. Its walls, fortified by large round towers every hundred paces, date back to the eleventh century, and enclose the grey city once known as "Avila of the Knights," but now from its memories of Teresa and its granite boulders, as "Avila of the Saints and rocks." The cathedral of San Salvador was built in 1091, and there, most probably, Anne went to pray before the gates of Carmel closed behind her. On August 1st she was clothed in the habit of a

---

[12] St. Teresa's niece.

Discalced Carmelite. The night of July 31st was passed inside the convent, whence she wrote to her cousins and others at Plasencia, signing herself "Anne of St. Peter," for at her own request this was to be her name, commemorating, so she thought, the name of her own patron on whose feast she had left home, together with that of St. Peter's Chains—a fitting day, as she reflected, on which to assume the livery of Our Lady and bind herself for ever to Mary's Son. However, before the ceremony took place on August 1st a letter arrived from St. Teresa, saying that the new novice was to be called Anne of Jesus—and as such she will from henceforth be known. Anne regarded this change of name as a special grace given to her by Our Lord.

When she received the religious habit she was in her twenty-fifth year; tall, but slightly built, with a smiling, open countenance, her features aquiline, and her complexion clear and pale. From the first day of her clothing she seemed to be quite at home, and the nuns of St. Joseph's declared that she fell into all their ways as perfectly as if she came from another convent, instead of from the world.

Besides the duties imposed upon her as a novice Anne of Jesus found many other opportunities of rendering service to the community: sometimes she helped in the kitchen, or relieved the older sisters in their household tasks. For the sick she had a thousand delicate little attentions, and often obtained permission to sit up with them at night.

Those who have been repulsed rather than attracted by the austerities Anne practised in the world will perhaps be relieved to find that during her first years at Carmel she suffered acutely from the very human trouble of hunger. St. Joseph's Convent, Avila, had been founded without revenues, and the nuns lived, literally, upon what was given to them as alms. Often enough, and especially when St. Teresa happened to be away, gifts either in money or in kind were less abundant, and the community lacked what was necessary.

Housekeeping in Spain to-day is much the same as it was in the fifteenth century, but it differs very considerably from customs obtaining in more northerly, and therefore colder, climates. There is no breakfast, and dinner in summer is at ten a.m., with a collation or supper in the evening. At Plasencia Anne had mortified her palate, but she had eaten sufficient to subdue the pangs of hunger. Now that she was a novice the devil no doubt added his solicitations to those of nature, and the desire to eat more than was provided became a really serious trial, and at the same time a source of great humiliation. As soon as St. Teresa returned to Avila and heard of Anne's trouble she told her saintly fellow-novice, Anne of St. Bartholomew,[13] to put a big piece of bread in Sister Anne's place. Long years afterwards when Anne of Jesus was prioress at Brussels she used to delight in telling this story to her novices, and she always concluded it by assuring them that her suffering at that time had been really severe, both physically and mentally.

---

[13] Anne of St. Bartholomew was the first lay-sister of the Reform. St. Teresa had at first intended to have no distinction of choir and lay-sister, but she found that it was impossible to carry out the recitation of the Divine Office if choir-nuns devoted themselves in turn (as was intended) to the cooking. Anne of St. Bartholomew, Aña Garcia, born sat October 1550, was clothed as a lay-sister on All Souls' Day, 1570. Later on she was made infirmarian, and St. Teresa died in her arms. She was of a retiring, timid disposition, though eventually she received the black veil of the choir sisters and was made prioress successively of several important houses. She died in the odour of sanctity on 7th June 1626, and was declared Blessed by the Church in 1917.

CHAPTER IV

MOTHER AND DAUGHTER

1570—1571

WHILE Anne was taking her first steps in religious life her holy Mother was at Toledo. Some time previously she had received an application for a foundation at Salamanca, Father Martin Gutierrez, S. J., having obtained the necessary authorisation of the bishop. Teresa had long desired to have a convent in that city, and while arrangements were pending she came back to Avila for about two months.

Nothing is more interesting in the lives of God's saints than to watch the drawing together of two souls destined to labour together for His glory. Even before Teresa de Ahumada in the maturity of her age met the young and brilliantly gifted Anne de Lobera their souls had been mutually attracted by divine grace. There is no record of their first meeting, but Teresa soon found that Anne's character far outstripped the reports she had received of it, "for," say the annals of the convent, "the Foundress discovered in the servant of God talents so exceptional and such consummate virtue that she destined her, there and then, not only for one of her most beloved daughters, but also as a sharer in her work, and as one who would bear on her shoulders the whole edifice of the Reform." Nor was the Holy Mother mistaken.

From the very first Teresa and Anne were like mother and daughter together. One day the young novice carried to the prioress a dress she had brought with her of rich black silk, asking her to make something of it for the Church. "Yes," said the saint, smiling, "it will do very well to make funeral drapery, which can be used when the sisters die. As for you, when you die you will not need it." Even during that first year while Anne was but a novice she was sent by the saint to Salamanca, where she took part in helping the new foundation.

A house having been obtained as a temporary convent, St. Teresa, with one professed Carmelite, Sister Mary of the Blessed Sacrament, took possession on the eve of All Saints, 1570, and Mass was said in the new Carmel the next day. Three professed religious from Medina del Campo were sent for and three novices from Avila, Anne of Jesus being one. She was put in charge of her two companions. Winter had already set in, roads were bad, inns few and far between, while the covered wagons which carried the nuns were anything but comfortable. The trio from Avila halted at Mancera, where the first two Friars of the Reform, Antony of Jesus and John of the Cross, had lately removed from Duruelo. The Holy Mother had spoken to the latter of the virtues of Anne of Jesus, and of the designs she had formed for her, and to Anne she had confided many particulars concerning the holy life of the Discalced Friar. When these two met that bleak November day they knew each other at once, and this was the beginning of a lifelong friendship. In later years Anne of Jesus, referring to this visit to Mancera, wrote: "The two Fathers told us of all that our Mother, Teresa of Jesus, had taught, and acquainted me with many points concerning the Reform."[14]

---

[14] With regard to this first meeting of St. John of the Cross and Venerable Anne of Jesus, Father Bruno in his life of the former says that it could not have taken place at Mancera, for St. John of the Cross left for Pastrana in mid-October, while Anne's journey was during November. The incident is taken from the Venerable Mother's deposition for St. Teresa's beatification, but the discrepancy is explained by the fact that, when under oath, Anne of Jesus spoke in general terms of all she knew,

MOTHER AND DAUGHTER

After bidding goodbye to the friars the three novices resumed their journey to the "Golden City," as Salamanca was called, on account of the colour of the stone of which it is built.

The house where St. Teresa awaited the arrival of the nuns was unhealthy, damp, and very small. There was no possibility of each having a cell, so the Foundress chose Anne of Jesus as her room-mate, and they spent many happy hours together. Often when the blessed Mother returned at night, after visiting the cells of the other religious, as the custom prescribed, she would, on reaching her own room again, sit silent and motionless with her eyes fixed on her young companion. Anne of Jesus noticed this, and one day she ventured to ask the saint why she did it. "Ah, daughter," was the reply, "I look at you because you are very dear to me." Then she would make a little sign of the cross on the novice's forehead and send her to bed. Referring to this time, Anne of Jesus wrote later of her holy Mother: "She treated me with so great confidence and familiarity that I knew almost all her affairs, either by witnessing them with my own eyes, or from her lips, or through writing traced by her own hand."

Together the mother and daughter received many favours from heaven. In their little room, just large enough to hold two beds and a small bench, the two were standing at the open window one sultry night, talking about a young girl in whom they were interested, whose youth, fortune and surroundings were a source of imminent spiritual peril to her. Moved with zeal and compassion, both religious began to pray for their friend, when suddenly out of the

---

and though she mentions that St. John of the Cross was sub-prior of Mancera at the time, she does not actually say that she *met* him there.

purple darkness flashed a flaming star, which fell headlong through the sky, while at the same time God gave them to understand that the young girl for whom they were praying was about to experience a serious spiritual fall. Teresa's tears mingled with those of Anne, but the latter's grief was so violent that in trying to restrain it she ruptured a blood vessel in her chest, an accident which caused her much suffering later on. For the moment, however, she seems to have been able to conceal what had happened from Teresa, for they still stood together gazing silently into the distant horizon. Presently the same star which they had watched falling rose gradually to its former place in the sky, where it continued shining with a steady light. After events justified their interpretation of this prodigy, for their young friend, after a lapse which caused public scandal, repented of her fault and became a Poor Clare.

It was while St. Teresa was at Salamanca in 1571 that she was rapt in ecstasy on Easter Sunday by the song of one of the novices, Isabel of Jesus (de Jimena). When, at the saint's own request, her fresh young voice began to sing:

> "Would that mine eyes could see Thee,
> Jesus mine!
> Would that mine eyes could see Thee,
> That Death would make me Thine!"

such a rapture of love fell upon the holy Foundress, that she dropped senseless amid her daughters, and had to be carried to her bed, where she remained for two whole days. The holy Mother, as her agony abated, poured forth her love of God in a beautiful elegy, known later as the "Gloss" or "Commentary" of St. Teresa.

It was Anne of Jesus who received her burning words

MOTHER AND DAUGHTER 41

and committed them to writing.[15]

In the early summer of 1571 troubles at Medina del Campo made St. Teresa's presence there imperative.[16] Before leaving she appointed Anne of Jesus Mistress of Novices, though she was still a novice herself, and recommended the prioress, Mother Anne of the Incarnation, to do nothing of moment without first consulting Anne of Jesus, in whose prudence the saint placed implicit trust.

In the following July, Father Pedro Hernandez, while conducting the canonical visitation at Medina, told St. Teresa that she had been appointed prioress of the Convent of the Incarnation at Avila (Mitigated Rule).

Anne of Jesus felt these changes more than any one else, for she had hoped to make her profession into the hands of the venerable Foundress herself, but God, who never refuses what is generously offered, took care to provide that His servant should not be satisfied in this. He went farther, and allowed her to think that she would not be allowed to make her vows at all. The haemorrhages from her ruptured vein became so violent and frequent that several of the nuns withheld their vote, deeming her unfit for profession in so severe an Order. The doctor was called in, but nothing he could do produced any improvement, so that the ceremony, which had been due in August, was indefinitely postponed. As the weeks went by Anne fretted more and more at the delay, till at last her confessor was moved to say: "If it is the Will of God that you make your vows, you will make them,

---

[15] The refrain of this poem is known to all who have heard of St. Teresa, who, trying to express her love, exclaimed:
"I die, because I cannot die."

[16] The Apostolic visitor had appointed Teresa de Quesada, a former nun of the Convent of the Incarnation, Avila, as prioress at Medina, but she soon left, and St. Teresa was appointed in her stead.

even should you become more seriously ill than you are at present. But if it is not His Will that you should be professed, why do you hanker after it?" From that day the poor novice's health began to improve. Anne had been losing sight of the end while striving to attain the means.

Her next idea was to make her profession as a lay-sister. Perhaps she had witnessed the favours bestowed by God on the saintly Anne of St. Bartholomew, and realised that hidden and menial work is no obstacle to the working of His grace. Perhaps, also, she hoped by means to escape being placed in posts of responsibility and trust. The matter was referred to St. Teresa, who promptly sent a formal order that Anne of Jesus had to make her vows as a choir sister, and the profession was fixed for October 22nd, the feast of two of Spain's virgin martyrs.[17] When the moment came for pronouncing her vows Anne walked with a firm step to the middle of the nuns' choir. The community and the many visitors assembled in the chapel listened to the solemn words with reverent attention, when suddenly, as she was repeating the formula for the third time, according to Carmelite custom, Anne was rapt in ecstasy. Unconscious of those around her, she remained pale and motionless, while rays of light darted from her face. All present were witnesses of this marvel, but the nuns tried to pass it off by referring to the recent illness of the newly professed, and declaring that she had fainted. God, however, bore witness to His newly-consecrated spouse, for Anne of Jesus recovered from her rapture for a sufficient space of time to disprove the statements made about her and then fell into another trance more prolonged than the first.

It was on account of this occurrence that St. Teresa, when the matter was reported to her, made the regulation

---

[17] St. Modia and her sister St. Nurtilo.

that for the future the ceremony of profession was to take place in the chapter room, where no strangers could be admitted, not even the ecclesiastical superior, the vows, made to the General of the whole Order, being received by the prioress as his delegate. This regulation was incorporated into the constitutions in 1581.[18] The formula of vows, as copied by Manriquez from the register of professions kept at St. Joseph's, Salamanca, runs as follows:

> "I, Anne of Jesus, make profession and promise obedience, chastity and poverty to God, Our Lord, and to the Blessed Virgin, Our Lady of Mount Carmel; and to the Most Reverend Father John Baptist Rubeo, Prior General of the Order of Our Lady of Mount Carmel, and to his successors, according to the Primitive Rule of the said Order, which is without mitigation, until my death.
> (Signed) Anne of Jesus."

After her profession Anne of Jesus continued to exercise her charge of Mistress of Novices, and so marvellous were the fruits of her training that the confessor, a celebrated lecturer at the University of Salamanca, questioned her one day about her methods. Her answer was worthy of one trained by St. Teresa: "I simply try to find out and to follow for each one the road along which the Spirit of God is conducting her. My own part consists merely in removing obstacles, or anything which might hinder the workings of God's grace in their souls."

The convent at Salamanca was founded without revenues, and in the beginning its poverty was extreme. This caused much anxiety to St. Teresa, who used to send what alms she could from Avila. However, Avila was also poor, and during the exceptionally severe winter of 1571-

---

[18] There is a public ceremony for the receiving of the black veil by a professed religious.

1572 the Salamanca community suffered terribly from the cold. Anne of Jesus did all that devotedness and mortified unselfishness could devise to help and relieve her sisters, but with all her efforts, suffering and privation could not be avoided. The hardest trial of all was that the nuns were without the abiding Presence of Our Lord, for the dampness of ceilings and walls was so excessive that it was not judged reverent to reserve the Blessed Sacrament. "I keenly felt what those sisters suffered there," writes St. Teresa in her Book of Foundations. Yet the nuns endured it all with joy, for she adds: "Some of them even told me that it appeared to them an imperfection to desire another house, since they were contented where they were, provided only that they had the most Blessed Sacrament."

Meanwhile, many favours were bestowed upon the nuns at Salamanca and upon Anne of Jesus in particular. The previous year St. Teresa, noticing Anne's gift of prayer, had said to her: "My daughter, it seems it is not you who prays, but Our Lord Who prays in you," and now, although mother and daughter were separated as to the body by many miles of mountainous country, their souls remained united. Thus, when on May 1st 1572 Teresa was rapt in ecstasy at Avila at the moment when Pope Pius V died, and he appeared to her and spoke of the Reform, Anne of Jesus, at Salamanca, saw her mother bathed in tears and heard her say: "O my daughter, we have just lost a great saint! His death will leave a great void in the Church."

Another day Anne's duty took her to the "turn" with some important message. Just as she got there the bell rang for the sisters' examen of conscience. Obedient to the Rule, which prescribes that at the sound of the bell "each one shall kneel down, wherever she may be, and straightway make her examen," Anne began her spiritual exercise. In the meantime the prioress was waiting for the answer to her message, and at last went herself to see what had detained her messenger. She found Anne of Jesus still on her knees and in so deep a rapture that nothing could recall her to herself. She remained thus till the following morning, then, realising what had happened, she hastened off to the duty of the moment.

On another occasion, when Anne was acting as hebdbomadarian[19] and all the nuns were waiting in choir for her to intone the *"Deus in adjutorium meum intende,"*[20] no sound was heard. After an interval of patient waiting the sisters turned round to find out what had happened and saw that Anne was in an ecstasy. The Office had to be recited without her, for the rapture continued for several hours.

So frequent were these occurrences that at last the prioress wrote to ask St. Teresa what was to be done. The saint's answer was worthy of her. "Try to divert Anne's attention," she wrote, "by occupying her in exterior duties. But once she is in an ecstasy, do not touch her, for I know the great harm that may be done if any hindrance is put to the free working of God's spirit." The office of portress was suggested as a suitable employment for the young sister, who herself wrote to the Foundress, begging her to ask God to cease showing her these external favours. For a time things went on much as before, and even when Anne was at the "turn," she was often rapt in ecstasy, but later on God withdrew His external favours for a time and then Anne suffered bitterness and desolation of spirit in a corresponding degree.

It was during this time that she had the consolation of

---

[19] In a public recitation of the Breviary, the hebdomadarian intones the beginning of the chant, and the first line of the Psalms. -Editor.

[20] "O God come to my assistance," from Psalm 69 (70). This verse begins every hour of the Breviary since ancient times. -Editor.

welcoming to the Carmel of Salamanca her cousin, Maria de Lobera, who received the habit in September 1572. As Sister Mary Angel she was delighted to have her holy cousin as novice-mistress. After making her vows on 22nd October 1573 Sister Mary Angel lived forty-one years at Salamanca, where she edified all her sisters by the holiness of her life. St. Teresa refers to her in her letter to Father Gracian, 11th March 1578.

CHAPTER V

FROM SALAMANCA TO VEAS

1571-1575

ST. TERESA'S anxieties about the unhealthiness of her convent at Salamanca were not ungrounded, and she had told the prioress to be on the look-out for another house. Towards the end of the third year a more suitable one was found, large and commodious, as were most of the houses of the upper classes in the town. On the other hand, the families living in them were usually poor, and very often rooms were let to students, who flocked to Salamanca in order to attend its university. The house chosen by the Carmelites belonged to Don Pedro de la Vanda, a nobleman of slender means and difficult temper, who gave St. Teresa much trouble, and on whose account the nuns, after her death, were obliged to remove elsewhere. As the house was entailed[21] a royal licence was necessary before it could be purchased. So many difficulties cropped up, and there were so many delays—the community all this time being deprived of the presence of the Blessed Sacrament—that Anne of Jesus, through Father Dominic Baliez, obtained an order from Father Pedro Hernandez, the Commissary-Apostolic, that St. Teresa should go herself to Salamanca to bring matters to a satisfactory' conclusion. Gathering together what money she could, the saint set out, notwithstanding the intense heat, and after many hardships

---

[21] In early modern English, an *entail* (Old French *taille*) means that a property is legally held in the possession of a certain family for a period of time. -Editor

arrived at Salamanca, only to find the proprietor absent. It was an annoying experience, and several of the saint's letters bear witness to her feelings at the time and her frankness in dealing with the situation.

The fact was, Michaelmas was the season in Salamanca for renewing leases, and the Foundress was anxious to get the community into their new quarters, so as to avoid being liable for the rent of their first house for another year. The enforced delay was utilised by the saint, however, in writing, in obedience to her confessor, at that time Father Jerome Ripalda, an account of the seven Foundations of the Reform. Anne of Jesus, who, as before, shared her holy Mother's cell, was the first to receive these precious manuscripts fresh from the pen of the writer.

The affair of the new Carmel was sufficiently advanced by mid-September for the solemn removal of the nuns to be announced for Michaelmas Day. Their new church was not finished, and the roof formed little protection against the torrential rain which fell uninterruptedly all during 28th September. At eight o'clock on that evening St. Teresa, standing in the porch of the church with Father Julian of Avila and the Licentiate Nieto, chaplain to the Carmel at Alba de Tormez, who had come to Salamanca for the ceremony, was discussing what had better be done. The saint complained interiorly to God: "Adorable Master," she sighed, "either command me no more to undertake works like this or put things right in this our hour of need." At that moment Anne of Jesus came up and said, in her emphatic way: "Your Reverence knows what time it is, and how many people are expected here tomorrow; will you not ask Our Lord to make the rain stop, so that we can arrange the altars?" "If you are so sure God will hear my prayers, ask Him yourself," answered her holy Mother, and Anne and her companions withdrew. Immediately the sky cleared and the stars shone out so brilliantly that Anne could not resist turning back to add: "Your Reverence might have asked Our Lord for this grace a little sooner!" St. Teresa watched her energetic daughter for a moment or two and then went off to her cell, laughing softly to herself.

By an early hour everything was ready and the installation took place. But the troubles of the community were by no means at an end, for de la Vanda, perhaps on account of his "indigestive condition," raised many complaints, so that St. Teresa was obliged to remain at Salamanca for five months. Much of her time was devoted to the training of her religious.

Anne of Jesus, in her quality of portress, one day admitted some of her own relatives who had called to see her. At the moment her holy Mother was in the speak-house, talking to a Jesuit Father. Anne gave the message: "One of my relatives is here, a stranger to me, who desires to speak to me." Without answering directly, the Saint turned to her visitor: "Did your Reverence hear what Anne of Jesus has just told me?" she said. "There is a knight here to whom she is related. She wants to let us know that her family is well connected, as if, forsooth, in religion, and especially among the Discalced, noble birth is of any account." The young sister received this reprimand in humble silence, while the Jesuit was left wondering which to admire most—the ingenuity of the Foundress in providing a trial for her daughter, or the simple humility with which her rebuke was received. But the holy Mother knew well the stuff of which Anne was made, and asked much where she knew much would be unhesitatingly given. Thus, on another occasion she told Anne to prepare a little spiritual discourse to give to the nuns during their recreation. Entering into her Mother's thought, Anne went to the community room betimes and arranged an impromptu pulpit. When the nuns had all assembled she got up quietly and was about to begin to speak, when St. Teresa, pretending to know nothing about it, stopped her, asking her aloud who had put such an idea into her head. Anne of Jesus sat down without a word. Presently her Mother's voice was heard again, this time reproaching Sister Anne because she had not spoken to the community as she had been told to do. The young religious was quite ready to obey, but the old chronicles do not relate whether or not St. Teresa let her give the discourse she had prepared.

In 1574 Father Baltasar Alvarez, St. Teresa's former confessor at Avila, was appointed rector of the University at Salamanca. He also acted as ordinary confessor to the Carmelite nuns, and soon recognised in Anne of Jesus a kindred spirit to her holy Mother, and acting on supernatural lights, he warned her of the many trials God had in store for her. Anne at the time was young and lighthearted, and at first made little of these prophecies, but one day, after St. Teresa had been talking to her about the difficulties connected with the foundation of a Carmel at Vas, Anne, in her turn, spoke of them to Father Baltasar. "I am well content, my child," was the holy man's reply, "that you are beginning to believe what Our Lord tells you by the mouth of His servants. Prepare yourself for the same experience with regard to the other trials I have predicted to you."

In the March of 1574 St. Teresa left Salamanca to found a new convent at Segovia, intending to return at once. She was unexpectedly detained until October, and then she went back, not to Salamanca, but to Avila. During the interval occurred one of the marvels of her life. Among the novices trained by Anne of Jesus was Isabel of the Angels, who had entered Carmel at Medina del Campo, but whom St. Teresa had transferred to Salamanca on account of complications concerning Isabel's family, for she was an heiress and had been early left an orphan. It happened that the young Carmelite fell ill, and Anne of Jesus, who nursed her tenderly, gives the following account of her holy death: "On St. Barnabas's Day, June 11th we went to the choir to hear Mass, leaving her [Sister Isabel] in a state of great depression. On our return we found her quite changed—an extraordinary joy had succeeded to her trouble of mind. Mother Anne of the Incarnation, our prioress, said to her: 'Blessed be God, Sister, you seem better. Why are you so full of joy?' 'Because to-day, Mother, my sufferings will come to an end,' she answered, 'and I shall go to enjoy the good I sigh for.'

"Mother sub-prioress[22] then asked her, 'Who told you that, Sister?' The invalid replied with a smile: 'What a question! Somebody told me, and it was somebody who had a right to say it.' The Mothers withdrew, and I, being her Mistress of Novices, remained alone with her. I said: 'How is it you are so sure that your exile will be ended to-day?' Then she confided to me that during Mass our blessed Mother Teresa had come to visit her and console her and giving her a blessing had said, while taking her face in her two hands: 'My child, do not be so foolish as to stop at all these scruples. Have, rather, a great trust in all that your Divine Spouse has done for you. God has great glory in store for you. Believe that even this very day you will enjoy it.'

"Isabel assured me that she already tasted the first fruits of that joy and that she felt so deep a peace in her heart that it might never have been a prey to anxiety of any sort. During matins two sisters watched beside her. Towards eleven o'clock, just as we were about to take the discipline, for it was a Friday, all of us, moved by an irresistible

---

[22] Mother Mary of Christ.

impulse, hastened to the infirmary. At once a blessed candle and crucifix were placed in the hands of the dying nun, and we began to invoke the Sacred Name of Jesus and to say the Credo, which she herself recited in Spanish. Hardly had she pronounced the last article when she sweetly expired. At the same moment her body radiated a heavenly beauty and supernatural splendor." The document adds that this phenomenon continued until the sister was buried, and was witnessed by the crowds who assisted at the requiem.

The day of Isabel's death one of the sisters at Salamanca wrote to Segovia a full account of what had happened. The recipient of the letter ran straight to St. Teresa's cell: "Mother," she cried, "now I understand why these last few days we have knocked in vain at your Reverence's door. You gave us no answer, and we found you looking as if you were dead. It was, as they have just written to say, because your Reverence was consoling Sister Isabel of the Angels at Salamanca." The saint could not deny this, but she tried to pass it off with some evasive remark. Meanwhile a letter from her had been received at Salamanca, mentioning things of which she could not possibly have had knowledge, unless she had been personally on the spot. The prioress showed this letter to Anne of Jesus, who answered at once that their holy Mother had certainly gone all over the house the day she came to console Sister Isabel. In a further deposition Anne of Jesus continues: "About a year later, when Mother Teresa sent for me to be prioress at Vas, I questioned her as to what had happened, and because she was very fond of me she told me that the facts [above related] were true. Then, not dreaming that she would die before me, I begged her to come and help me at the hour of my death. She replied: 'I promise you to do so, if God will allow it, for things like that are not in my power.' I asked her again if she had told Sister Isabel that God had great glory in store for her in heaven.

'Yes,' she answered, 'for His Divine Majesty showed me that this sister had merited as much during the five years of her religious life as many others do in fifty years of strict observance.'"

On 11th August 1574 Anne of Jesus received her obedience for the new foundation at Veas. The news caused her much distress, for she was very happy at Salamanca, but when, as usual, she took her trouble to Our Lord He consoled her, and her soul found peace. The new convent was not to be opened till the following January. Obedient to what had been recommended to her by her superiors, St. Teresa did not come to Salamanca to fetch Anne of Jesus, but met her at Handovers, a small town not far from Avila. Anne and her companions were escorted by a Hieronymite Father, preacher to Philip II, whose business took him along the same route.

Together he and Anne conversed of the things of God, and the young Carmelite made such a deep and lasting impression on her companion that he resolved to embrace the Reform. Later on he visited Anne of Jesus at Veas, and on her advice became a Discalced friar, taking the name of Antony of the Mother of God. After some years the holy man was seized with the desire of preaching the Gospel in pagan lands. Again he consulted Anne of Jesus. She assured him that his wish was pleasing to God, and that He would ask of him the sacrifice of his life. Two years afterwards, when Carmelite friars were asked to evangelize New Guinea,[23] Father Antony volunteered and was accepted. A small vessel bearing the missionaries set sail with a fleet of trading ships 20th March 1582. When they were a few days out of harbour the small vessel collided with a larger one

---

[23] Jingo Ortiz de Retas took possession of New Guinea in the name of the King of Spain in 1545.

and foundered, all on board perishing except two of the crew. Thus was the prediction of Anne of Jesus verified.

To return, however, to 1575. When the little party of nuns from Salamanca reached Handovers they sought hospitality in a convent of the Mitigated Observance. St. Teresa was tired and ill, and had to go straight to bed. Meanwhile the prioress of the Calced nuns prepared a meal for her guests, but when she pressed them to partake of it they insisted on waiting till leave had been obtained from St. Teresa. The latter afterwards scolded her sisters, not only for what had every appearance of incivility, but for want of submission to the local superior. Anne of Jesus, who knew that her holy Mother intended to make her prioress at Vas, thought this an excellent opportunity of showing how unfitted she was to be placed in authority. "Mother," she said, "it is because we are but recently professed that we make so many blunders. It is really a pity to take us so soon from the noviceship and to put us in a position of responsibility." The holy Foundress knew well what was in her daughter's mind, and answered promptly: "Obedience teaches us everything. St. Francis and St. Dominic began with those God sent them. Let us try to be perfect, that is all that matters." It was nevertheless true that Anne was not then thirty years old, and had been professed only a little over three years, so that, to make her prioress, St. Teresa had been obliged to apply for a dispensation from the then recently promulgated Decrees of the Council of Trent.

After a short rest the travellers went on towards Toledo, where two more religious were to join them for Vas. It was here that a day or two later Anne of Jesus on the morning fixed for their departure, prayed earnestly while St. Teresa went to receive Holy Communion, that she might share some of the graces which God showered on her holy Mother. Possibly Teresa was made aware of her daughter's prayer, but, at any rate, she had no sooner returned to her place than she turned towards Anne, saying: "Quick, Sister, go and put some nuts in a sack, for we are to start almost immediately." Anne left the choir to obey, but she had hardly got a few paces from the church, when she heard her Mother's step behind her. Teresa was urging her again to make all haste. Surprised beyond measure at what seemed to her a want of recollection, Anne turned the matter over more than once in her own mind, thinking that God had given a strange answer to her prayer. The next morning Anne herself received Holy Communion, and Our Lord unravelled the puzzle about her holy Mother by saying "This is what pleases me so much in her; she is always occupied with my interests."

The story of how God wonderfully prepared the way for a foundation at Vas is told by St. Teresa in her Book of Foundations, and must not be repeated here. The saint, in her account, tells of the mysterious dream sent to Catherine Godinez, the temporal foundress, about twenty years before she had ever seen a Carmelite nun. After Catherine had been saluted in silence by some religious, whose habit was totally unfamiliar to her, one of them, more beautiful than the rest, embraced her and presented her to another, older nun, saying: "This one is your Mother, and it is her Rule that you must follow. The other nuns are your sisters, and the Order is my Order." After that the Rule was read, and then one of the nuns coming forward, said: "Daughter, I want you for this house. Upon this Catherine awoke, full of joy, determined to give herself to God. Three years later, on the feast of St. Joseph, 1558, she put on the distinctive costume of a beata. Maria de Sandoval,[24] her younger sister, then about thirteen, a pretty and lively child, objected very strongly to being seen about Vas with her sister in semi-religious garb.

Catherine prayed much for the high-spirited girl, and about a year later, when the two sisters were together at Mass, Our Lord showed Himself in the Sacred Host to Maria, offering Himself to her as her Spouse. Maria was conquered, and from that day the two sisters rivalled each other in their works of penance and charity.

After the long delay described by St. Teresa, all the difficulties having been overcome, Catherine wrote to the Saint, then at Segovia, to tell her she had taken a house, and was furnishing it for the nuns. It happened that an application for a foundation at Caravaca, a town some distance east of Vas, reached St. Teresa about the same time as Catherine's letter, and the Foundress determined to establish the two Carmels during the same journey. Vas was to be founded first, as the letters patent for Caravaca had not been obtained.

Everybody knows, nowadays, the mistake St. Teresa made in thinking that Vas was in Castile, and not, as it actually was, just within the border of Andalusia, where she had been forbidden to make any foundation.

Her letters referring to the subject are quite conclusive. The Saint set out, therefore, in all good faith, taking with her sufficient religious for the two new foundations. From Toledo the little party, escorted by Julian of Avila and Antony Gaytan, went on to the Carmel at Malagon, where

---

[24] It is the custom in Spain for the eldest daughter to adopt her mother's surname. The others are known by their father's name. Catherine Godinez married Sancho Rodriguez de Sandoval, a wealthy nobleman of Vas, a small town, situated on the borders of Murcia, Toledo and Jaen.

a postulant was received for Vas. Her brother, a priest, offered to join the caravan. The next halt was at Almodovar del Campo, where St. Teresa had business connected with the foundation of a priory for Discalced friars.

Towards the middle of the day the party stopped at a roadside inn to get some food, for they had brought no provisions with them. It happened that there was nothing in the house but a couple of eggs, which the landlady had put aside for her own supper. St. Teresa was fasting, and faint from fatigue and hunger, but the good lady was by no means willing to sell. Two of the priests pleaded with her in vain. At last Anne of Jesus came to the rescue, and after a few tactful words the two eggs were put into her hands for "the good Mother." Anne never forgot this act of charity, and whenever opportunity served she would send a medal or a pair of scapulars to the landlady who, on her side, often sent vegetables, especially asparagus a favourite vegetable of their confessor, St. John of the Cross, to the nuns at Vas, and always treated well any Carmelites who passed that way.

Once Almodovar was left behind, the route lay over the rugged Sierra Morena, and the travellers met with hardships of many kinds. Whenever it was possible halts were arranged for at the less frequented villages, and St. Teresa always tried to manage that the priests who accompanied her should be able to say Mass. At one such spot, after Father Julian of Avila had said Mass, there was no more altar wine, and no large particle for a second Mass. Much distressed, St. Teresa turned to Anne of Jesus: "Ask God that enough may be found," she said, "for I cannot bear to think that the Church should lose the benefit of the Holy Sacrifice." Anne had hardly time to obey before altar-breads and sufficient wine were found ready at hand; no one knew whence.

In the mountain passes all had to travel on mules. One

day the hired guides lost their way, and the party found itself suddenly at the brink of a precipice. St. Teresa invoked St. Joseph, and at the same moment the voice of an old man was heard crying out: "Stop, stop! or you will perish," and adding instructions about the way to follow. Though the mules were urged in the direction indicated, the path was so rough and precipitous that everyone's attention was occupied in traversing it. After a short time, however, a safe and easy road was reached, and the guides, relieved from further anxiety, turned to thank their rescuer. Hither and thither they rode, but nowhere could he be found. Meanwhile St. Teresa, with tears of consolation in her eyes, was saying to Anne of Jesus and her other companions: "Truly, I am at a loss to know why we let these men go to look for our benefactor; for it was my Father, St. Joseph, and they will not be able to find him."

Another, and more marvellous intervention of Providence was experienced by the little caravan as they drew near to Vas. After descending the southern slopes of the Sierra Morena the nuns travelled in a covered wagon until they reached the river Guadalimar, which had to be crossed by a ford. This necessitated a halt, for all had to get out and ride through the water on mules. While waiting inside the wagon until mules could be brought from a neighbouring farm the nuns suddenly found themselves transported to the opposite bank, wagon and all. "Hardly had we reached the brink of the river," wrote Anne of Jesus afterwards, "than we found ourselves on the other side." The people of Vas, distant six or seven miles to the south-west of the ford, had come out to meet St. Teresa and her daughters, and when they saw this prodigy take place before their very eyes they were filled. with astonishment and reverence. The principal gentlemen of Vas, making their horses caracole in honour of the nuns, escorted the whole party to the parish church. There the clergy were waiting in surplice and stole, together with many noble ladies of the neighbourhood, among them Catherine Godinez and Maria de Sandoval. After a short interval for prayer the Carmelites were conducted in solemn procession to the house of the latter, where they were to live until their new convent was ready. This was on 15th February, 1575.

The joy of the two sisters was unbounded, especially when Catherine recognised by the nun's habits those she had seen in her dream. When all the visitors had departed and Catherine and Maria were alone with the nuns they lifted their veils, and Catherine at once recognised Anne of Jesus as the one who had read the Rule to her and claimed her as her daughter. She went up to salute her future superior, but Anne presented her to St. Teresa, telling Catherine that she alone was her Mother and Foundress, and that it was Mother Teresa whom she must obey.

About a week later a house adjoining the principal church in Vas, and formerly belonging to the parish priest, was ready for the nuns, and they made their solemn entry on the feast of St. Matthias February 24th. The same evening Catherine and her sister received the Carmelite habit. It was the former's thirty-fifth birthday, and she received the name "Catherine of Jesus," her sister becoming "Mary of Jesus."

The new foundation was dedicated to St. Joseph of Our Saviour, and the two novices made over their fortune unconditionally for its maintenance. Touched at such generosity, St. Teresa said to them: "What will you do, if we do not want you and send you away?" "In that case," was the unhesitating answer, "we will serve you as *tourières*,[25] and if you will not even feed us, we will beg our bread for the love of God."

---

[25] Out-Sisters, not bound by inclosure.

After the clothing had taken place St. Teresa appointed Anne of Jesus prioress, and left all decisions concerning the settlement of the house to her, herself obeying her with great exactness and humility. It was a lesson which Anne of Jesus never forgot. From the very first she made a compact with Our Lord, promising that if He would look after the temporal affairs of her convent she would devote herself to all that more directly concerned His service, and God certainly came to her assistance in marvellous ways.

CHAPTER VI

FIRST TRIENNIUM AT VEAS

1575-1578

S T. TERESA stayed about three months at Veas—a period which brought her much sorrow, but also much consolation, and which saw the beginning of the troubles which ended, after the Saint's death, in the complete separation of the two branches of the Carmelite Order, Mitigated and Reformed.

The first link in the long chain of events was forged at Veas, where St. Teresa met for the first time Father Gracian, in religion, Jerome of the Mother of God. This remarkable man was born at Valladolid the same year as Anne de Lobera, 1545, and he pronounced his vows as a Discalced Carmelite on 25th March, 1573. He was on his way to Madrid two years later, on business concerning the Order, when he made a detour to visit St. Teresa at Veas, for up to that time he had only known the Foundress from her letters. He arrived at Veas on 1st April 1575. After St. Teresa had opened her soul to him in confession she had a vision in which Our Lord appeared standing beside her, with Father Gracian at His right. He took the right hand of each and clasped them together, saying: "Here is he whom I wish thee to hold in My place as long as thou livest. I desire that you both have the same way of seeing things, for thus it behoves it to be." It was this which made St. Teresa trust the young friar as she did. Later on she made a vow to obey him in all things, provided it was not against her conscience to do so. The autograph of this vow was long preserved at the Carmel of Brussels, and is now among the treasures of the Carmelites of Chichester. Father Gracian was detained three months at Veas, and this was no doubt permitted by God so that he might become better acquainted with St. Teresa and Mother Anne of Jesus. In the latter he recognised the same spirit as he found in her holy Mother. Anne, on her side, grew to love and trust her youthful Ecclesiastical Superior, and throughout all the trials that befell them in later life the two remained firm friends and loyal children of their saintly Foundress.

While he was at Veas Father Gracian gave the Carmelite habit to the priest who had travelled with the nuns from Malagon. Julian of Avila about the same time asked to be made a participator in the prayers and good works of the Order. Wishing to do honour to St. Teresa's travelling companion, Father Gracian asked all the nuns to come to the grate for the ceremony, wearing their white mantles and holding lighted candles. The young Provincial then preached for an hour on the beauty and holiness of the Carmelite life. The sacristan had passed through the "turn" to be blessed two baskets, one containing a complete new habit, the other a small scapular. Father Julian had no intention of becoming a friar, and when he saw the coarse habit laid out and heard the glowing panegyric of Father Gracian he thought St. Teresa must have been inspired from heaven to make him a Carmelite. Great beads of perspiration broke out upon his forehead at the mere thought of being bound to such a life. However, his discourse finished, Father Gracian took up the scapular and invested Father Julian with it as a symbol of his affiliation to the Carmelite Order. Afterwards both priests and nuns had a good laugh over the fright of St. Teresa's friend.

It was during this time that news came to Veas from Caravaca about the nuns there being subjected to the Order of the Knights of St. James of Compostella, which obliged St. Teresa to postpone the foundation. She purposed going to

Madrid, but Father Gracian obliged her to go to Seville instead. Her obedience was rewarded by a vision in which Our Lord told her she had done well to obey, and that the work of the Reform and the proposed foundation at Madrid would succeed all the better for it. The Provincial, therefore, left for Madrid on 20th April, leaving St. Teresa to spend another month at Veas, quietly preparing for her journey to Seville. One morning letters arrived from Palencia and Valladolid, telling that the MS. account of her life had been taken before the Inquisition.[26] This news gave the Saint considerable anxiety. "In writing the book I had no anxiety at all," she said to Anne of Jesus, "but now I fear I may inadvertently have used inaccurate expressions which the Holy Office may condemn. For myself personally I do not mind, because God knows that I have always acted straightforwardly. But I am very distressed for the sake of others."

Anne of Jesus had too great trust in her Mother to be upset, and answered at once: "If your Reverence asks God to bring good out of this trial, and to make known that you acted loyally in everything, I am convinced that He will do it. Therefore what is the use of worrying?" St. Teresa was only partially consoled by these trustful words, but the next morning during her thanksgiving after Holy Communion Our Lord reassured her, and she went straight to her coadjutrix. "Give thanks to God, daughter," she said (Anne of Jesus herself relates the story), "for what you told me yesterday has already come to pass. At the moment of my Communion Our Lord consoled me, saying, 'Do not be

---

[26] This was the copy she had lent to the Princess of Eboli, who was, however, not friendly to the Saint. As the life was only in MS. and not intended for publication there was no reason for submitting it to the Inquisition. The Princess of Eboli had sent it through spite.

troubled, for this is my cause.' By this I understand that the inquiry, far from being hurtful to any of our convents, will, on the contrary, benefit them greatly." This prediction was verified twelve years later, when, after the Saint's death, Anne of Jesus received her writings back, fully approved by the Holy Office, so that she could get them printed. Meanwhile the days of happy intercourse between Mother and daughter slipped by all too quickly. One day when they were conversing together St. Joseph appeared to each of them separately, and humility forbade either making known to the other what she saw. However, St. Teresa, anxious to leave at Veas some souvenir of her visit, got a painter to represent the Saint in a large picture, just as she had seen him. Anne of Jesus at once recognised the likeness between Saint Joseph as she had seen him and as he was painted. It told her that her Mother had had the same vision as herself. St. Teresa seems to have been aware of it all the time, for she said to the sisters, when sending for their prioress to receive the picture: "She will be able to say whether or not the painting is like the original."

At last the day dawned for the Saint's departure for Seville. It was Wednesday, 18th May 1575, the day on which for the last time, Anne of Jesus was to see her blessed Mother in the flesh.

They corresponded, it is true. But the next few years were full of troubles and persecution for the Reform, and St. Teresa exacted that all her letters to Anne of Jesus should be burnt, she herself burning those she received from Veas, as well as from elsewhere. Only a few fragments have escaped, but these are redolent of the holy affection which bound together the Foundress and her coadjutrix.

Before leaving Veas St. Teresa performed an act trivial in itself, perhaps, but none the less symbolic. Just as the Saint was getting into the covered two-wheeled cart which was to take her and her companions to Seville she turned back to Anne of Jesus. "Daughter, let us change mantles," she said. "Take mine, which is new and suitable for one of your age; yours, which is old and worn out, will suit me perfectly. Thus did Anne receive the mantle of her blessed Mother, and with it, no doubt, a double measure of her spirit.

After St. Teresa's departure for Seville the young prioress devoted herself to training six novices whom her Mother had received. Shortly afterwards the daughter of a distinguished family in La Mancha presented herself as a postulant. Anne of Jesus admitted her to the noviceship under the name of Jane of the Kings. The young girl proved of so difficult a character and was so unsuited to the life of a Carmelite, that no instructions or private counsel seemed to have any effect upon her. Anne of Jesus put this down to her own sins and imperfections, and one day when she was thus blaming herself before Our Lord in the Blessed Sacrament she clearly heard the words: "Take the habit off her, if she is not what she ought to be; others will come in her place." "What, Lord," answered the distressed prioress, "dost Thou not wish the first religious I have received to dwell in Thy house?" And Our Lord deigned to reply: "Hast thou not noticed that when a seedling begins to grow its first leaves fall off, and then others develop which give it strength and beauty? Thou wilt experience the same before thou leavest this convent. Go into the garden, and thou wilt find a seedling with four shoots; the first leaves are dead, the shoots fresh and green. If thy first leaves wither, others will flourish. Take the habit away from this novice. I will give thee four others instead, as thou wilt see."

In spite of these consoling words Anne hoped against hope that the novice would correct herself, and the dismissal was postponed. A week later Anne's former confessor,

Father Rodriguez, brought his niece to Veas, where she wished to become a Carmelite. She received the habit on 11th June 1576 and was called Magdalen of the Holy Ghost. Her health proved to be exceedingly delicate, and in great anxiety Anne of Jesus consulted Our Lord as to whether she should be allowed to remain. "Let me fashion this stone," was Our Lord's answer, "for I will place it in a prominent place." Later on Sister Magdalen founded the Carmel at Cordova. On the prioress's feast day, 26th July, a second postulant was admitted, who received the name Luise de San Salvador, and on 1st December a third, Sister Eleanor-Baptist of Jesus, who afterwards became prioress at Veas, and later on founded the Carmel at Valencia. Mindful of Our Lord's promise, Anne of Jesus made up her mind to dismiss Jane of the Kings the day after Sister Eleanor-Baptist's clothing. That same evening a fourth postulant came to ask admission. This was Frances de Sandoval, daughter of Sancho Rodriguez de Sandoval, one of the brothers of the two temporal foundresses of Veas.

Her mother belonged to a noble Spanish family, Guerra de Luna, and led the life of a saint. She had five sons, and much wished for a little girl, and for this intention begged the prayers of her holy sisters-in-law. Her desire was granted. A little girl was born to her and baptised Frances. She grew up in simple faith and piety, and after she became a Carmelite wrote an account of her early years, which gives a charming picture of Spanish home-life in the sixteenth century.

"My mother," she writes, "inspired her children with great devotion towards the patrons they had been given in baptism. When each one's feast came round it was kept with great rejoicings, Mass being said for the child who bore the name of the Saint of the day. In order to inspire her sons with a love of the Rosary she used to recite it aloud. In each corner of the room knelt a boy, she herself being in the centre with the youngest beside her. As for myself, before I was four years old my mother taught me to say nine Hail Marys in honour of Our Lady that I might always bear Jesus in my heart. When I was still quite little, about three or four years old, I used to go at my mother's bidding and kneel before a large and beautiful statue of Our Lady with the Child Jesus in her arms, and say:

"'Mother of God, I want to be spouse to Thy Son: As to the rest of men, I despise them, every one.'"

"At other times my mother would say: 'Run to the Mother of God, daughterkin, and salute her reverently.' Then I would stand before the statue and recite these lines:

> "'Mother of God and Virgin true,
> You love me, and I love you—
> We love each other, just we two!'"

One day, when Frances was twelve years old, her mother, having to go out on the eve of Candlemas Day, told her to see to the alms she was accustomed to distribute every Feast of Our Lady. The child faithfully fulfilled her mother's injunction. Shortly afterwards she heard the voice of another beggar and asked one of the servants to give him something. The girl went to do as she was told but found no one there. Again Frances heard the voice and again she sent the servant to give relief but no one could be seen. Nevertheless, Frances still heard the pleading voice, but though several other servants went to look no one could be found. Unconvinced, the young girl at last went to the door herself, holding some money in her hand. Then Our Lord appeared to her in shining garments. "The alms I want," He said, "is the offering of thine own heart and soul." "Lord, I give them—they are Thine," cried Frances in return; and from that moment she lived only for Christ her Lord. She spent much time in prayer and penance, cut off her beautiful hair, and always dressed in plain grey satin. Her father watched this change with consternation, and one night, disappointed pride getting the better of him, he entered his daugher's room and shook her roughly, declaring that she had left off loving him. He even threw her to the ground, spurning her with his foot. Then, his mood changing, he offered her his whole fortune if she would but marry according to his wishes. For answer the gentle Frances threw her arms round her father's neck. "My Lord and dear Father," she said, "I am grown up now; why do you still treat me as a child who only cares for toys? I implore you not to press this upon me any more." At that Sancho Rodriguez was so enraged that he treated his daughter even more roughly than before, when suddenly a beautiful young man appeared, who, leading Frances into another room, prevented her father from following. It was his daughter's Guardian Angel. Touched by grace Don Sancho fell on his knees earnestly begging pardon of God, and promising never again to hinder Frances from becoming a nun. Then, like the good husband and father he really was, he went to find his wife. After telling her the whole story he added with characteristic vehemence: "Even if our daughter wants to dress herself in a mat I will not prevent her. Let us pray that God may not punish us for resisting so long."

At last the day came when Our Lord Himself conducted His chosen spouse within the walls of the Carmel at Veas. It was 2nd December, 1576, and Frances-herself tells the story:

> "The first Sunday of Advent," she writes, "finding myself towards evening alone in my room, I was all at once enveloped in a bright cloud and heard a voice saying: 'Come with Me if thou dost wish to enjoy My company!' At the same moment I felt Our Lord, for it was He, take my hand. He led me to the wall of our garden and lifted me over to the other side. He did the same at the Carmelite Convent. Having seated me on the top of

the convent wall He passed inside then took me in His arms and set me on the ground.

"Then He led me to the refectory where the nuns had just sat down to supper.[27] A few minutes before they had taken the habit off a novice in whose place Our Lord had promised the venerable and saintly Mother Anne of Jesus four others. His Divine Majesty placed me in the middle of the refectory and I asked the community, for the love of God, to give me the habit.

"All rose from table, and came and embraced me. Reverend Mother Anne of Jesus told me I seemed to her too young and delicate, and that she would send me back to my father, whom she would not pain by keeping me against his will. Then, gazing fixedly at me, she added: 'Besides, what do you know of religious life?' All I know is,' I answered, 'that it is my most earnest wish to be a religious. There alone is life and happiness for me.' Then I added, 'Madam, when children are very little all they seek after is their food. When they receive it they stop crying, but if they were asked what they wanted they could not say. It is the same with me. I cannot explain what religious life is, but all I desire is to be a nun. Perhaps, when I have grown up as a religious I may be able to explain things better.'

"As I was saying this our blessed Mother Anne of Jesus (it was herself who told me this) saw Our Lord standing beside me, and heard Him say: 'This is the fourth novice I promised thee.' Then she clasped me tight in her arms. 'If your father were the King of Spain, and every mountain in his kingdom were of precious stones,' she exclaimed, 'I would not give one bit of you in exchange for all those riches.'

"The nuns, seeing the affection blessed Mother Anne

---

[27] An autograph account of this is preserved at Jaen, wherein it is related how astonished the community were at the sudden appearance of an outsider in their midst.

of Jesus lavished upon me, showed me, in their turn, all sorts of kindness. At last the happy day came when our venerable Mother gave me the habit. While she was dressing me I raised my eyes to look at her and saw Our Lord seated in her heart, whence He gave me His blessing. The same thing happened when I made my profession."

This paper is signed "Frances of the Mother of God," that being the name by which Frances de Sandoval was known in religion.[28] There was always a special tie of affection between Anne of Jesus and Frances of the Mother of God. The night before the young sister was to pronounce her vows she was praying in her cell, when a sudden and strange noise coming from the corner of the room startled her. Looking round she saw the evil one under the form of an enormous wolf, who threatened her, saying: "You shall not make your vows. I can easily prevent it." Rigid with terror the young novice could only call aloud for help. Sister Lucy of St. Joseph, her cousin, came in haste to see what was the matter. "Oh, sister," Frances cried, "take me to our Mother for I cannot move a limb." Sister Lucy, fearing to disturb the prioress, for by this time it was about one o'clock in the morning, refused to do anything of the kind, when the door opened, and Anne of Jesus came in. "My child," she said, "what is the matter?" "Oh, Mother," the trembling novice replied, "I wanted to come to you and I could not walk a step, and Sister Lucy refused to help me." The prioress sent Sister Lucy back to bed, and then again asked Frances what was the matter. "Look in that corner, Mother," she cried, "and you will see for yourself." The demon-wolf was still there but such apparitions held no terrors for the

---

[28] When Manriquez was writing his life of Venerable Anne of Jesus Frances was still alive, and she supplied him with several interesting details incorporated into this narrative.

holy prioress. "What are you doing here, evil wretch?" she said, "In the name of Jesus Christ I command you to go back to hell." Then she led the still trembling and exhausted novice to her own cell and made her lie down on her bed. The holy Mother passed the rest of the night on her knees beside her afflicted child: "Sleep in peace, dear child," she said, "for never again shall such sights terrify you." In fact as soon as Frances found herself lying on her venerable Mother's bed all her fear left her and her nerves became composed.

"I might have been in paradise," she said afterwards. Yet it troubled her to see her venerable prioress so long on her knees, though a mysterious feeling kept her from making any remonstrance. Some time afterwards when speaking of this to her, Anne of Jesus replied: "Even had you asked me I should not have left my place at your side, for I saw Our Lord standing at the head of the bed, and He kept His sacred hand upon your forehead."

Frances made her profession on 21st January 1578 and lived to be eighty-four.[29]

While these events were happening within the Convent Anne of Jesus was also busy helping the Discalced Friars to found a house between Veas and Granada. A suitable one having been established under the name of "Mount Calvary," or "Calvario," the prioress sent some furniture from the convent, and, as neither nuns nor friars had any money to pay for the house, it was decided to borrow the necessary sum—400 ducats. One day, while this matter was under discussion, word was brought to Anne of Jesus that there was an old man living in Veas, of miserly habits, who kept a sum of 400 ducats sewn into different portions of his

---

[29] She was, therefore, among the aged religious who lived on during the period when it was forbidden to receive novices at Veas.

garments. She sent for the man and persuaded him to part with his money, giving him a receipt in due form by which she promised to repay both capital and interest.

The house was accordingly bought and prepared, but day after day the old miser came up to the convent demanding to see the prioress, to whom he bewailed the lightness of his garments, and his foolishness in exchanging good coin for a useless bit of paper. So persistent were his visits and complaints, that, to get rid of him, Anne of Jesus bade her nuns pray to St. Joseph for wherewith to refund the debt. Almost at once, a shepherd, Diego Garcia, presented himself at the convent turn. He had come, he said, to beg the Mother Prioress to intercede for him with the Friars of Calvario where he wished to enter.

Anne of Jesus saw at once that he had the Carmelite spirit and promised to do what she could. Thereupon Diego offered her 400 ducats—the price he had just realised by the sale of his sheep and goats. Giving thanks to God the prioress accepted the gift and immediately sent for the old miser and paid her debt. The shepherd became a lay-brother, Diego of St. Basil, and lived and died a holy and exemplary religious.

It happened that there was no water supply at Calvario, and the friars desired to obtain possession of a neighbouring well used by the cottagers who lived near it.

The cottages were bought up and Anne of Jesus, who seems to have been the leading spirit throughout the whole affair, gave notice to the tenants to quit. The order appeared a cruel one for the poor people had nowhere to go, but the prioress insisted: they must go that very day. Out of respect for the Servant of God the order was obeyed. All packed up their little belongings and went away. Two hours later the cottages collapsed; had the inhabitants remained not one would have escaped alive. The event was the more remarkable because the houses were solidly built and not in need of repair. Praise of "the holy prioress" was heard on all sides for all attributed to her the saving of so many lives.

CHAPTER VII

LIFE AT VEAS BEHIND THE GRATE

1578-1582

WHAT Anne of Jesus had done for the priory of Calvario pleased St. Teresa immensely. She wrote to Father Mariano about her quite jubilantly (21st October 1576). But trouble was not far off.

Legal action was brought against the nuns for putting up a grate in the wall between their convent and the church. Veas was only a small place and it was difficult to obtain preachers, so with the consent of the clergy, the nuns had had a window put in whence they could follow the services in the parish church. Their real choir was on the ground floor, but they had fitted up a room contiguous with the Church on the first floor as an oratory, and Sisters often obtained leave to watch before the Blessed Sacrament there during the night. A certain lay official, or syndic, considered the opening of the window an abuse, and without informing either the clergy or the nuns, obtained leave to wall it up. Of course the permission thus secured was invalid but that troubled Alphonso de Montalbo not at all. He exhibited his permit to his friends on his return from Madrid, whither he had gone in person to obtain it. "Take care what you are doing," said one, "you risk much by interfering with these holy women. By trying to deprive them of the consolation of hearing the word of God, who knows whether your eyes may not be closed instead of the grate." Montalbo only laughed at this, and raising his voice for all to hear, he cried aloud: "Bear witness, all you who are present. In three days either the grate or my eyes shall be closed."

The friends of the Carmelites went round at once to tell

the nuns what was going on, for so far they were in ignorance of Montalbo's intentions. Mother Anne of Jesus assembled the community, and after laying the matter before them, told them to pray about it. Before dismissing them she asked each in turn if she had anything to say. One of the youngest, Sister Magdalen of the Holy Ghost, who left an account in writing of the whole affair, said that she thought there was no need to be afraid, because God would defend them. The same evening Montalbo was seized with sudden illness of which he died on the third day. God had "closed the eyes" of the man who ventured to persecute His chosen spouses. The whole town was struck with the coincidence, which they considered as a warning from God that His religious cannot be attacked with impunity. Anne of Jesus ordered special prayers for the repose of the soul of their enemy, for she regarded his death as an effect of God's Mercy, since He sometimes punishes sin in this world instead of in the next.

The letters of Sister Frances of the Mother of God give further details of the affair.

> "One day I went into our venerable Mother's cell," she writes, "and when she noticed me she rose and spoke to me with great respect. Feeling I was quite unworthy of this reverence I threw myself at her feet, saying: 'How is it that you, who are my Superior, can speak to me with such veneration?' 'Ah, my child,' she answered, 'how can I not honour and love those whom God regards as the *light of His eyes*, whereas I am but dust. Listen, but do not speak of this to anyone. On Sunday morning when the syndic was exhibiting the letters he had obtained from Madrid, I said to Our Lord during my thanksgiving after Holy Communion: O Jesus, wilt Thou allow those souls who have left all for Thy love, and who day and night are occupied solely in loving and serving Thee, to be deprived of the only consolation they enjoy, that of

hearing Thy Divine word? Our Lord fixed the dazzling beauty of His eyes upon me and answered: Thou and the souls under thy care are the light of my eyes. Dost thou think then that Alphonso de Montalbo can touch thee? Could he make me blind? No, Lord, I replied. Very well, Our Lord continued, still less can he close up your grate."[30]

Mother Frances adds:

"Our venerable Mother also told me that, since that vision, she has had to do violence to herself not to manifest to her religious all the respect and love she bears them."

Among other great gifts bestowed by God on Anne of Jesus was that of reading the hearts and consciences of her religious daughters, a gift she often made use of to help them in their spiritual needs. Sometimes when instructing her novices she would say: "I had committed such or such a sin, and as I was afraid to confess it, I managed like this." One day Sister Frances said in her simple, direct way: "But, Mother, the sin you have just named is the very one I am in trouble about, how can you say that you committed it?" At this the holy prioress began to smile, and answered, "Well, since you are my daughter, must I not look upon your sins as though they were my own?" Incidents like this were of frequent occurrence. Nevertheless, some souls under her guidance resisted this means of grace. One especially presented herself as a postulant with several grievous sins

---

[30] The grate in question was still used in 1809, but during the Peninsular War Veas was sacked by the French. The only building that escaped was the new Carmelite Church built by Mother Mary of St. Joseph, who died in odour of sanctity in 1709. When the nuns were obliged to leave their Convent in 1810 they carried her body with them and placed it in the crypt of the Church she had built, asking her to protect it. It was the only building of note in Veas left intact.

on her soul. Her outward conduct appeared irreproachable, and as she regularly received the Sacraments with the rest, she was in due time clothed with the habit of a Carmelite novice. But black despair and bitter remorse preyed upon her soul to such an extent that at last her health gave way. The doctor was called in and declared that the Last Rites must be administered.

Anne of Jesus, enlightened as to the cause of this strange sickness, for the novice was of a healthy and robust constitution, prostrated herself in prayer to gain this erring soul. As she remained thus, bathing her crucifix with her tears, grace penetrated the heart of the dying novice and she sent an urgent message, begging that the prioress would come to her cell. A few minutes later a priest was sent for and everything was made straight. Even her body was cured, and when the doctor came again he could hardly believe the evidence of his own senses. The sister lived in good health for several years and was noted for the fervour of her religious observance.

St. Teresa knew of, and approved, the relations of trust and affection existing between Anne of Jesus and her spiritual daughters. Writing from Toledo to Mother Mary of St. Joseph at Seville, 2nd March 1577, the Saint says: ". . . The prioress of Veas writes to tell me that her nuns make their confessions to one priest, to whom they speak of nothing but their sins, so that he hears the whole community in half an hour. She adds that this plan ought to be observed elsewhere. The sisters are perfectly contented and attached to their prioress, since they treat of their souls with her. . ."

Yet on occasion Anne of Jesus could be strict as well as kind.

A sister who continued her work for a moment after the bell had rung for some community exercise was severely reprimanded. On one occasion the prioress said, "How dare you not obey, Sister, when you hear the voice of God. She who is not faithful in little things will most certainly not be faithful in greater ones." So deep was the impression made on the religious to whom these words were addressed that fifty years later she declared that they were always fresh in her mind. Another time it happened that some workmen had left in the enclosure garden a large heap of big stones. The prioress desired the sisters to remove them to another spot, she herself taking part in the work. When all was done and the nuns were contemplating with satisfaction the result of their toil their indefatigable Mother gave a fresh order. Every stone was to be carried back and the heap remade in its original position. "Why are we doing this, Mother?" asked one. "In order to learn," replied the holy prioress, "that obedience does not ask 'why?' but executes quietly whatever is enjoined."

Another day the venerable Mother had a little saucepan put on one of the steps of a staircase in constant use. It was very much in the way, but no one ventured to remove it. Some days passed. The offending saucepan was still on the staircase when at last one of the nuns could not endure the sight of it any longer. She waited for the prioress to come along, and then asked: "Mother, what is this saucepan doing on the stairs?" "What is it doing?" replied Anne of Jesus, "It is telling us how unmortified you are. Since your Charity finds it inconvenient where it is you had better carry it hung from a cord round your neck until I decide otherwise." And so it was done.

To those who could bear it the holy Mother meted out harder tests. A certain sister who was an expert seamstress was told to cut out and make up some simple garment. When it was finished she took it to her superior. Anne of Jesus hardly looked at the work but told her to unpick the whole and make it over again. This was done six successive times and each time the sister began again with the same promptitude and diligence she had put into her work at first.

But all the daughters of Anne of Jesus were not cast in the same heroic mould. A lay-sister, whose duty it was to send the corn to the mill, found it more convenient to drop the sacks filled with grain from the window of the granary instead of carrying them downstairs. When Anne of Jesus came to know this she forbade it to be done. Nevertheless, when the day came round again the sister, either from habit or inadvertence, flung out the heavy sack as usual. As she did so, her arm fractured in two places. So severe a punishment was enough, and as soon as the prioress heard of the accident she hastened to console the injured sister, though pointing out at the same time the merit and safety of exact obedience.

Since St. Teresa's time the gaiety of Carmelites has become almost proverbial. Her letters tell of the songs and rhymes composed by the nuns for community feasts. Anne of Jesus was, in this, no way behind her holy Mother, and at Veas many a pleasant hour was spent in innocent games or improvised dialogues, in which the sisters vied with one another in dramatising some incident from the lives of the Saints, or inventing some other form of recreation. An ancient MS. relates how Anne of Jesus shared in all this.

> "As to our venerable Mother, she set us an example, and took great delight in watching the joy and simplicity with which the sisters went through their parts, because she felt convinced that their souls gained much merit and spiritual advantage thereby."

One favourite game was that of "Martyrs," and the holy prioress, carried out of herself one day by her desire of suffering for Christ, cried out: "Is it possible that I shall have to die in my bed like a coward?" One of the sisters, in writing to St. Teresa, repeated this remark and the Saint wrote back assuring her coadjutrix that she would not die in her bed—words which proved prophetic. In prayer, penance, and innocent recreation the months passed quickly away, and the novices who had been received during St. Teresa's stay at Veas made their profession into the hands of Anne of Jesus. God blessed her dealings with these young souls, not only interiorly, but by many striking miracles, all of which are well authenticated. Catherine of Jesus (Godinez), after her profession, was put in charge of some alterations which were carried out during the Lent of 1577. Part of the original house was being pulled down, and as Sister Catherine, standing at the top of an adjoining staircase, was noting down what had still to be done, the whole structure gave way. The young religious was flung to the ground, stairs and roof crashing down on the top of her. The community were reciting vespers, but the workmen who hurried to the spot, sent word to the prioress of what had happened. All hastened to render what help they could. Sister Catherine, terribly injured, was placed gently on a board and carried to the infirmary. At first she gave no sign of life, but the doctor, hastily summoned, found her still breathing, and so set her broken limbs. For several days the poor sufferer lay in intolerable agony. She was quite conscious, and united her sufferings to those of Our Lord on the Cross. At last the doctor gave up all hope of her recovery and declared it was useless for him to come again. Thereupon Anne of Jesus exclaimed: "I know for certain there is a remedy for God is still in His heaven. It will cost Him no more to cure her than it did to create her." Assembling the community, she went with them to the choir, and had the Litany of the Saints recited.

    Bathed in tears the Servant of God prostrated herself on the ground, saying again and again: "By Thy sacred merits, Lord Jesus, cure her!" Then, signing to the nuns to follow her, she took in her hands the crucifix given to her by St. Teresa, and which she always carried on her breast, and went to the infirmary. "My child," she said, "why do you not get up, and come and help us to sing the office of tomorrow's feast?" "Ah, Mother," replied the cripple, "I should like nothing better if my poor bones would only allow it." "Do you not believe that Our Lord can, with a single word, knit together the broken bones and entirely take away your sufferings?" "Yes, yes, I believe it," answered Sister Catherine repeating the words several times. "Very well," replied her venerable Mother taking her hand, "in the name of Jesus Christ, whose image this is, and in virtue of holy obedience, I tell you to do so. Get up and dress yourself." Catherine at once rose from her bed and dressed herself without any help, then in the sight of all present she began to walk. The prioress, noticing that she put her hand against the wall to steady herself, pretended to be displeased, "Do not walk like a little child," she said, "there is no need to lean on anything." The obedient religious immediately walked across the room—she was cured, completely and permanently.

Sometime afterwards her niece, Frances of the Mother of God, asked her how she had had the courage to get up when she knew that both her legs were broken. Her aunt replied that when her venerable Mother took her by the hand Our Lord did so too, and that at the same moment she experienced a shock through her whole system, not of pain, but of relief, which told her she was cured. Anne of Jesus attributed this miracle to the heroic obedience of her daughter, but everyone else put it down rather to the sanctity of the prioress. The holy Carmelite friar, Bartholomew of the Kings, signed a written document in which he states that Our Lord once appeared to Anne of Jesus, and by the contact of His divine hand on hers, communicated to her the power of healing bodily ills. To this was added a remarkable gift of turning sinners to repentance, and of reading consciences, as has already been recorded.

During her first year at Veas it happened that a priest in the town had been led into serious sin. Anne of Jesus sent for him on some excuse of business, and spoke to him so persuasively that his repentance, and the public expiation he made for his wrong-doing, completely effaced the scandal he had given.

One feast of Corpus Christi, always a great day in Catholic Spain, the Governor of Veas, Pedro Garcia Milian, whose duty it was to prepare everything for the solemn procession of the Blessed Sacrament, determined through vanity rather than devotion, to break the record in the magnificence displayed. This gentleman had a brother a Jesuit who was accustomed to visit the Carmelites, and relying on this circumstance, he asked the Prioress to undertake the making of the portable throne, used when the Blessed Sacrament is carried in the monstrance for long distances. Anne of Jesus willingly undertook the work and a day or two before the feast the Governor called upon her in person to offer his thanks. Pleased alike with himself and with his preparations he said to her in a tone of triumph, "For once at any rate we shall have a magnificent feast." "The feast God likes best," quietly responded the religious, "is the humble purification of our own hearts by a good confession, so that we may receive Him in Holy Communion." The words went home, and, Pedro, to the edification of all, received the sacraments as Anne of Jesus had suggested. A few months later he was taken ill, and died in most Christian dispositions. Mother Magdalen of the Holy Ghost writes:

"On the occasion of this death our venerable Mother wrote through me to the Reverend Father Garcia Milian, to condole with him on the loss of his brother. She spoke of the consoling dispositions of the deceased, adding that, by a special favour of heaven, someone had seen his soul enjoying the bliss of heaven. While writing this at her dictation I was so astonished that I looked up at our Mother. Her countenance was radiant with heavenly beauty, so that I knew at once that the person of whom she spoke was herself."

Later on one of Pedro's daughters entered at Veas, and was known as Mother Mary of St. Paul.

However, all whom Anne of Jesus reproved were not so friendly towards her. At great cost to herself she had succeeded through her friends, among the clergy and others, in putting a stop to some public scandal. The guilty parties, full of resentment, bided their time. Several weeks later Anne was laid up by illness, and they sent as alms for the invalid a tempting-looking dish to which poison had been added. Quite unsuspicious the holy prioress took a little, and almost instantly the symptoms of violent poisoning ensued. The doctor, hastily summoned, managed to save her, but for the rest of her life the poison remained in her system, and from time to time gave rise to painful ulcers. It was when one of these was being dressed by Sister Mary of the Incarnation at Madrid that Anne of Jesus told the above story, suppressing the names of those concerned.

Another story of the marvels worked by her prayers throws light on the dangers which attended travelling in the sixteenth century. A man and his wife being on a journey their way led through Veas. On the outskirts of the town a libertine attempted to carry off the woman by force, and the husband in trying to save her killed him. The case was brought before the municipal magistrate, and the traveller, poor and a stranger, was condemned almost unheard. His wife, distraught with grief, did all she could to save him, but in vain. The very morning fixed for the execution arrived, when she heard of the wonders wrought by the prioress of the Carmelites. In a voice broken with sobs the poor woman told her tale to Anne of Jesus. After a moment's prayer the prioress wrote a few words on a sheet of paper which she charged the sacristan to take at once to the Governor. The accused man was already standing beneath the gibbet amidst a crowd of people assembled to see him die. The sacristan despaired of reaching the Governor in time, when suddenly a venerable old man took him by the hand, crying out: "Way! Make way, for the messenger of the Mother Prioress!" The crowd fell back instantly, and the two passed quickly to where the Governor was standing. Hardly had the latter glanced at the note than he felt himself impelled to suspend the death sentence and order a fresh inquiry.

This time the true facts of the case were made evident, so that the charge of murder was withdrawn, and the poor man and his wife went on their way rejoicing. As for the venerable old man he was never seen again; but Anne of Jesus told her nuns that it was her good Father, Saint Joseph.

More than once men "wanted" by the Inquisition took sanctuary in the Carmel. On one such occasion, it happened that the door from the church into the enclosure was open, and seeing no one about, the poor refugee slipped in. Advancing a little way into the convent he met the prioress, and told her of his trouble. She might not allow him to remain in the cloister nor would she refuse him sanctuary, for the officers of the Inquisition were already knocking at the door. Quick as thought she shut the offender up in the sacristy, telling him to recommend himself to God, while she herself went to take counsel with Our Lord in the Blessed Sacrament. As if in answer to the holy Mother's prayer a Franciscan priest came into the church and asked to see the prioress. She begged him to go at once to the sacristy, where the fugitive throwing himself on his knees, implored the friar to hear his confession. His offence, whatever it was, was at once put right, the officers of the Inquisition were informed, and priest and penitent left the church together. The friar was afterwards fond of relating this story as an illustration of the kindness and ready wit of the venerable prioress.

Needless to say, all these wonders were not wrought without much cost to the Servant of God herself. She added bodily penance to her prayers for others and humbled herself before her community in all sorts of ingenious ways, prompted by her own resourceful devotion. In addition to this the evil one did all he could to hinder her work, often appearing to her under some terrifying form.

CHAPTER VIII

WORK FOR THE ORDER AT VEAS

1575—January 1582

IN ORDER to understand what part Anne of Jesus played in the dispute between the Mitigated Carmelites and the Discalced it will be necessary briefly to recapitulate the story.

St. Teresa had been authorised by the General, Father John Baptist Rubeo, to found as many convents of nuns as "she had hairs on her head," and, moreover, to found two priories for friars who were to follow the same kind of life as her nuns. In course of time he granted leave for the foundation of some more priories, but always on the distinct understanding that none should take place outside the province of Castile, and, secondly, that the Discalced Friars should on no account set themselves up as a distinct province, but should remain under the jurisdiction of the provincial of Castile.

The establishment of the Congregation of Mantua in Italy, and of Albi in France, towards the end of the fifteenth century, had led to such troubles (those concerning Albi were not at an end at this time) that Father Rubeo would not risk a similar rift in Spain. Circumstances altogether unforeseen placed Father Jerome Gracian, a learned young friar of only a few years' profession, at the head of the province of Andalusia under the title of "Visitor Apostolic" with extensive faculties. While engaged on a visitation of the priories in that part of Spain he took the opportunity of establishing there several houses for Discalced friars, as well as a Convent of Discalced nuns at Seville. He thought, rightly or wrongly, that his power as Visitor entitled him to supersede the definite instructions of the General, and he committed the mistake of leaving the latter entirely in the dark as to what was being done. When Father Rubeo at length received bitter complaints from the Calced friars in Andalusia he was naturally very angry. He wrote repeatedly to St. Teresa for an explanation, but the letters were delayed, with the result that, when a General Chapter was assembled at Piacenza in May 1575, not a word of explanation from either St. Teresa or Father Jerome Gracian was forthcoming in reply to the recriminations of the Andalusians.

The General produced a copy of the faculties he had granted, with the restrictions already mentioned, and the Chapter ordered the closing of the priories founded without the General's sanction, and enjoined St. Teresa to choose a convent for her future residence, forbidding her to make further foundations.

Father Gracian, relying on what he considered his superior powers, and on the support of the King and the Papal Nuncio, Hormaneto, took no notice of the ruling of the Chapter, but went so far as to constitute the Discalced friars into an autonomous province on his own authority. This was in the autumn of 1576. A Visitor, sent by the Chapter, was refused the Exequatur by the Royal Council. This went on easily enough as long as the Nuncio lived, but Hormaneto died the following year, and on the arrival of his successor, Monsignor Sega, who, like the General and his Chapter, had no accurate knowledge of the real state of affairs, active steps were taken against Father Gracian and the leading Discalced friars. At the same time expired the term of office of the Provincial of Castile, Angel de Salazar, who on the whole had been favourable to St. Teresa, and his successor, Gutierrez de la Magdalena, caused Father John of the Cross, confessor to the Convent of the Incarnation at Avila, to be seized and taken prisoner to Toledo, where he was confined for more than eight months in a narrow, stifling cell, and subjected to barbarous treatment. He escaped in a truly miraculous manner, during the octave of the Assumption 1578.

The Provincial also acted harshly towards the nuns of the Incarnation who had ventured to elect St. Teresa as prioress. Mother Frances of the Mother of God gives part of one of St. Teresa's letters to Anne of Jesus at this time, in which the saint says:

> "It is but too true the Fathers of the Mitigation are doing their best to wreck the Reform. For the love of God, unite your prayers, I beg of you, to those of my dear daughter, Catherine of Jesus, since you both treat so familiarly with the good Jesus, and ask Him to help us and to enlighten us as to what we ought to do and what steps we ought to take. For this end, have the Litany recited in choir for a fortnight and add one hour's prayer to the customary time.
>
> "Then let me know, dear daughter, what lights God gives you, both you yourself and also my daughter, Catherine of Jesus."

Anne's answer after she had taken counsel with God in prayer was that St. Teresa should write to the King, begging him to take the Reform under his personal protection. At this time both Provincials were Friars of the Mitigation, and their sympathies, very naturally, were against the Reform. The Provincial of Castile was anxious to meet Anne of Jesus and make the Visitation of the Carmel at Veas.

In a letter in which he addressed her as "Chief of Prioresses" he endeavoured to prove that St. Teresa's work was but "a lopped branch of the Tree of Carmel." The Servant of God wrote back a vigorous defence of her holy Mother, and represented that, as Veas was in Andalusia, the Provincial of Castile could not be received there as the Canonical Visitor.

Unfortunately the Discalced friars made a great mistake in assembling in Chapter (autumn 1578) and proceeding to the appointment of Superiors. For neither of these acts had they any power whatever. Not only did the Nuncio annul their proceeding, but he imprisoned—that is, he relegated to special priories—the recalcitrant friars. It had been decided at their meeting to send some from their ranks to Rome to negotiate matters; one of those chosen was Peter of the Angels of whom Anne of Jesus, when she heard the news, remarked: "He is going to Rome barefooted, but he will return shod."[31] This prophecy was fulfilled, for Father Peter, meeting with much kindness at the Viceroy's Court at Naples, did not get as far as Rome, but abandoned the stricter life of the Discalced friars for that of the Mitigated. The intended negotiations, therefore, led to no result, and the affairs of the Discalced were at their lowest when, through the good offices of their staunch friend, the Count de Tendilla, the Nuncio was induced to set up an unbiassed Committee of Inquiry. After hearing both sides this committee advised the separation of the Discalced friars and nuns from the Province of Castile, and their organisation as a separate province. Both the Nuncio and the King supported the plan, but it was opposed by Salazar, it is difficult to say on what grounds. Naturally, the General, now Father Caffardo, followed Salazar's advice, as did also, just as naturally, the Cardinal Protector of the Order, Buoncompagni, the Pope's nephew.[32]

---

[31] Some writers attribute this saying to St. John of the Cross.

[32] The "Cardinal Nephew" (Cardinale Nepote) is the Prefect of the Secretariat of Briefs, the name being due to the fact that from the Middle Ages till the seventeenth century, the prefect of the department was regularly either a nephew or some other relation of the Pope. Gregory XIII's family name was Buoncompagni.

The Discalced friars decided, therefore, again to send two of their number to Rome to lay their side of the matter before the Holy Father. By St. Teresa's advice the mission was entrusted to Father Juan de la Roca and Father Diego of the Trinity, who were to keep the purpose of their expedition a profound secret. After consulting with ecclesiastical authorities it was decreed that the two Fathers should, for the journey, put off their religious habit and wear secular clothes.

Financial aid was secured through some of St. Teresa's friends and from her convents. The prioress of Valladolid gave 400 ducats, and Anne of Jesus raised the same sum. St. Teresa asked the two envoys to call at Veas on their way to Alicante, the port of embarkation, and tradition says that Anne of Jesus, for greater security, herself sewed the 400 ducats into the lining of the travellers' cloaks.

Father Juan de la Roca assumed a family name, Don José Bullon, and he and his companion were supposed to be lawyers journeying to Rome to obtain a dispensation for the marriage of Don Francisco Bracamente, a gentleman of Avila, who furnished the disguise besides contributing 400 ducats towards general expenses.

The two envoys had to stay about a year in Rome, but they were eventually instrumental in obtaining all that the Discalced friars asked for. St. Teresa, deeply touched at all that Anne of Jesus had done to support the work of her Reform, wrote from Avila, probably in 1579.[33]

> "... My daughter and my crown! I cannot thank God enough for the favour He did me in drawing you to the

---

[33] The Stanbrook Edition gives this letter under the date 1578. St. Teresa was at Avila till June 1579, and on July 27th of that year she wrote to her brother, Luis de Cepeda: "Fra Juan de Jesus (de la Roca) has reached Rome."

religious life. For as His Majesty, when He delivered the children of Israel from Egypt, set before them a column which guided and illumined them by night, and sheltered them during the day, so He seems to have done for our Order—and your Reverence, my dear daughter, is the column which enlightens and defends us. All that you have done for these Fathers has been most judicious, and your devotion and generosity prove that God dwells in your soul. May the Master for whom you have done it reward you, and may He grant to these efforts the success befitting them!. . ."

There seems to be a reference in this letter, only part of which is extant, to a vision granted to St. Teresa earlier in the dispute, most probably in July or August 1577, and which she communicated to Father Gracian:

". . . I saw a violent tempest," the Saint wrote. "As the children of Israel were persecuted by the Egyptians, so shall we be persecuted; but God will enable us to pass through the sea dry-shod, and our opponents will be swallowed up by its waves. . ."

The time was at hand when the latter part of this vision was to be fulfilled. The two envoys of St. Teresa gained a hearing from Cardinal Sforza, who persuaded the Pope to adjudge the case himself in a consistory of Cardinals. To this Gregory XIII consented. Almost all the Cardinals spoke in favour of the Discalced, especially Cardinal Montalto, afterwards Sixtus V, who was such a good friend to the Reform. On 22nd June 1580 a Brief was granted separating the Discalced Carmelites from the Calced, and giving leave to the former to establish a Province of their own, subject to the General of the whole Order.

While these affairs were being settled in Rome, life went on peacefully for the community at Veas. Towards the end of December 1578 St. Teresa asked St. John of the Cross, who had, after his miraculous escape from Toledo, been named prior at Calvario, near Granada, to call at Veas on his way there from Almodovar. Anne of Jesus and her community received him with all the honour due to one who had suffered so severely in the cause of the Reform. In order to entertain him the prioress told one of the nuns to sing some verses she had composed for the approaching festival of Christmas. Instead of doing so, the Sister, perhaps under an inspiration of grace, sang a verse of her own in praise of suffering. Hardly had she got through the first two lines when St. John made her a sign to stop. The nuns, who were all present, were astonished to see the holy friar seize the projections of the grate with both hands. A rapture had come upon him, and, in spite of his efforts to the contrary, his body was raised into the air. For a whole hour God held him thus in close embrace, much to the edification of Anne of Jesus and the whole community. On coming to himself Father John told them that the one word "suffering" was sufficient to raise him to the heights of prayer.

It is on record that the holy man had come to Veas intending to discourage Anne of Jesus from prayer leading to rapture, and that God had shown him in her presence that the gift of ecstatic prayer cannot be refused against His good pleasure. The armchair in which the Saint was sitting when the rapture came upon him was long preserved at Veas. Portions of it are now at the Carmel at Jaen, and Brussels possesses a large fragment. The nuns, when they knew St. John better, used to call him among themselves "God's goldfinch."[34]

St. John not only approved Anne's method of prayer, but allowed her to receive Holy Communion daily—a very rare privilege at that time. So far as can be ascertained it was

---

[34] St. John of the Cross used to walk two Spanish leagues every week to visit Veas from Calvario.

during the Christmastide of 1578 that the saintly prioress was favoured with a vision of Our Lord's Birth at Bethlehem. On the eve of the Feast of the Circumcision she exhorted her religious to prepare themselves to receive a drop of the Precious Blood shed by the Infant Jesus in that mystery. On the morning of the Feast she saw the Divine Child in the Sacred Host, and heard Him say: "I will give thee not only a drop of my Blood, but all of It, together with my body and soul." During the evening a small statue of the Infant Jesus was enthroned in the nuns' recreation room, and Anne of Jesus, kneeling before it, consecrated herself to her Infant Lord, and then invited each of the nuns to do the same. Sister Frances of the Mother of God being the youngest was the last to make the act, and she experienced great consolation while doing so. The next day she went to thank the prioress for the happy evening, adding: "To judge by the effects His Divine Majesty produced in my soul, dear Mother, it seems to me that the Infant Jesus was really among us yesterday." "He was there," replied Anne of Jesus, "surrounded by millions of seraphim. His Divine Majesty caressed each sister according to the degree of faith and love with which she approached Him. Love and serve our good God, my child, and you will see what great graces He will bestow on you. But I do not know why I should speak to you of these things," added the holy Mother, "when with other sisters, who are holier than you, I can say nothing."

Early in 1579 Father Gracian was released from the censures and penalties he had incurred, and St. Teresa received permission to visit her convents again. In the June of that year St. John of the Cross was named prior of Baëza, one of the newly sanctioned foundations. He had foretold this appointment to the nuns at Veas, and Anne of Jesus gave her saintly confessor all the help she could, even sending to Baëza all the furniture that could possibly be done without. God showed His Fatherly care for the nuns at Vas by working a wonderful miracle there on Christmas Eve, probably in 1579. Sister Luise de San Salvador had been confined to her bed for nine months, and was in such a state of weakness that four sisters had to lift her, while the infirmarian made her bed. The latter was Sister Catherine of St. Albert, about whom St. John of the Cross once wrote:

> "If you were aware of the treasure you possess in Sister Catherine of St. Albert you would kiss her very footprints. One could hardly believe except through having personal intercourse with her that, in the unhappy times in which we live, there could be a soul serving God with so much fidelity and living in such close union with Him."[35]

While matins for Christmas Day were being chanted, Sister Catherine was alone with the invalid, who kept asking to be carried to the upper grate so that she might share in the office of that great Feast. "I dare not take you," answered the infirmarian; "the doctors have forbidden us to lift you, even to make your bed." But the look of disappointment on her patient's face made her add quickly: "I will go to Mother Prioress, and if she gives permission I will do what your Charity desires." Anne of Jesus was not a little astonished to see Sister Catherine coming into the choir, and was quite startled when she learnt her errand. However, after a moment's prayer she replied: "Go, my daughter. Carry Sister Luise to the grate, but do not forget that I wish you to bring her to me afterwards, perfectly cured." "But, Mother," whispered the frightened infirmarian, who had little expected such an answer, "how can I do that?" "Put some

---

[35] It was to Catherine of St. Albert that St. John once said in speaking of his imprisonment at Toledo: "No single grace of those God granted to me there could be purchased by many years in prison."

mattresses on the floor by the grate," was the answer, "and lay the invalid upon them. Then with great faith, ask the Divine Infant to give us the cure as a Christmas present, for it is certain that His Majesty is more eager to give us favours than we are to ask them."

Without another word Sister Catherine fulfilled her obedience and then knelt down beside Sister Luise to pray for her cure. As Matins proceeded the latter felt herself growing stronger. At the end of Lauds Sister Catherine stood up, and was preparing to carry the invalid back to her cell. But Sister Luise motioned her to one side. "No, no," she said, "there is no need for that any more. I am better than you are yourself," and wrapping herself in a blanket she executed a dance of delight. Then the two descended together to the lower choir, as Anne of Jesus had enjoined. The community had not dispersed, and when they saw the miracle God had worked they remained yet a little longer to thank Him for this truly royal Christmas gift. Sister Luise lived fourteen years after this in perfect health, and was able to practise all the austerities of rule without inconvenience.

Thus, between joy and sorrow, the anxious days of waiting passed, and so great was St. Teresa's faith that by 5th May 1580 she mentioned in a letter to Father Gracian her desire to found a house at Madrid. The Papal Brief authorising the erection of the Discalced friars and nuns into a separate province reached Spain on the Feast of the Assumption that year. The President of the first Chapter was to have been the Bishop of Seville, but as he died almost immediately it became necessary to send to Rome for a second nomination. Gregory XIII appointed the great Dominican, Pedro Hernandez, but he also was taken away by death. A third nomination included two names, Father Juan de las Cuevas, prior of the Dominicans at Cordova, and Alberto Aguayo, one of his friars. The Brief containing these appointments arrived on 4th January 1581. After all necessary formalities had been fulfilled Father Juan de las Cuevas summoned the delegates of the Discalced friars to a Constituent Chapter at Alcala de Henares. There, on 3rd March, he declared the separate Province of the Discalced canonically erected.

When St. Teresa heard the good news, she felt that her work on earth was accomplished. She was already much broken in health, and, raising her eyes to heaven, she exclaimed, "Now, O Lord, I am no longer needed here below, summon me when Thou wilt."

All during the February and March of that year the holy Foundress had been busy settling the Constitutions of the Discalced nuns, which had to be submitted to the newly-formed Chapter.

After the friars had elected Father Gracian as Provincial he presided over the Chapter of Affairs, and the Constitutions for both friars and nuns were approved and promulgated. St. Teresa's joy was intense. In her account of the foundation at Palencia she refers to it as follows:

"I consider the joy I then experienced as one of the greatest I could receive in this world. For more than twenty-five years my life had been one long chain of troubles, persecutions and sorrows endured for the cause of the Order. To tell them all would take too long, my adorable Master alone knows them. Hence, when I saw everything brought to a happy ending I felt my heart vibrate with a joy only to be appreciated by those acquainted with my former troubles."

The Generals of the Carmelite Order continued to be elected from the ranks of the Mitigated, but there was never any further friction with the Discalced. Troubles arose for the nuns, as will be seen, but these had nothing to do with the Calced Carmelites.

For the moment all was joy and peace. The friars, assembled in chapter at Alcalá, sent to Veas, at St. Teresa's request, the two delegates who had been to Rome in order to thank in person, on behalf of the newly-erected Province, Mother Anne of Jesus, who had done so much towards bringing matters to a satisfactory conclusion. As the prioress entered the speak-house (i.e. parlour) to receive her visitors, the two friars greeted her with the words sung to the triumphant Judith by the people of Bethulia: "Thou art the glory of Jerusalem; thou art the joy of Israel!" This characteristic message from her dearly loved Mother did not disturb her saintly daughter, who knew well to whom all honour belonged. Together with the friars and the nuns she at once chanted a Te Deum in thanksgiving for the graces God had bestowed upon the Order.

St. Teresa, in spite of her desire to sing her *Nunc dimittis*, made good use of the new arrangements for inaugurating further foundations. A Carmel was founded at Soria and another at Burgos, the latter being the last which the Saint superintended personally. She was also corresponding with the authorities at Madrid, and settling about a foundation in Andalusia. This was to be at Granada, the old Capital of the Moors, where she sent Anne of Jesus to make the foundation in her name.

VISION ON THE FEAST OF THE CIRCUMCISION
1578

CHAPTER IX

THE FOUNDATION AT GRANADA

July 1581 to August 1582

IN 1581 St. Teresa wrote to the community at Veas when the second term of office of the prioress expired telling them not to elect her again as she was wanted elsewhere. The election took place in July and the nuns chose Mother Catherine of Jesus (Godinez) as prioress and appointed Anne of Jesus to no office of any kind, so that she took her place in the community as a simple sister. While the Choir-nuns were busy with their voting Sister Catherine of St. Albert was rapt in prayer, and saw in a vision a number of souls in a far distant country waiting for Mother Anne of Jesus, by whose means they were to be converted. The holy lay-sister told her late prioress what she had seen, but at the time Anne of Jesus did not attach much importance to it.

Several years after her death, however, Mother Beatrix of the Conception,[36] writing from Salamanca on 27th October 1641, says: "I have found two papers in the handwriting of our blessed Mother [Anne of Jesus]. The first, written in France, contains the following words: 'A year before the death of our Mother [St. Teresa] it was known that I should come into these parts.'" The account of Sister Catherine's vision is appended to a MS. copy of the history of the foundation of Granada, made by Father Diego de Guevara in 1585, together with that of a letter written by St. Louis Bertrand to St. Teresa in 1560, in which he tells her that, "before fifty years have passed [her] Order will be one of the most illustrious in the Church of God." This prophecy

---

[36] Beatrix de Zuniga.

is still in process of being fulfilled. In the late sixteenth and early seventeenth centuries Anne of Jesus was one of God's chief instruments in bringing it about.

For six months, July 1581 to January 1582, Anne lived in retirement at Veas. The nuns, with the willing consent of their young prioress, consulted the Servant of God, as before, on spiritual matters, and Mother Catherine of Jesus went to her frequently for comfort and advice. Outsiders also continued to call at the convent to ask help from the former prioress in their various needs. It happened that during this time a young girl named Juana Calancha presented herself as a postulant, asking to be received as a lay-sister. From her seventh year this poor girl had been tormented by the Evil One, but her pretended ecstasies and the wonders she worked had acquired for her the reputation of unusual sanctity. Even her confessor, and the Bishop of Jaen, by whom she was recommended to the nuns, had been deceived. Anne of Jesus, enlightened as to the state of Juana's soul, did all she could to prevent the nuns from giving her their votes, but all in vain. Father Gracian, whose permission had to be obtained before Juana could receive the habit, only consented unwillingly, and against his better judgment.

On the day of her clothing Mother Anne of Jesus called the young girl aside and asked if she was feeling happy. "I am perfectly at home," answered the novice, adding that while she was being dressed in the habit of Our Lady of Mount Carmel the Infant Jesus had clothed her in a rich mantle. That night after matins, while the nuns were in the choir, the new sister novice was suddenly raised into the air, as though rapt in ecstasy. On seeing her many of the community were moved to tears of devotion. Anne of Jesus was not present, having retired to her cell at the conclusion of the Office. An irresistible impulse of the Holy Spirit made her return in haste. She seized the would-be ecstatic by the feet and led her away, saying severely, "Sister, we have no need of your ecstasies here, but we want your help in washing the dishes."

As the same sort of phenomenon was repeated during the next day or two, Anne of Jesus counselled the young prioress to confine Juana in a cell next to her own, on the plea that her extraordinary gifts required complete solitude. The advice was followed. About eleven o'clock one night the prioress, while praying in her cell, distinctly heard the words, "Watch! it is time."

At midnight a great noise and incoherent voices were heard outside the window of the unhappy novice's cell. Sister Catherine took her little lamp and went to see what was the matter. As she opened the door she perceived a sickening odour and on advancing into the room she saw Juana in conversation with the Evil One, who fled at the prioress's approach. After saying a few words to the novice the distressed prioress went for comfort and counsel to Anne of Jesus. Together they decided to dismiss Juana, and sent word to her confessor that, as she had no vocation, he had better come and take her home. The next morning the decision was put into execution, and, not long after Juana's return to the world, she was examined by the Inquisition at Murcia and received a severe sentence. Happily this opened the poor girl's eyes. She entirely renounced her evil ways, and gave unmistakable evidence of her sincerity by undertaking a journey to Veas on purpose to thank Anne of Jesus for being instrumental in delivering her from the thraldom of Satan.

With regard to the newly-erected Province of the Reform matters were progressing very satisfactorily. Father Gracian, unable to cope with all the business himself, named two Vicars Provincial, whose authority was only valid in their respective districts whenever he himself was in the other. Father Diego of the Trinity was appointed to this office in Andalusia, and in the October of 1581, after visiting the Priory of the Martyrs at Granada, he proceeded to Veas to lay before Anne of Jesus a proposal for immediately founding the projected Carmelite Convent in the ancient Capital of the Moors. Influential citizens had promised help, he said, and the time for the foundation was ripe.

Although ninety years had passed since the capture of Granada in 1492 the city was still backward and poor, so that at first Anne of Jesus did not put much faith in Father Diego's assurances; moreover, as she herself says in her account of the foundation, she was sure that the Archbishop of Granada would not give permission for the founding of an unendowed convent, seeing that there were already a great many nuns there who had hardly enough to live on. However Father Diego recked little of such matters, and declared that the Licentiate Lacuna had promised abundant alms for the foundation of the convent, and that Father Gaspar de Salazar, S. J., who had corresponded with St. Teresa in 1577-78 about becoming a Discalced friar, had promised to obtain the Archbishop's permission. Urged by these repeated assurances, Anne of Jesus begged the community at Veas to pray that God would make known His Will in the matter, while she also recommended the whole affair to Him in earnest prayer. The result is best told in Anne's own words: "The Lord heard our prayers," she writes. "He gave me to understand that, though for a time human assistance and favour could not be relied on, the foundation must nevertheless be made as others had been, by putting trust in Divine Providence, and that He would have the house under His especial care, for He would be well served therein."

The holy prioress adds that these words were made

known to her one morning after Holy Communion, when, for more than three weeks, she had been resisting the persuasions of Father Diego, and that at the same moment all her hesitation vanished. She immediately called the portress, Sister Beatrix of St. Michael, saying: "Know that God wants this foundation at Granada to be made, so summon Father John of the Cross, in order that I may make known to him, as my confessor, what His Divine Majesty has revealed to me."

The saintly confessor came immediately, and when he had heard all Anne of Jesus had to tell he advised her to communicate with the Vicar Provincial. The very same day all preliminary arrangements were decided on. Father Diego was to return to Granada to look for a house suitable for the nuns, and Father John of the Cross was to set out at once for Avila with letters for Father Gracian and St. Teresa, who was begged to come in person to superintend the new foundation.

Father Diego gave an order to this effect written by his own hand, but Anne of Jesus could only have pleaded for it as a favour, for the foundation at Granada had been proposed many years previously, and St. Teresa had repeatedly told her coadjutrix that she would be the one to superintend it. In the early days at Veas, when Teresa and Anne were living together in closest intimacy, the latter often urged her Mother to send Mother Brianda of St. Joseph to found a Carmel in Madrid, but the saint would reply: "Do not weary yourself making plans for what will not come to pass. You will go to Granada, and after that you will make the foundation at Madrid. Have faith, and be assured that, from the latter, will spring many other foundations, where you will be able to exercise your courage and satisfy your zeal."

Yet in spite of this it is certain from St. Teresa's letters that she hoped to go to Madrid herself, and more than once was on the point of doing so when some unforeseen circumstance prevented it. It is, nevertheless, equally certain that the holy Foundress looked to Anne of Jesus for help in her arduous work. "See, my dear Sister Anne," she would say, "they call me Foundress, and I bear that name, but in reality the title belongs to you, and God is reserving you for important work." Sometimes, Anne of Jesus would write and tell the saint some good news about the progress of the Reform, then St. Teresa would say to the community she happened to be with at the time: "Anne, Anne, you do all the work, and I get all the credit." Yet in spite of the mutual love and trust of these two great souls the foundation at Granada was to bring a last purification of the affections for the one, and perhaps the bitterest cross of her life for the other.

St. John of the Cross left Veas for Avila 13th November 1581, the very day Anne of Jesus had received the divine locution spoken of above. This was the first time he had been to that city since his imprisonment, so it is easy to imagine what a welcome he received. By the 28th of the same month Father Gracian's sanction had been obtained, and St. Teresa was speeding St. John of the Cross on his return journey. That same evening she wrote to Seville asking Mother Mary of St. Joseph to send two nuns from her community to Granada, adding: "and I trust you not to choose the worst."

It was just at this time that the Saint had undertaken to go to Burgos where another new foundation had been promised. According to her custom the Foundress consulted God in prayer to find out which of the two houses should be begun first. "My daughter Teresa," was the answer, "let both foundations be made. Send someone to Granada in your name; the work there will easily be accomplished. Go yourself without delay to Burgos." Though Father Gracian had urged the saint to go to Granada he must have left her complete freedom of action, for she wrote to him on 30th November telling him what arrangements she had made. It is in this letter that the first hint occurs of a misunderstanding between the holy Foundress and her coadjutrix, though the words of St. Teresa prove that she had perfect trust in the obedience of her saintly daughter. At Villanueva there were more lay-sisters than were needed, five to be precise, and the prioress had written to St. Teresa proposing that two should be sent to Granada. The Saint agreed, and laid the matter before Father Gracian. "The prioress of Villanueva is right," she says, "and it is well to have them [the two lay-sisters] as the foundation at Granada is so promising. But she further adds: "Anne of Jesus will not like it, as she wished to control everything herself. If you approve, will you be firm about the matter, for no better nuns could be found."

For the moment all went well, and St. John of the Cross bore back with him to Andalusia all the necessary documents for the opening of a new Carmel, besides affectionate letters from St. Teresa. Later on, when Father Gracian put Anne of Jesus under obedience to add to the Saint's Book of Foundations the history of that of Granada, the Servant of God wrote: "To see myself at a foundation without my holy Mother seemed absolutely impossible, and I could not bear to think of it. You can imagine what I felt, therefore, when, on the Feast of the Conception of the Blessed Virgin, I saw the nuns arrive at Veas without her. They brought me a letter from her in which she said she would have come solely for the sake of giving me pleasure, had she been free, but that our Great God wished something else of her; and, as to the rest, she was quite sure that all would go well at Granada, and that the divine Master would let me feel His powerful help."

The nuns who accompanied St. John of the Cross on his return journey were Mother Mary of Christ, who had shortly before resigned the office of prioress at Avila in favour of St. Teresa, Sister Antonia of the Holy Ghost from the same community, and Mother Beatrix of Jesus, St. Teresa's niece, from Toledo. When Saint John had been pleading with the Saint to accompany him herself, she not only told him of Our Lord's command that she should go to Burgos, but added: "Besides, the success of the undertaking is as safe in the hands of Anne of Jesus as it is in mine. Where she is, my presence is not at all necessary." The holy friar shared the Foundress's high opinion of her coadjutrix, for at the time he was Anne's confessor, and his estimate of her has been preserved: "Anne of Jesus," he used to say, "resembles Teresa in everything; she has the same spirit of prayer, the same capabilities, the same method of government."

Thus heartened by the trust of her beloved Mother, and encouraged by St. John of the Cross, Anne of Jesus wrote to Father Diego, who was at Granada, asking him to press forward the arrangements for the new convent. But his task had been no easy one, nor did the many offers of assistance materialise. Worst of all, the archbishop refused permission for the foundation, declaring that his diocese was so poor that he would like to close the convents already existing, and that nothing would induce him to sanction the opening of a new one. Strangely enough, this refusal was ignored by Father Diego, and two influential citizens of Granada, Don Luis Mercado and the Licentiate Lacuna, persuaded a third, whose name is not given, to let his house to the nuns. "It does not take much to support ten religious," Anne of Jesus had written, and she and the sisters were eagerly awaiting the summons to set out.

Matters stood thus on 13th January 1582. That evening

THE FOUNDATION AT GRANADA 109

Anne went, at the usual hour, to make her prayer, her subject being the words of Our Lord to St. John the Baptist: "For so it becometh us to fulfil all justice" (St. Matt. iii, 15). Suddenly, while she was in deep recollection a terrible noise arose, heard, apparently, only by herself. "It is the devil," she thought; "the order for our departure must have arrived." The disturbance grew to such a pitch that the Servant of God seemed about to faint. The young prioress, who saw that something unusual was happening, was about to send for a restorative, when Anne of Jesus made a sign that she was not ill, but that a sister had better go down to the Turn. Sure enough, there was a courier from Granada, and no sooner had he handed in the letters from Father Diego than a terrific storm burst over Veas, and Anne of Jesus was suddenly taken ill. It was Saturday, and the dispatches bade the nuns leave for Granada on the following Monday. All Sunday Anne lay ill and suffering; she could not even go to Holy Mass, though her cell was next to the choir. However, she would not let the preparations be interrupted, and by three a.m. on Monday she and her companions were actually on their way. That evening a halt was made at Dayfuentes, and Father Peter of the Angels and St. John of the Cross, who accompanied the nuns, took counsel with Anne of Jesus regarding the best means of overcoming the reluctance of the Archbishop of Granada to receive them. It was decided to send St. John on beforehand to ask for the required licence.

His Grace, Don Juan Mendez de Salvatierra, received the Saint very badly, and he returned to Dayfuentes without having accomplished his purpose. During the night a terrific thunder-storm occurred, and, as the travellers learned afterwards, the prelate's house was struck by lightning, part of his library burnt and several of his mules killed in an adjacent stable. The archbishop was so terrified at a phenomenon unheard of at that time of the year, that he took it to be a supernatural warning, and two days later authorised in writing the foundation of the new Carmel. But this did not end the trouble, for that same day the landlord, learning for the first time that his house had been rented for a convent, absolutely refused to allow the nuns to enter it. Father Diego was in great distress. Every hour brought the Carmelites nearer to Granada, and they would find no roof to cover them after their long and tiring journey through the cold and wet. Finally Don Luis de Mercado persuaded his widowed sister, Ana de Peñalosa, to set aside some rooms in her house for the use of the nuns and to arrange a little oratory where the Blessed Sacrament could be reserved.

In order to keep their arrival secret the little caravan came into Granada at three o'clock in the morning of 20th January, the feast of SS. Fabian and Sebastian. Aña de Peñalosa was awaiting them at her door, and all went at once to the little chapel, where Anne of Jesus intoned the "*Laudate Dominum.*" Although Father Diego and the other priests would have had the bell rung, and Mass said at once, Anne of Jesus begged them to desist until formal leave had been obtained. Towards seven a.m., in answer to a letter she had dispatched to His Grace, telling him of their arrival and begging leave to have Mass, etc., the archbishop sent his vicar-general, Antonio Barba, to welcome the nuns and grant all their requests. The vicar-general then celebrated High Mass, St. John of the Cross being deacon, and Father Peter of the Angels subdeacon. During the day many visitors thronged the new convent, declaring that the nuns were saints, and that God had visited their country in sending Carmelites there.

God had, indeed, watched over the nuns during their journey, which was not accomplished without several narrow escapes, and as the travellers drove through

Guardahortuna, a suburb of Granada, Anne of Jesus said to her companions, "We have a sister here." Later on a postulant entered from that district. For the first six or seven months the nuns lived in great poverty, and were very much cramped for room, so that, although as many as two hundred young girls presented themselves as postulants, not one could be received. Sometimes the little community even lacked food. The townspeople, under the impression that Aña de Peñalosa supplied all that was needed, gave very little in the way of alms, so that they had not sufficient beds and coverlets to go round, and used to take their rest in turns, some sleeping on mats in the choir while the others were in bed. But as all these privations were borne silently, and Aña de Peñalosa always saw the nuns with smiling faces (as she was "temporal" foundress they lifted their long veils while conversing with her), the kind lady never guessed the straits in which her guests lived. Still more carefully were their needs hidden from their many illustrious visitors and the distinguished ecclesiastics who came, unsolicited, to preach in their little chapel. Among the latter was the rector of the Jesuits, who used to say: "I need no books for my instruction. My conversation with Mother Anne of Jesus is enough."

On account of the poverty of the community and the lack of sufficient accommodation, Anne of Jesus, with the consent of Father Diego and St. John of the Cross, sent back the two lay-sisters who had come from Villanueva, and wrote to Mother Mary of St. Joseph about sending back the two choir nuns from Seville. The lay-sisters were dismissed without St. Teresa's permission, the harassed prioress of Granada having sent off a long letter to her holy Mother, explaining the difficulties she was in, and begging that Father Gracian might come to Granada to put matters on a better footing. The letter, so far as is known, is no longer extant, but the overburdened prioress must have complained to the Saint, that the letters she received from the Provincial were not properly addressed. When one is in "a peck of trouble," as was the case at Granada just then, even trifles seem unbearable. But the holy Foundress, when she thought fit, could hide her kindness under severity, and she answered her daughter by one of those "terrible letters" which made her faulty correspondents tremble, though their Mother's admonition left no bitterness. The vigour of its reprimands, and the perfect freedom with which it is penned, show "the confidence that St. Teresa had," as one of her daughters of today puts it, "in the humility and obedience of Mother Anne of Jesus. It is a saint's letter to another saint."

St. Teresa wrote from Burgos, 30th May 1582, and addressed her letter to the whole community at Granada, though parts of it apply only to the prioress. A few extracts must suffice here:

"Jesus!

"May the holy Spirit be with your Reverences!

"I am amused at the outcry you are all making against our Father Provincial, while at the same time you have neglected to acquaint him with how things are going on at Granada, since the one letter in which you told him the foundation had been made. You have treated me in the same way. . . News came in a letter from the Prioress of Seville that you had bought a house costing 12,000 ducats.[37] As you are so prosperous it does not matter much that your patents are so restricted. But you are so clever at Granada in evading obedience that I feel greatly hurt, for your behaviour will seem bad to the whole Order, and

---

[37] Perhaps this refers to the first house proposed, the negotiations for which fell through. The nuns did not obtain a permanent lodging till August 1582.

such liberties may become the custom, for the prioresses will always be able to find some excuse.

"Knowing the circumstances of these gentlemen, it was most indiscreet of your Reverence to take so large a party to their house. Then, when these poor little things[38] had hardly arrived, you sent them back at once. I do not know how you had the heart to do it... Knowing that you would have no house of your own, you should not have brought the nuns from Veas... The affair has been mismanaged from the first. Our Father... must have been at Villanueva when those poor sisters returned. I am deeply grieved by the thought of his pain and humiliation. You might have sent them to Veas until you had consulted our Father, for you had no permission to restore them to their own community, since by his order, they belonged to your own. Yet you put them back under his very eyes! You alone are to blame, as you did not tell our Father whom you were taking from Veas, or whether you had any lay-sisters, and made no more account of him than if he had not been your Superior. It is so desirable that the Veas nuns return there that, did I not fear giving you occasion of offending God by disobedience, I should send you a formal order to dismiss them, for, as regards the Discalced nuns, I represent the authority of Father Provincial."

The letter goes on to reproach Anne of Jesus for showing partiality towards the nuns from Veas, and concludes with an admonition regarding detachment, and indifference to titles of respect.

To properly understand this incident in the life of the Venerable Mother, it must be remembered that regular exchange of correspondence between Granada and Burgos was impossible in winter. At least three months would have elapsed before a letter sent from either city could be

---

[38] The two lay-sisters from Villanueva.

answered from the other, and in the case of Father Gracian there was the further difficulty that he was constantly moving from place to place preaching, and letters might very easily have failed to reach him.

Anne of Jesus fulfilled her holy Mother's injunction of letting the letter be read by the Mother Subprioress and Saint John of the Cross. The latter was aware that Anne had acted under the personal advice and supervision of Father Diego of the Trinity, her Vicar-Provincial. The saint had a very high opinion of Anne of Jesus. He used to speak of her as "a seraph of love and prayer," and formally declared that the work of the foundation at Granada had been well done.

Moreover, Saint Teresa at the moment of her death was allowed by God to visit her faithful daughter in Granada, on which occasion she entrusted her with several admonitions for other Convents of the Reform. It was also during the early days at Granada that God favoured not only the prioress, but the other nuns with unusual consolations whenever they were in the Presence of the Blessed Sacrament.

"May God make my Discalced nuns very humble, and obedient and submissive," the Saint had written, and Anne of Jesus would have been the first in eagerness to attain this ideal.

The Abbe de Montis, who wrote a life of the Servant of God in 1788, at the request of Mme. Louise de France, then a Discalced Carmelite in the Convent of St. Denis, near Paris, refers to the omission of St. Teresa's letter of 30th May 1582 in the life of Venerable Mother Anne of Jesus by Manriquez (1631), calling it an "error of judgment."

> "The saints, and even the greatest saints," he says, "are not saints in the eyes of the Church because they never committed any fault, but because they humbly acknowledged their faults, because they wept over them, and detested them before the Lord, however small they

were, with as much sorrow as if they had been enormous crimes, and because they made use of these same faults as warnings, in consequence of which they watched over themselves more closely, and advanced by that means with greater fervour in the way of perfection."

Perhaps the Saint's own words to Mother Mary of St. Joseph on an earlier occasion may help to explain her severity towards her coadjutrix: "The misfortune is that the more I love, the less can I put up with any fault."[39]

---

[39] A letter written by Mother Magdalen of the Holy Ghost, the year after Anne of Jesus died, throws some further light on this painful incident. "The religious who arrived for the foundation of Granada," she says, "lodged in the house of Don Luis de Mercado, and Doña Aña de Peñalosa, his sister. It was a year of great drought. Needs were many, privations numerous. Upon this, came two old lay-sisters sent by the Prelate [Father Gracian] from Villanueva de la Jara. Our holy Mother [Anne of Jesus] judging that an increase of two unnecessary persons would inconvenience our hosts, did not allow these sisters to enter [the enclosure] at Granada, but begged those who had brought them to take them back to Villanueva. This measure brought our holy Mother many reproaches and scoldings. Nevertheless, the superior and others judged that, considering the state of affairs, she had acted very prudently. Our Mother St. Teresa thought the same, and that the decision had been well made."
It is not known where the information contained in the concluding sentence was obtained.

THE CARMEL AT GRANADA
BACK OF HOUSE, SHOWING ORANGE-TREE UNDER WHICH
ST. JOHN OF THE CROSS USED TO PASS; AND CHAPEL,
SHOWING STATUE CARVED BY HIM

CHAPTER X

LIFE AT GRANADA

August 1582 to 1586

IN SPITE of the poverty of the first beginnings at Granada, Anne of Jesus herself left it on record that she received supernatural assurance that "nothing would be wanting." Our Lord made this known to her while she was pondering the words of Ps. 90: "He shall overshadow thee with his shoulders, and under his wings thou shalt trust." Writing four years later, the venerable Mother bears witness to the influence for good which emanated from the Carmel of Granada, and then goes on to say:

> "To the favours already mentioned which Our Lord granted to us, He added another, greater than all the rest—we felt sensibly that He kept us company in the most Blessed Sacrament of the Altar, and this feeling was so strong, that it made His Presence almost palpable. We all experienced the same sweet consolation, and it was so ordinary an occurrence, that we spoke familiarly of it to one another. We used to say that never, in any other place, had the Blessed Sacrament produced the same effect. This intimate sense of the Presence of our Divine Spouse amongst us dates from the very moment when He was enclosed in our tabernacle. It lasts still for several of us, even as I write, though the feeling is not so strong as it was during the first seven months."

In August 1582 Father Gracian arrived at Granada, and when he saw the cramped quarters occupied by the nuns he at once set about finding them a house of their own. He succeeded in renting one from Don Alfonso de Granada y Alarçon, which was not very convenient, but more so than the few rooms lent them by Aña de Peñalosa. That good lady continued to help the nuns by constant alms, and God rewarded her generosity by raising her to a high state of prayer. "One day, when Mother Anne was profoundly recollected in prayer," writes Mother Teresa of Jesus (Princess of Croy, then a Carmelite at Brussels), "she saw in God two persons who were very dear to her, Father John of the Cross and Aña de Peñalosa. In her astonishment she cried out, 'How can this be, Lord?' and He answered, 'Those whom thou lovest in Me, thou wilt find in Me.'"

Shortly after the nuns had removed into their new house the prioress became dangerously ill. The doctors despaired of saving her life, and so violent were the attacks of her malady that her confessor, St. John of the Cross, had to stay in the convent all night, waiting to administer Holy Viaticum. As soon as Anne of Jesus had received Our Lord she begged to be left entirely alone. It was the night of 4th October 1582 and hardly had the sisters retired, when the dying prioress saw beside her bed a religious clothed in the Carmelite habit, but so surrounded with glory that her features could not be clearly distinguished. Writing afterwards of what took place, Anne says:

> "On looking at her more attentively I said to myself, 'I know this nun.' She, on her part, smiled and drew nearer to me. But the nearer she came, the less could I make out her features, because the brilliant light which came from her whole person prevented me from seeing her clearly. It was especially bright across her forehead. As I gazed upon her, there came into my heart a great love and esteem of our holy vocation, and a great appreciation of even its tiniest details. I understood the value which each small regulation contains. An ardent desire took hold of me to tell all the sisters how small a thing it would be to give one's life for the safeguarding of the least of our observances and of the great glory in

store for us if we are faithful to them."

Though Anne of Jesus did not know it, her blessed Mother, then at Alba, had that very hour passed to the embrace of her Divine Spouse, and at the moment of her death had come to console and cure her faithful daughter. When the vision ceased, Anne summoned the two sisters who had come to Granada from Avila and told them what had taken place, adding "No doubt Our Lord is about to call me to Himself. That is why I tell you this, so that you may be obliged to esteem, and see faithfully practised, what gives so much glory to God and wins for us so great a reward." She then asked that Father John of the Cross might be sent to her, as she desired to tell him of her vision and consult him about certain abuses which had been made known to her by her heavenly visitor. The holy prior did as he was requested, and very soon letters were dispatched to certain Carmels, where some indiscreet devotions had been adopted, which were dropped at once when the holy friar's letters were received. The next morning Anne of Jesus found herself better, much to the astonishment of the doctors who had attended her, and a few days later she was able to get up. The sequel will be best given in her own words.

> "I was beginning to get up," she writes, "when we received the news that God had called our holy Mother to Himself. At once I understood that it was she who had appeared to me, but my sorrow was so great I could not go on reading the letter that had been sent to me. All at once my understanding was penetrated with the words: 'The Church did not cease to exist when St. Peter and Paul were martyred, neither will our Order now come to an end. On the contrary, it will spread even more than before, because I shall be able to help you better from heaven.'
>
> "Thereupon my soul became profoundly recollected, and I was so much comforted and encouraged that I

consoled all our sisters by what I was able to tell them."

The prioress sent word of her recovery to Salamanca, but without mentioning that her cure was due to the intercession of her holy Mother. "Thanks be to God," she wrote, "I am very well. I enjoy much better health and have fewer cares, for His Divine Majesty does all in this house."

From this time till her death St. Teresa often visited her faithful daughter, and all that Anne of Jesus undertook was done at her bidding and under her guidance and protection, while each year brought her some special favour on 15th October.[40]

Already at Granada many young girls of the best families were waiting for admission. Six received the habit with the usual solemnities, and the ceremony caused a great stir throughout the city. It happened that both the parents of the first to be received, Sister Mariana of Jesus, died shortly after their daughter's clothing. Rumour asserted that grief had caused their death, and in consequence several families forbade their daughters even to visit the nuns. Those who were received, however, were as happy as the day is long, and four of the first six lived to give juridical testimony concerning the heroic virtue of their beloved prioress. One of them relates her zeal for correcting faults, even exterior ones such as raising the voice too much at recreation. Another tells how these admonitions left no sting behind, since it was plain to see that the holy Mother spoke from a heart filled only with divine love. At recreation time the conversation turned often on prayer, and one day when all the community were together, their prioress was rapt in ecstasy. "We were struck with admiration," writes an eye-

---

[40] It is to be noted that the year St. Teresa died was the very year of the reform of the calendar, so that the day after October 4th was reckoned as the 15th. Hence the Saint's feast is now kept on October 15th.

witness, "on seeing her countenance glowing with a heavenly radiance." After a short interval, turning to Mother Mary of Christ, who was subprioress and mistress of novices, she said: "I have just been recommending our dear novices to Our Lord, and asking Him to make them great and holy religious, and He deigned to reply: 'Do thou mould them into shape, then I will gild them!' Oh, how much those words have consoled me."

As at Veas, so at Granada, Anne of Jesus had the gift of prophecy and of healing. She often spoke to the nuns of what was passing in their hearts. To a young girl who was about to get married she declared it was God's will that the engagement should be broken off, so that she might become a Carmelite. The girl entered Carmel, and her intended husband found another bride, but hardly had the marriage taken place than he fell ill and died.

A more pleasing incident than this gives at the same time a glimpse of the interior of a Carmelite noviceship. While the six novices already mentioned were together, it chanced that Anne of Jesus had to keep her bed.

> "In order to give her a little amusement," says one of them, "our Mistress told us to prepare a little feast. As it happened to be St. Hilarion's Day 21st October, to whom our venerable Mother had a great devotion, we thought we would get up a procession of hermits going to visit the saint in a hermitage, which we had contrived near our Mother Prioress's bed. One of the novices represented St. Hilarion, and we dressed her up as an ancient solitary, with a long beard made of hemp. Just as we reached the hermitage the candle which one of the novices was holding in her hand set fire to the hermit's beard, and in spite of our haste to put it out, the flames scorched the sister's cheeks and burnt off her eyelashes and eyebrows. We were all dreadfully distressed, for, the very next day, that particular novice had to go outside the enclosure for

the examination [a canonical formality previous to her profession], and all her family had already come to Granada from Lucena for the occasion. Our holy Mother, seeing us in such consternation, sat up in bed as well as she could and said, 'Do not be distressed, dear children, for God will come to our aid. Let Sister Catherine (the novice who had personated Saint Hilarion) come to me, and someone go for a little honey.' While one of us ran for the honey, our Mother took the novice's head in her hands. That instant all traces of burn disappeared, and Sister Catherine's face seemed even more beautiful than it had been before the accident. She was able to attend the canonical examination next day, and we all saw in the event a miracle which God had been pleased to work through His faithful servant."

Nor was Catherine the only novice favoured in this way. Another of the six became very ill; every moment was expected to be her last. The infirmarian had already sent to the woollen vestry for a habit in which the dying novice was to be buried. Instead of giving what was asked for, the sister in charge went in haste to Anne of Jesus. "Mother," she said, "why is your Reverence letting this novice die?" The prioress looked up with a smile, "So you think that is in my power, do you?" "Yes, Mother." "Very well, let us go to her." Arrived at the bedside of the sick novice, the venerable Mother bent over her, saying, "See, dear sister, they are asking me why I let you die, and urging me to restore your health. That is what I have come for." Then she gently stroked the invalid with her hands, and in a short time the crisis passed and she began to recover. As soon as the novice was strong enough she was admitted to profession, "after which," the narrative concludes, she lived more than twenty years in religion, and died a great saint."

Such happenings as these were frequent at Granada, but, on the other hand, the devil did his utmost to disturb the nuns, and turn them away from the pursuit of perfection. Many a time Anne of Jesus made aware of this, came to the help of her sisters. Once while she was talking to a nun on spiritual subjects she saw the devil circling round her head under the form of a ball of fire. The young sister, half dead with fright and with the struggle against temptation going on in her soul, threw herself into the arms of the prioress, who instantly soothed her and told her not to be afraid. At the same moment the devil departed, leaving behind him an intolerable stench. Another time, about eleven p.m., while Matins was being recited, a violent and prolonged knocking was heard at the convent gate. The portress got up to go downstairs, but Anne of Jesus signed to her to stay. The knocking continued, and some of the nuns, in their fear, looked round towards their prioress and were horrified to see a viper coiled up in the middle of the choir. "Go on quietly with the Divine Office," the holy prioress said, at the same time making a sign to one whom she could trust to take the creature up and cast it out of the window. The sister obeyed at once, and "the devil," so the old chronicle runs, "furious at being treated with such contempt, vented his rage on the Turn so violently, that it sounded as if it would be broken to pieces."

After living about ten months in the house procured by Father Gracian the prioress was desirous of obtaining a freehold property, where a proper convent could be established. It was St. Teresa herself who obtained this home for her daughters. Anne relates the whole transaction as follows:

> "After the death of our Mother, Teresa of Jesus, they sent to me at Granada a portion of the sheet on which she was lying when she breathed her last sigh, as well as pieces of her veil and tuck. They were all stained and scented with the oil which still flows from her sacred body. As I knew our Mother so intimately, I treasured

these precious objects with great devotion. About this time the Duchess of Sesa wrote to me from Baéna to say that her eldest son, Don Juan de Guzman, whose wife was the Marchioness of Ardales, had been given up by the doctors, and was reduced to the last extremity. She despatched a messenger to me in great haste, in order that we might all pray for the sick man. I was so touched at the poor lady's distress, that I at once asked our holy Mother to help us to obtain a complete cure. At the same moment I felt inspired to send some of the relics I had just received, so that they might be placed on the invalid, yet I durst not do this without consulting the Father Rector of the Jesuits, who was then my confessor. It was only a short time after our Mother's death, and no one, as yet, had had recourse to our relics, and she was almost unknown.[41] The Rector, Father John Jerome [Ripalda] answered that I ought to send the relic as soon as possible. It was a small portion of our Mother's habit, and I slipped it into my letter to the duchess. As soon as it was placed upon the young man he was miraculously cured, as they hastened to write and tell me.

"These ladies professed so great gratitude towards us that they offered to give us, free of cost, the premises belonging to them which the Grand Master had formerly. occupied in Granada, in order that we might build our convent there. Their pious design could not be immediately realised, on account of certain lawsuits which were pending, but some time afterwards we were able to take possession of the buildings on the payment of a small sum of money, which was to be made over to Don Luis de Córdoba."

The Grand Master here referred to was the famous Gonsalvo de Cordoba, known as "El Gran Capitań," who

---

[41] St. Teresa's chief work had been in Castile. Anne of Jesus was speaking of Andalusia.

drove the Moors from Granada in 1452.[42] His house was in a central position, opposite the Franciscan friary in the Calle San Matias. Its windows command magnificent views of the neighbouring country, and from one of the terraces the "Desert" of The Martyrs can be seen.

The Carmelites at Granada still live in the Grand Master's House, but their church was not built in the lifetime of Anne of Jesus. The nuns reverently preserve the little parlour and grate used by the venerable Mother and her first companions, as well as the narrow corkscrew stairs, up which St. John of the Cross used to climb when he went to visit the nuns, or to take them a few sardines, to eke out their scanty provisions. At that time there was only a temporary chapel dedicated to St. Peter, where St. John of the Cross often said Mass. He was clever with his hands and made a large statue of the Infant Jesus, which he gave to the prioress, who placed it in the middle of the altar. It is of gilded wood, the right hand being raised in blessing, the little finger apart, as if asking something. The saint often used to say to the nuns. "Do you know that He is saying to you with His little finger, 'O soul, give Me thy heart?'" Today the Carmel of Granada is one of the finest and most spacious in Spain.[43] Beside the entrance is a carving in white marble of the workshop at Nazareth, with the inscription

---

[42] Don Gonsalvo de Córdoba married Doña Maria Manriquez, and was commander-in-chief of the armies of Isabella of Castile. When he was campaigning in Italy two brothers of St. Ignatius Loyola fought under him and lost their lives. During the siege of Granada the Queen's tent caught fire and her entire wardrobe was consumed. Don Gonsalvo sent to Córdoba for Doña Maria's trousseau to replace it.

[43] This paragraph was written before the disturbances of 1931.

"*Erat subditus illis.*"[44] The fine church was built by Mother Louise of St. Joseph, who died in 1638, but it suffered devastation during the revolution of 1836, and its only remarkable treasure to-day is a series of pictures, probably by Alonso Cano, representing scenes from the life of St. Teresa, and evidently suggested by the prints executed in Antwerp in 1613, under the direction of Anne of Jesus.

Soon after her daughters were settled in their new home St. Teresa gave them unmistakable marks of her love and protection. On the Feast of St. Joseph, 1583, the sisters were all assembled in the choir when they heard the whirr of wings, as though a dove was flying about the chapel, and then a clapping of hands. In the latter Anne of Jesus recognised a familiar action of her holy Mother. She reminded the nuns of this, and they exclaimed: "As tomorrow is the Feast of our Father St. Joseph, our holy Mother has come to invite us to recollection," and when the time came they went to bed happy in that thought. But their prioress felt certain that there was something more than this, so she sent a message to the sacristan, bidding him search the chapel to see if any stranger was hidden there. No one was to be found. Finally Anne of Jesus sent him to try the door, and to his astonishment he found it closed, but not locked. A miller who frequently came to the convent had brought the keys to the turn that evening, saying that he had locked the door. He had meant to return, no doubt, and secure some of the rich ornaments put out for the feast, but the nuns never saw him again.

Many other favours were worked for the nuns or their friends by St. Teresa, but only one or two can be recorded here. It happened that the bubonic plague was raging at Granada, and two lay-brothers of the Monastery of the

---

[44] "He was subject to them." -Editor.

Martyrs died of it. Within a week their prior, St. John of the Cross, was stricken down by the same malady while actually saying Mass at the convent.

He was too ill to go back to the sacristy, and a mattress had to be brought, on which he was carried to the outquarters.[45] Anne of Jesus and her community stormed heaven for the life of so valued a father and friend, and a relic of St. Teresa having been sent to him, he was instantaneously cured at its first application and able to return to his monastery.

The Servant of God herself was the next victim. She retired to her cell, giving orders that no one was to come in to attend her. Two of the older sisters, disregarding this injunction, went in to her carrying a relic of their holy Mother, which they applied to a large and much inflamed tumour, the first symptom of the dreaded plague. Shortly afterwards the prioress fell into a peaceful sleep, from which she awoke perfectly cured.

It was while Anne of Jesus was at Granada that St. John of the Cross completed his explanation of the Spiritual Canticle, dedicating it to her.

His manuscript bears the title:

> "Explanation of stanzas treating of the exercise of love between the soul and Jesus Christ, its Spouse, dealing with, and commenting on certain points and effects of prayer, written at the request of Mother Anne of Jesus, Prioress of the Discalced Carmelite Nuns of St. Joseph's Convent, Granada, 1584."

The Spiritual Canticle represents the soul as pursuing her Beloved, Who, after wounding her with His love, abandons her in order that she may herself seek Him.

"Where hast Thou hidden Thyself

---

[45] Rooms outside the enclosure occupied by laymen who served the nuns as sacristan, porter, etc.

> And abandoned me in my groaning, O my Beloved?
> Thou hast fled like the hart,
> Having wounded me.
> I ran after Thee, crying, but Thou wert gone."

It is a high testimony to the elevated state of prayer bestowed by God on Anne of Jesus that St. John of the Cross did not hesitate to dedicate to her a treatise so mystical and sublime. In the editions of the Spiritual Canticle published between the years 1627 and 1909 part of St. John's words were omitted. After saying that he is passing over the more ordinary states of prayer, the Saint adds:

> "This I do for two reasons. . . the second is that I am addressing myself to your Reverence, at your own bidding, for you have received from Our Lord the grace of being led on from the elementary state, and led inwards to the bosom of Divine Love." And again a little farther on, ". . . though your Reverence is ignorant of scholastic theology you are by no means ignorant of mystical theology, the Science of love . . ."

It was largely due to the encouragement unfailingly given her by St. John of the Cross that Anne of Jesus laboured so unceasingly to obtain the publication of St. Teresa's writings.

When speaking in the Spiritual Canticle of raptures and ecstasies, St. John dismisses them with a few words, saying, ". . . I do this the more readily because our Mother, blessed Teresa of Jesus, has written admirably on this matter, whose writings I hope to see published soon." Part of Anne's work at Granada was seeing St. Teresa's works prepared for the press. The Constitutions were printed in the Saint's lifetime, towards the end of 1581, but her other works did not appear until 1585. A letter written by Anne of Jesus 9th September 1584 to her cousin, Mary Angel, at Salamanca gives us a glimpse of the prioress's life. "I am very busy these days, my dear Sister," she writes, "with professions, the purchase of houses, and the getting together of a sum of money which must be paid in cash in order to avoid a hundred and one annoyances that I fear will befall us from this Don Luis de Cordoba, who is another Pedro de la Vanda for his melancholy humour... The sisters at Veas have shown how simple they are in electing me lately as their prioress, seeing that I can hardly get through my work here at Granada..."

The election referred to was not confirmed by the Provincial, but in 1585, when a foundation was to be made at Malaga, Anne of Jesus was named by her superiors as prioress of the new house. This time it was the authorities at Granada who intervened, for they had no mind to lose one who seemed so powerful with God. It was finally arranged that all should be superintended from Granada, and that Mother Mary of Christ should go as prioress to Malaga, accompanied by two sisters from Veas and two from Granada. One of the former was Sister Catherine Evangelist, who had been received after Anne of Jesus had left Veas, and contrary to her earnest advice. Warned supernaturally of trouble to come, the Servant of God would not have accepted Sister Catherine for Malaga, had not St. John of the Cross insisted on her doing so.

It seems to have been in 1585 that Anne of Jesus was again brought to death's door, this time by a mystical malady—the wound of divine Love. So violent were the transports that seized upon her when in prayer, that the bones of her chest became dislocated, and she could only lie on her bed in great pain. Once more St. Teresa appeared to her, and passing her hand over her chest, left her whole and well. Nevertheless, during these first years at Granada St. John of the Cross put Anne's devotion to a severe test. One day, after hearing her confession, he told her she was not to go to Holy Communion again until he gave her leave. The humble religious said nothing, and for the next two days knelt on in her place when the others went to Communion.

The nuns were puzzled, and with great simplicity asked their holy Mother if anything was amiss. "My daughters," she replied, "I do not receive Holy Communion because our Reverend Father Prior has forbidden me to do so." A few days later leave was given for her to resume her Communions, and she presented herself once more at the grate. But Anne's heart was beating so violently with joy in receiving her Lord once more, that it seemed to leave her body altogether in order to hide itself in that of her divine Spouse, to whom she had offered it as a place of rest. It is a well-attested fact that during the remaining forty years or so of her life the beating of her heart was imperceptible both to herself and to others.

Several who have recorded this prodigy heard of it from the lips of Anne of Jesus herself, and St. John of the Cross, to whom she gave a full account of what she had experienced, answered: "Do not be astonished at what has happened, my daughter. When little birds see the dawn breaking they exhaust themselves in singing the praises of their Maker. So has your heart spent itself, so great was your joy in receiving Him." On the first anniversary of the death of the holy prioress, in the panegyric preached before the whole court of Brussels, Father Francis de Vivero referred to this wonderful occurrence. He had himself spoken, he said, with two sisters who had lived in the close intimacy with Anne of Jesus, and they had more than once assured him that they had themselves often placed their hand over the left side of the Servant of God and had never felt the least pulsation from her heart. As Manriquez puts it: "If she had a heart, she no longer felt it . . . its pulsations were the pulsations of perpetual prayer."

Many another time during her years at Granada the saintly prioress was reduced almost to extremity by the ardour of her love of God. Doctors could do nothing to alleviate her, and when St. John of the Cross was called in his invariable answer was : "What do you expect ? Your Mother is ill with divine love." One of these crises occurred on Christmas Night, 1585. St. John of the Cross was hastily summoned by the anxious nuns, but the prioress bade them all proceed with the Midnight Office. When it was over she called the community to her cell, and assured the nuns that she was not going to die. Then she recited aloud some verses she had composed in honour of the Infant Jesus. They run as follows :

Show Thyself here, Beloved, I give Thee this heart of mine, Take what is Thine.	Sal aca fuera, Querido Daremoste el corazon, Y tu tomards posesion.
Show Thyself here, Beloved, Leave now Thy Mother's womb, From Thy Father's high throne in Heaven Come down to disperse our gloom.	Sal aca fuera, Querido, Ya del vientre de tu. Madre Abaj o de las alturas Que alli tienes con tu Padre.
Who so faileth to see Thee, His heart will not be Thine, At least, Lord, take mine.	Que no te entrega nadie Hasta verte, el corazon: Y tu tomaras posesion.

    Together with the gift of contemplative prayer God favoured his faithful Servant with the power of reading the future, and of knowing what was happening at a distance. The brother of one of the community, Don Diego Velasco, was struck down by a fit of apoplexy, and when the news reached the convent Anne of Jesus assembled all her nuns to pray for his recovery. She herself remained on in the choir long after the others, wrestling with God, as it were, to obtain this grace. At last she took hold of Sister Mary of the Cross's hand, and said: "Rejoice, your brother is safe. Our Lord has granted me this grace, but see what it has cost me!" A heavy perspiration bathed the holy Mother from head to foot, so intense and prolonged had been her supplication. Almost at the same moment messengers arrived to say that Don Diego had taken a turn for the better, and after a few days his health was completely restored.

Another day, during High Mass, when the words of the Credo—*cujus regni non erit finis*—were being chanted, Anne of Jesus raised her heart to God, saying: "O Lord, what joy Thy friend and servant, Teresa of Jesus, used to have whenever she heard these words." And as if in answer, she heard a voice within her soul reply: "Her praises, too, will have no end," words which gave her coadjutrix to understand that her beloved Mother would one day be canonised. This happy event took place about forty years later, on March 16th, 1622.

In the spring of 1586 Sister Catherine of Jesus, who had been re-elected prioress at Veas, when the superiors refused to confirm the election of Anne of Jesus, had been failing in health. As she felt unfit to fulfil her duties, she wrote to Granada, begging that some one might be appointed to replace her. "Die in peace, dear Mother," wrote Anne of Jesus in reply, "and do not worry about the future. God will provide." She was one of her first novices, and had a truly happy death. St. John of the Cross gave permission for Mass to be said in an oratory within the cloister, where she could assist at the Holy Sacrifice, and she had many other consolations, including a visit from St. Teresa. On the eve of her death she begged the nuns to sing St. John's Spiritual Canticle, and when they, in turn, begged for a last word of advice, the holy young prioress replied : "Die often during your lifetime, and then it will not be hard to die when the time comes." Spring is early in Spain, and the invalid kept constantly asking whether the trees were budding again. God had told her that He would call her to Himself when Nature clothed herself again in green. At last, on the Feast of St. Matthias, her birthday and profession day, her pure soul winged its flight to God.

This holy death was very consoling to Anne of Jesus, who had just passed through a heavy trial. A few months after the foundation at Malaga she had been suffering from a feeling of sadness and oppression which she could not shake off, and had written to Mother Catherine at Veas:

> "Pray much, my daughter, for the convent at Malaga. Some great misfortune threatens it... If our holy Father, John of the Cross, were here, I would ask him to go there. As he is a saint he might be able to hinder what the devil is doing."

Father John was away at Lisbon, attending a Provincial Chapter (May 1585), but even on his return he was unable to go to Malaga. Meantime Sister Catherine Evangelist ended by losing her reason, and flung herself headlong out of one of the windows of the convent. The shock, or the prayers of the venerable Servant of God, to whom this sad event seems to have been revealed beforehand, brought the poor sister to her senses. She received the Last Sacraments with every sign of devotion. Nor did the incident leave a bad impression on the inhabitants of Malaga, for within a very short time some desirable postulants presented themselves and were received. The demon, however, baulked of his prey, wreaked his vengeance on Anne of Jesus. Accompanied by other devils, Satan appeared to her one night under a terrifying form, crying out: "Here is the she-wolf, Aña de Lobera[46] who

---

[46] Lobera means relating to a wolf, from lobo, wolf.

torments us. Let us torment her in return." But the purehearted religious calmly replied, "For many years now I have borne the name 'de Jesus,' not 'de Lobera.' Why do you not give me my proper name—Anne of Jesus?' "That is a name we cannot speak or bear to hear," was the savage reply. "Every time it is pronounced our torments are renewed, and it is because you bear that name graven in your heart that we cannot do you as much harm as we should like." While saying this the demon seized upon the holy prioress, and lifting her up to the ceiling of her cell, threatened to let her drop. But Anne ceased not to call upon the Holy Name, so that the devils, deprived of all power over her, were forced to put her back upon her bed. Vanquished by the repeated aspiration, 'Jesus!' the enemy of souls at length retired, and then Our Lord Himself visited His faithful servant, bringing peace and joy.

Another miracle of 1585 was the famous one in which Anne of Jesus saw St. John of the Cross in danger and saved his life when he was travelling back to Granada from Lisbon. Her prayer for her spiritual Father had been so intense, that the wound in her chest reopened and some of her ribs were dislocated, but St. Teresa visited her that same night and cured her completely. Much later than this the holy prioress told Father Hilary of St. Augustine, that God allowed to St. John of the Cross and herself mutual knowledge of their interior graces and privileges, which they afterwards communicated one to the other, always finding their experiences to agree. Indeed, the venerable Mother had relations of a similar kind with other holy men and women, of which one or two examples must suffice. Among the novices received at Granada was Sister Juliana of the Mother of God, Father Gracian's sister. One day a rumour reached the Carmel that the Father Provincial was dead, and the whole community were plunged into grief, though none so deeply as Sister Juliana. Moved at the young sister's distress, Anne of Jesus had, as usual, recourse to prayer. After a few minutes she called Sister Juliana and assured her that her brother was not dead, but was actually, at the time she was speaking, saying Mass in a place which she named. Later on Father Gracian confirmed what the prioress had said. He told Anne of Jesus that St. Teresa had not left him unconsoled after her death. On the First Sunday of Lent, 1583, she had appeared to him and said: "We in heaven and you on earth must be united in purity and love; we in rejoicing, you in suffering. What we enjoy on high through the Vision of God you must strive to attain on earth through the most Blessed Sacrament. Tell all my daughters this." It has been seen that Anne of Jesus had a most ardent devotion to the Blessed Sacrament. Occasionally during her thanksgiving after Holy Communion an urgent message would be brought from the Governor of Granada or some other exalted personage, which the portress felt obliged to deliver at once. "Tell them not to trouble," the prioress would answer, "and that all will go well." When the persons concerned called afterwards at the convent to thank Anne of Jesus for her advice or prayer she often recollected nothing of what her visitor was referring to. Her message had been sent subconsciously, while her faculties were absorbed in prayer. Often she would gently reproach the portress for letting this happen: "God forgive you, Sister," she would say; "but I beg of you if ever I say anything foolish, do not go and repeat it at the turn, for then people would think that nuns do not speak the truth."

In the early days of the foundation Father Peter of the Angels, who had on his way to Rome in 1578 exchanged the Rule of the Discalced for that of the Mitigated, came to live in Granada. There he sold his white mantle, and Anne of Jesus out of respect for Our Lady's habit, sent the convent sacristan to buy it back. Moved by grief at the defection of one who had been prior at Calvario, and who had acted as confessor to the Carmelite nuns at Veas, she wrote Father Peter a letter, telling him of her sorrow at what he had done, and warning him that he would not long enjoy the finer habit in which he had clothed himself.

"The great affection I bore you," continued the holy prioress, "and which I still feel towards you, makes this change of yours affect me deeply. Alas! your eyes have been blinded to the great good which you have abandoned. Before acting you ought to have consulted Our Lord in prayer and asked counsel of those who loved you. But you would neither see nor listen to anyone. All that is left for you to do now is to recommend your soul to God's mercy."

This letter touched Father Peter so profoundly that he went up to the convent to see Anne of Jesus, meaning to speak to her of his spiritual state. But at her express desire he was refused admission, and though influential friends in Granada begged the prioress to relent, she only answered: "Let him take care never to set foot in our convent, for God may inflict a heavy punishment if he does."

This state of affairs grieved the now repentant friar deeply, and he wanted to be received back among the Discalced. One day on passing the Carmelite Church he noticed that the door was open, and he said to his companion: "Let us go in and pray." They did so, and Father Peter received so much light and grace, that the sorrow awakened in his heart for leaving the Reform caused him to shed such torrents of tears that he lost his eyesight. A few days later he died in admirable sentiments of patience and penitence. When Anne of Jesus heard what had happened she said to those who brought the news: "I knew what awaited him if he entered our convent, and that was why I refused to see him. Blessed be Our Lord, who has punished him in his body in order to spare his soul, for, after all, he was a great servant of God and a good religious."

After her election for a second time as prioress at Granada Anne of Jesus received several novices who, later on, became the glory of that Carmel and left precious testimony concerning the sanctity of the servant of God. One of these was Catherine of the Incarnation, who writes:

> "I never had the least intention of entering a Carmelite convent. Yet one eve of the Annunciation as I was praying in the Cathedral of Granada I felt suddenly inspired to consecrate myself to God in the Carmelite Order. So strong was my desire to do this that it seemed as if nothing on earth could prevent me. I kept my own counsel, however, about what I intended to do, until the very moment when I presented myself to be received. But what had happened in the interval?
>
> "Mother Anne of Jesus had assembled her chapter, proposed my admission and received the Sisters' votes. I was actually accepted before I had made known my intention of entering. Astonished and delighted, I thanked God for so unlooked for a grace, which I rightly regarded as miraculous, and due to the holiness and prayers of Mother Anne of Jesus. Never since the first moment I entered religion have I had the least temptation to regret what I have done."

Another novice was Doña Maria Machuca de Alfaro, daughter of a Licentiate of Granada, who was a member of the Royal Court of Chancery.[47] Maria was received in 1585, but was so delicate that when there was a question of admitting her to profession the nuns did not give her their votes. The Mistress of Novices, Mother Beatrix of St. Michael, was very distressed at this, for she recognised the

---

[47] Doña Maria was not able to bring the dowry usually asked, and it was of her that St. John of the Cross said to Anne of Jesus who hesitated about receiving her on account of the extreme poverty of the nuns: "Is it possible, Mother, to set aside such ardent desires and withhold this spouse from God for a matter of four reals more or less?" A Spanish real equalled about twopence halfpenny.

excellent qualities of Sister Mary of the Cross, for that was Maria's name in religion. Finally Mother Beatrix made up her mind to appeal to the prioress.

"Dear Mother," she said, "what is to be done? Why does not your Reverence tell this novice to get stronger? We shall lose her, if she does not get better soon, for the nuns want me to send her away." The venerable prioress only smiled at her vehemence, and said calmly: "Do not worry, Mother; the novice will get well. She will make her vows and will be as much a religious as I am."

The prophecy was amply fulfilled. Sister Mary of the Cross lived to earn her name. Her first grief was the departure of her beloved prioress for Madrid, which took place early in 1586. Seeing the poor novice bathed in tears at the thought of the coming separation, Anne of Jesus called her aside one day, saying: "Be brave, dear child, for God has many trials in store for you." Moreover, she promised to befriend Sister Mary of the Cross's brother, who wanted to join the Reform, but had been refused on account of weakness of sight. The venerable Mother spoke for him, and he entered later on at the Priory of St Hermenegild, in Madrid.

Sister Mary of the Cross made her vows in October 1586. She became Mistress of Novices at Granada, and was sent in 1595 to found a Carmel at Ubeda, where she died in the odour of sanctity in 1638. All her life she had had a most tender devotion to the Blessed Sacrament. When her infirmities prevented her from visiting Our Lord in the Tabernacle she one day complained of this to Our Lord, begging Him to enable her to do so. At that very moment she saw from her bed a large candle burning beside the altar with an unusually pure and radiant flame. As she was wondering how it came to be there, Our Lord said to her: "It is your soul. It shall burn constantly before Me as you wish, even when illness keeps you a prisoner and prevents your visiting Me."

Such were the daughters of St. Teresa received and trained by Anne of Jesus. Before she left Granada God granted her yet another favour. In the ancient palace of the Grand Master were several disused turrets, and Anne of Jesus was accustomed to retire to one of these in order to pray undisturbed. The room where she usually went faced what was called by tradition the "Holy Hill." Often, as the prioress knelt at her devotions, she was conscious of a sweet-perfumed breeze blowing gently towards her from the Holy Hill, though she could perceive nothing on it which could give rise to such an experience.

A few years later the relics of Christian martyrs, slain by the Moors, were discovered on the "Holy Hill," much to the consolation of the people of Granada. The nuns then recalled what Anne of Jesus had frequently told them of the sweet-smelling wind which had issued from that spot, and had no difficulty in believing that God had made known to His faithful servant the resting place of the relics of His saints.

CHAPTER XI

THE FOUNDATION AT MADRID

1586-1589

AFTER St. Teresa's death numerous miracles were worked through her intercession, and on 1st January 1586 a formal diocesan inquiry into the heroicity of her virtues was opened and her sacred remains exhumed. The body of the Foundress had been taken from Alba, where she died, to Avila. During the time that elapsed before its restoration to Alba three royal commissioners were sent to open her tomb—namely, Paul de Lacuna, who had been so active in the foundation at Granada, Francisco de Contreras, a member of the King's Council, and Diego de Yepes, afterwards Bishop of Tarazona and author of the first published life of the Saint. Twice already, since her death in 1582, had Teresa's body been examined. It was fragrant and incorrupt, and exuded a sweet-perfumed oil, which had been instrumental in working many cures. It was chiefly this marvel which occasioned the official investigation, which was carried out under the Bishop of Avila. When the commissioners' report reached Philip it soon spread farther, and Cardinal Quiroga, who had during her lifetime opposed St. Teresa's project of founding a convent in Madrid, now made it his business to obtain, not only Carmelite nuns, but a monastery of friars also. For this purpose the cardinal wrote to Father Nicholas Doria, who had succeeded Father Gracian as provincial. The proposal was accepted at once for both foundations, but the house for the friars was opened first. It was, at the king's request, dedicated to St. Hermenegild, a Spanish martyr in the Arian persecution, and was opened on 25th January, 1586. For the coming of the nuns a little more preparation was necessary. Father Nicholas wrote to St. John of the Cross and to Anne of Jesus at Granada, appointing the latter prioress of the new foundation and bidding her choose the sisters she thought best suited for the undertaking. St. John, as vicar-provincial, was to accompany the nuns with a suitable escort.

St. Teresa herself seemed to sanction the arrangements of her coadjutrix, for just at this time a letter of hers to Anne of Jesus, which had accidentally escaped being burnt according to the directions of the Saint, was discovered at Granada. It exhaled the same sweet perfume already associated with St. Teresa's virginal body, or her spiritual presence, and from it exuded such a quantity of fragrant oil, that it seemed, as Anne of Jesus wrote long afterwards, "as if the note paper had been recently soaked in oil." This precious letter was lovingly treasured at Granada, and was the instrument of many miraculous cures. It seems to have been written about 1579, for it contains words of encouragement to Anne of Jesus about Granada, and also a reference to Madrid, which runs: "The foundation of Granada ought to produce much good, but that of Madrid will be more important than all the rest."

About the middle of July, the nuns were ready to set out. Anne of Jesus took with her St. Teresa's niece, Beatrix of Jesus, and a lay-sister called Anne of Jesus. They were joined at Malagon by Sister Agnes of St. Augustine, and Sister Mary of Jesus, while from Toledo came Sister Guiomar of Jesus and Sister Mary of the Nativity, the last being appointed sub-prioress. Like a true daughter of St. Teresa, Anne of Jesus took with her only what was strictly necessary, together with a small tabernacle, a statue of Our Lady and a little handbell. She carried the bell herself, and rang it at all community hours, so that even during the journey religious exercises went on as usual. The distance from Granada to

Madrid is about 100 Spanish leagues, and the route lay over the same mountains and valleys which she had crossed in the opposite direction when travelling to Veas with her holy Mother eleven years previously. It is not known whether Anne of Jesus halted at Veas; her Mother's letter of 1582 had reproved her for undue attachment to the religious of that Convent, and perhaps her faithful loyalty kept her from calling there. At any rate, the first incident of importance chronicled about the journey occurred when they were near Malagon, and reads like a page from the life of St. Teresa herself.

The river Guadiana was in flood, owing to heavy summer rains. At the sight of the swollen waters the nuns wondered how they could get their wagon across. St. John of the Cross, who was on horseback, did not hesitate, however, to lead the way. The nuns could hardly believe their eyes as they watched his horse pick its way on the surface of the swirling waters. Not even were the fetlocks wet, as the nuns proved for themselves, when their own conveyance, following the Saint's lead, got safely across. Another halt was made at Toledo, a convent of poignant memories for Anne of Jesus, who had lived there with her holy Mother. On 6th September the travellers reached Illescas, famous for its shrine of Our Lady. A few hours more would have taken them into Madrid, but the nuns heard that a cavalcade of nobles and gentlemen was coming out to meet them, and waited until it was dark before going farther. That night, as soon as the nuns and their escort were on the open road, a brightness as great as that of noon shone round about them, while a delicious perfume enveloped them as they went along. It was Saint Teresa, making her presence felt in this mysterious way, though only St. John of the Cross and Anne of Jesus were privileged to see her. Some of the nuns were genuinely alarmed, but their prioress soon comforted them. "Do not be astonished, daughters, at what is happening," she said, "for our Mother is travelling with us. She has told me of the joy which this new foundation is giving her, and has bidden me have fresh courage because this undertaking will give great glory to God: Since this is so, we may rejoice." The miraculous light accompanied the nuns until they reached the gates of Madrid. By the express wish of the Empress Maria, widow of Maximilian II of Austria,[48] the nuns were received at the house of her major-domo, Don Gracia de Alvarado, where Father Nicholas Doria and other friars were waiting to welcome them. Here the nuns stayed for about a week. When enclosed nuns are given leave to travel, the law of enclosure is entirely suspended for the time being, hence, when the Empress Maria summoned the Carmelites to visit her at the Franciscan convent where she was staying, they made no difficulty about complying, and were received with every mark of gracious affection and respect. One of the ladies-in-waiting, Yolande de Salazar, was so impressed by the holiness of the nuns that she begged to be accepted as a future postulant. Meanwhile, Father Nicholas Doria had found a small house for the nuns near the Gate of San Luis, and it was arranged that they should take possession of it on the night of 16th September. St. John of the Cross busied himself chiefly with domestic details, bringing with him on the day fixed a saucepan and other kitchen utensils. When the nuns set out about five p.m. they had with them one Juan de la Ciguela, a native of Soria, who was to act as sacristan. Anne of Jesus named him Brother John of the

---

[48] Maximilian II was head of the Holy Roman Empire, and therefore bore the title of Emperor. His wife, the Empress Maria, was sister to Philip II of Spain. It was in her train that St. Aloysius Gonzaga went to Spain in 1581.

Cross, and bade him prepare a room in which Mass could be said next morning. Nothing loath, the young man set to work to remove a dividing wall between two small rooms, so that together they might serve as a chapel. Standing on a ladder, he loosened the bricks and passed them to a nun stationed below, who, in her turn, passed them on to other nuns who stacked them in an outer court. Suddenly the ladder slipped, and with it Brother John. His leg, caught in one of the rungs, was badly fractured and loud groans broke the profound silence. It was one a.m., and there was no one to fetch a doctor. Anne of Jesus quickly tore her handkerchief into strips and two nuns knelt down to bandage the broken limb. No sooner was this accomplished than Brother John rose up perfectly cured and able to continue his work. In his own account of this incident, written later when he was a priest, John says: "Before morning I succeeded in getting everything ready for the chapel. I could not help saying to the Carmelites, when Anne of Jesus was not there: 'Ladies, this is indeed a great miracle!" They replied: "Brother, God is wonderful in His Saints!"

On the morning of 17th September, Mgr. Neroni, vicar-general of the diocese, came to say the first Mass at the new Carmel and to perform the ceremony of the enclosure. The Carmel was dedicated to St. Anne, in accordance with the express desire of the Empress Maria, who had made handsome gifts of Church furniture in memory of her beloved daughter, Anne of Austria, fourth wife of Philip II, who had died in 1580. The same evening Father Nicholas Doria presided over the elections. Anne of Jesus was appointed prioress, Mother Mary of the Nativity sub-prioress, while Sisters Guiomar of Jesus and Beatrix of Jesus were elected discreets.[49] God attested the virtues of His servants in various ways.

One night no oil was to be found for the sanctuary lamp, and it was too late to buy any. The sisters drained their lanterns and gave what they could to the prioress, who set her lantern before the choir grate to do duty for a lamp. To make up to Our Lord for "this poor little light" Anne of Jesus spent the greater part of the night in prayer before the Blessed Sacrament. When the Sacristan arrived next morning with a fresh supply he was greatly surprised to find the sanctuary lamp full of oil and burning as brightly "as a four-ply wick." No one had entered the Church after he had locked up, so the oil was looked upon as having been miraculously supplied.

A more talked of miracle was the unsolicited cure of Count Tiburcio, one of the members of the Empress's Court. Although seriously ill, he had, out of devotion to Our Lady and affection for her Carmelite daughters, risen from his sick-bed to be present when the Empress first received Anne of Jesus and her companions. Some days later his life was despaired of, and his disconsolate wife knelt beside him through the night, waiting to receive his last sigh. All at once he turned towards her, quite conscious, declaring that he was perfectly well. "The seven religious whom I saw with the Empress have been here around my bed," he told her, "and with them an eighth, whose face I did not recognise, but who wore the same habit. This one came close to me and showed great compassion for my sufferings, then left me completely cured." The count sent at once for his confessor, Don Antonio de Capolis, to whom he related his wonderful

---

[49] *Discreets.* The title given to the Sisters who keep the keys of the box containing the convent documents, etc. (Chest of Three Keys), and act as Counsellors to the prioress.

experience, afterwards sending him with a generous alms to the new Carmelite convent. Anne of Jesus in her deposition concerning the miracle says: "I gave him [Don Antonio] a likeness of our Holy Mother for the count, who cried out on seeing it : 'That is the religious who came and cured me.'" Don Antonio became later Bishop of Oristano, in Sardinia. He was still living when the process of beatification of St Teresa was drawn up.

Such favours from heaven drew many postulants to Carmel. The first received was a near relative of Father Nicholas Doria. She entered on 4th October, and took the name of Sister Catherine of St. Francis. Another was a protegee of the Empress, who, after a short probation, was found unsuited to the life of a Carmelite, so that, in spite of the recommendations she brought from Court, she had to be dismissed. Yolande de Salazar entered on 21st November. She received the name of Mary of the Incarnation, and the Empress entered the enclosure to assist at the clothing of her lady-in-waiting. The royal lady afterwards questioned the prioress about her former protegee, telling her that the girl had a reputation for sanctity throughout the town. "Madam," answered the humble religious, "God watches over our houses, and He enlightens the prioresses as to what it is best to do."

About a year later, in October 1587, Catherine Doria made her vows, and with the large dowry she brought the nuns were able to take a larger house in the parish of San Sebastian, whither they removed in the following spring. Miraculous marks of God's favour did not fail to attend them in their new home.

The licentiate, John de Tegida, lent the nuns a cart in which to remove their furniture. On the way his driver, a Moorish slave, had a bad fall and broke his arm. Instead of taking him to a doctor Brother John of the Cross conducted the wounded man to the convent, where he had a long interview with Mother Anne of Jesus. The Moor left the parlour perfectly cured and promised to seek baptism. After due preparation he was received into the Church, and the licentiate granted him his freedom. God was not long in rewarding this generous act. Shortly after, Doña de Tegida fell ill and was given up by the doctors. However, her own faith in the efficacy of the prayers of Anne of Jesus prompted her to ask that something that the saintly prioress had used might be sent for her comfort. In reply Brother John was dispatched with a scapular which Anne of Jesus had formerly worn. The sick lady applied it to her person and was instantaneously cured. The very next day she was up at the convent in time to assist at Mass, and afterwards thanked her benefactress. As some acknowledgment of this signal favour the same lady sent, on the following Feast of Corpus Christi, a handsome pair of candelabra, furnished with thick wax candles, requesting that they might burn during the Exposition of the Blessed Sacrament kept up during the octave. When all was in readiness Brother John, as sacristan, went to light up, but seeing that the candles sent by Doña de Tegida nearly touched the wooden ceiling, he hesitated, and went to ask Anne of Jesus what was to be done. "Brother," she replied, "light them just as they are. God, Who is here present, will let them burn for His glory, without any harm to us." So the candles were lit, and to the surprise of all who witnessed the prodigy, the flames, although they actually licked the boards of the ceiling, left not even so much as a trace of smoke.

Nor was it only in external things that God watched over this new foundation. A young girl whose name was Mariana ardently desired to become a Carmelite, but could not obtain her father's consent. One day she went to the convent and having on some pretext or other obtained that the enclosure door should be opened, she slipped inside and begged Anne of Jesus there and then to give her the habit. Naturally, after such an irregular proceeding the prioress hesitated to comply, but at the same moment St. Teresa appeared to her and told her that Mariana would tender great service to the Order, but that, on pain of losing her, she must be received at once. A special chapter was assembled, and the votes being in the girl's favour, she was clothed in Our Lady's habit and received the name of Mariana of the Angels. Hardly was the ceremony over when her brother arrived to take her home. When he understood that she had entered of her own accord he was wise enough not to insist. Sister Mariana lived as a perfect Carmelite, and later on was sent as foundress first to Talavera and afterwards to Lerma.

St. Teresa also came to the rescue of another novice who was going to be dismissed on account of her poor health. Anne of Jesus was much distressed at what she believed to be her duty, as the votes had been adverse. St. Teresa, however, appeared to her and said: "Do not grieve: this novice will make her vows, and will become an excellent religious." Needless to say the profession took place. The sister lived to a ripe old age, and assisted at the foundation of the Carmel at Consuegra. But St. Teresa did not always act like this. A young girl of noble birth had received the habit and was known as Sister Baltasar Baptist. During her noviceship she became very ill, and all hope was abandoned. During a sort of coma which came upon her Anne of Jesus pleaded for her life, laying her face, in imitation of Eliseus, on the face of the dying novice. By degrees strength returned to the young sister, but not sufficient for the austerities of Carmel. Enlightened by God with regard to the novice's true vocation, Anne of Jesus made all arrangements for Baltasar Baptist to enter a less strict Order. She passed from Carmel to a convent of Franciscans, where she served

God in good health for many years.

A pleasing story is told of the veneration in which Anne of Jesus was held by the Empress Maria. The latter used to visit the convent, her royalty giving her the right of entering the enclosure. On one of these occasions a courier arrived with letters from her son, Archduke Albert[50] but, without opening the packet, the Empress put them aside and continued her conversation with the saintly prioress.

One of the ladies-in-waiting ventured to say that the letters might contain important business, and called for immediate attention. "That may be," replied the Empress, "but I do not care to lose a single moment of my time with Mother Prioress." As for the Infanta Isabella, she was devoted heart and soul to the Carmelites, and particularly to Anne of Jesus. While yet but a child she had been blessed by St. Teresa, who traced the sign of the cross over the radiant little princess, saying: "God bless you, my child, and enable you to fill your high calling worthily," a blessing which bore abundant fruit as the years went by.

One of the first results of Isabella's visits to the convent at Madrid was her enrolment in the scapular of Mount Carmel. The ceremony took place in the convent chapel, and the Infanta cherished this bond of union with her beloved Carmelites until the day of her death. She often spoke of the nuns to her royal father, and it is recorded that the grave and reserved Philip professed great admiration for Anne of Jesus and her nuns, and openly took their part before his Court.

Testimony from contemporary priests, religious, and

---

[50] The Archduke Albert married the Infanta Isabella, daughter of Philip II of Spain by his third wife. The government of the Spanish Netherlands was ceded by Philip in 1598 to Albert and Isabella as joint sovereigns. When spoken of together they are referred to as "The Archdukes."

bishops confirms the impression that even during her lifetime Anne of Jesus was regarded as a saint. St. John of the Cross spoke of her as "our Mother," and often said to Sister Mary of the Incarnation (Yolande de Salazar), "You are happy in having such a superior; she is a seraph incarnate," while Luis de Leon, the Augustinian friar, to whom Anne of Jesus entrusted the revision of St. Teresa's writings, said more than once: "If prayer, meditation and knowledge of spiritual things all came to be lost, they could be recovered in Anne of Jesus. She, without having studied theology, knows more than I do, for all my years of professorship." One of his religious who frequently preached at the Carmel of Madrid held the same opinion. "The prioress's knowledge is not of this world," he used to say, "but from heaven. I doubt whether her equal can be found upon earth." Similarly Diego de Yepes, later on Bishop of Tarazona, a frequent visitor at the convent, one night said to Brother John, who was accompanying him home: "Walk beside me, Brother John. I think more of your service of Anne of Jesus than you could of my being confessor to the king, and prior of the monastery of St. Jerome."

Testimonies like this could be multiplied, but they would become wearisome. These are sufficient to show in what high esteem Mother Anne was held. One would think that no breath of evil or calumny could touch her. But God had other designs. Before telling of these, however, some further testimony which God gave to the sanctity of His servant must be recorded. One evening the nuns had said Compline and were about to make the customary visit to the Blessed Sacrament when the prioress stopped them. "Do not make the visit to the Blessed Sacrament till I tell you," she said. While the nuns waited in choir a loud noise was heard, and each religious felt herself struck, as by a man's hand, on the shoulder. They were naturally much frightened and turned to the prioress for an explanation. "Do not be alarmed, daughters," she replied; "our good friend the Marquess del Valle has just died and has come to ask our help. It was on this account that I put off our visit to the Blessed Sacrament, so that we might have more to offer for him." Next morning news was brought that the Marquess del Valle had expired at the very moment when Anne of Jesus had been speaking of him.

Something similar happened with regard to Luke Gracian, eldest brother of Father Jerome. Anne of Jesus saw him pass into Purgatory and recommended him at once to the prayers of the nuns, though news of his death did not arrive till later. A still more striking story is that connected with John Baptist de Baëza. This gentleman was a great friend to the Carmelites in Seville, and being in Madrid on business, he soon came to know and esteem Mother Anne of Jesus, and each morning he heard Mass in the convent chapel. It happened that urgent matters of State were entrusted to him by Philip II, which necessitated an immediate journey to Segovia. On the morning of his departure news came from Seville that his wife was not well. Hastily recommending her to the prayers of the Carmelites, he arranged that Mass the next morning should be said for her recovery.

The following day Anne of Jesus gave directions for a Requiem Mass to be said for her, and while it was in progress the King's secretary, unaware that de Baëza had already left Madrid, came to look for him at the convent. In answer to his inquiry for whom the Requiem Mass was being celebrated, he was told it was for the wife of his friend. Much moved, he put aside all other business and rode post haste to Segovia. John Baptist was much astonished to see him, and still more astonished to learn the reason of his coming. "I am infinitely grateful to you," he said, "but there must be some mistake. The good nuns, doubtless, misunderstood my instructions." But it was not so. A few days later letters reached Segovia from Seville stating that de Baëza's wife had died precisely at the hour when the Requiem Mass was begun for her at the Carmelite chapel in Madrid.

As with outsiders, so with her own. Her namesake, the lay-sister, had a great desire one Holy Week to spend her time in recollection, but her occupations being more than usually heavy at that time, she kept her longing a secret between herself and God. According to custom the prioress washed the feet of the entire community on Holy Thursday. As the venerable Mother bent to kiss the foot of the white-veiled Anne of Jesus all the nerves of her instep contracted, and for three days the sister could hardly bear to put her foot to the ground. Seated in a corner of the choir, she was able to give herself to contemplation as she had desired. She always attributed this to the prayers of the prioress, for on Easter Sunday, though no remedies had been applied, she was able to go about her work just as usual.

It is a well-attested fact that St. Teresa frequently appeared to Anne of Jesus while she was at Madrid, curing her maladies, admonishing her of any practice that might open the door to the least relaxation, and consoling her in various ways. The sweet perfume which always accompanied the Saint's presence was perceptible to others, but it was only the prioress who saw and conversed with her.

By such ways as these did God prepare His faithful servant for the trials He was about to send her. Among other consolations was that of superintending the first printed edition of St. Teresa's writings. The work of editing these was, as has been said, entrusted to Father Luis de Leon, and when his task was accomplished he dedicated the volume to

Anne of Jesus and the Carmelites of Madrid in a long preface, which shows unmistakably the high esteem in which he held the Holy Foundress of the Carmelite Reform and her saintly daughter, and his appreciation of the part Anne of Jesus was playing in the rapid development of St. Teresa's work.

CHAPTER XII

TROUBLES CONCERNING THE CONSTITUTIONS

1585-1594; 1613-1621

NEVER has great work been done for God or heroic sanctity attained apart from the Cross, and in the life of Anne of Jesus that sacred Tree planted deep roots. Her mental sufferings were bitter and prolonged. They were connected chiefly with matters concerning the internal government of the Discalced Carmelite nuns, and had little to do with external affairs.

To understand what follows it is necessary to go back to 1562. In that year St. Teresa began her foundations, and had the authority of the Pope to draw up suitable Constitutions for her nuns. This the Saint did, and her Constitutions were approved by the General of the Order, Father Rubeo. He, with the necessary alterations, adapted them for the Discalced friars, although, owing to the different orientation of their life, which contained a large proportion of apostolic work, the friars were never able to put them completely into practice. When the Chapter of the Discalced at Alma was at hand, St. Teresa discussed the question of Constitutions for the nuns in a series of letters exchanged with Father Jerome Gracian (1581). In the course of eighteen years experience had shown that many details required adjustment. There were some points upon which St. Teresa laid great stress. In any difficulty that arose she always endeavoured to get the very best advice that could be obtained; this was so in legal matters, medical matters, architectural matters. It was so also in matters of conscience and spiritual guidance. She herself used to consult the Dominicans in theological matters, the Jesuits in matters of direction, and many other saintly priests, both secular and religious, in matters of spiritual science. She wanted her nuns to have a similar latitude, and therefore it was necessary to secure for the prioresses the right to call in directors and confessors. As to the latter, it was, of course, imperative that they should have faculties for hearing the confessions of nuns, and these could only be granted by the ecclesiastical superior of the respective convents.

St. Teresa knew, personally, all the prioresses of her convents, and the majority of her nuns, and could therefore exercise a kind of supervision on this point. Father Jerome Gracian, the first provincial of the Discalced, not only seconded her views, but being inclined to lay stress on revelations, visions, and other mystical phenomena, fostered among the nuns a rather exaggerated mysticism, with the result that many theologians and directors were called in, so that, in the words of the chronicler, there were in some convents "more directors than nuns," and the parlours and confessionals were constantly occupied for the purpose of spiritual conferences.

St. Teresa, Anne of Jesus, and some others of the leading prioresses who possessed the gift of discernment of spirits could be trusted to use the privilege granted by the Constitutions to the advantage of souls. Father Jerome Gracian, while under the influence of St. Teresa, was an excellent superior, although she frequently found it necessary to admonish him, as may be seen from her letters. He was beloved by many of the friars and by all the nuns on account of his gentleness and amiable character, but often after St. Teresa's death he was not wholly trusted. In many ways he was an idealist, and spent a large portion of his time in preaching. When the time came for a change of superiors there was a swing of the pendulum, and the power passed into the hands of Father Nicholas Doria, a man diametrically the opposite to Father Gracian.

Father Doria was a native of Genoa, and during the dispute with the Friars of the Mitigated Observance, had rendered great service to St. Teresa and the cause of the Discalced. He was a man of great practical energy, austere and tenacious. With his brother he managed a big banking business in Spain, where Philip II held him in high favour, but at the call of God Nicholas renounced all prospect of worldly advancement, and about the fortieth year of his age asked for and received the habit of the Discalced Carmelite friars. In many of her letters St. Teresa speaks of him in terms of high praise, and he was elected a definitor in the Chapter of Alcala. Father Jerome Gracian sent him soon afterwards to found a priory at Genoa, for it would have been impossible for two men of such opposite temperaments to work harmoniously together.

One of Father Doria's first acts as Provincial was to send Father Gracian, in his turn, to Portugal, for in the previous three years the Reform had greatly increased, many priories and convents having been founded in all parts of Spain, inclusive of Portugal, which was then under the Spanish Crown. Furthermore, Father Doria feared that the rules laid down at Alcala in 1581 were not sufficiently detailed to ensure absolute uniformity among religious belonging to different races and living under different climates and social conditions. Therefore he undertook the task of centralising the government far more than it had been up to that time. While subdividing the Discalced "Province" into four sections, he, without having taken the chapter into his confidence, elaborated a scheme which placed all power, even in the minutest details, in the hands of the provincial, that is, himself, assisted by a consulting body of six friars, of whom St. John of the Cross was one. Moreover, he greatly increased the austerity of the Order, and curtailed or withdrew what little spiritual freedom had been left to the individual. This new form of government came, not only as a surprise, but as a severe blow to the entire Province, and although in some respects it was mitigated on recourse being had to Rome, it proved a heavy yoke as long as Father Doria lived, that is, until 1594. The Carmelite nuns were concerned, inasmuch as they, like the friars, were under the "Consulta." Besides this, they clearly foresaw that, sooner or later, their Constitutions, the work of St. Teresa as approved by the Chapter of Alcala, would be revised and brought into line with those of the friars. Under these circumstances Anne of Jesus, as the leading prioress since the death of St. Teresa, considered it her duty to keep intact the legacy of her Holy Mother. At that time Father Doria was ordinary confessor at Madrid, and she asked him whether it would not be well to get the Constitutions of the nuns confirmed by a Papal Brief. He answered in the affirmative, but the sequel shows that he must have had in his mind his own revised Constitutions, whilst Anne of Jesus was referring to those left to the nuns by St. Teresa.

Before applying to Rome, Anne sought further advice from eminent theologians, and then, with the support of St. John of the Cross and Father Gracian, but without again consulting Father Doria, who was then vicar-general, she sent the Constitutions to Rome for approval. Pope Sixtus V appointed the Cardinal of Santa Severina[51] to inquire into the matter, with the result that all that the nuns asked for was granted in a Brief dated 5th June, 1590. But Father Doria delayed the promulgation of this Brief, and Pope Sixtus dying in the meantime, the whole affair had to be again referred to Rome.

---

[51] It was customary at that time to name Cardinals after their titular Church, his family name was Santorio.

TROUBLES CONCERNING THE CONSTITUTIONS

It happened that another provincial chapter was due. It was held in May 1591, and during its sessions the question was again discussed of reducing all regulations for the nuns to exact conformity with those of the friars. St. John of the Cross and Father Gracian strongly opposed the measure, but to no avail, and Father Doria was free to establish his reforms.[52] Through Philip II he had petitioned the Pope, then Gregory XIV, for a Brief sanctioning his amendments to the Constitutions. This was granted on 25th April, 1591. Friendly relations were resumed between friars and nuns, but the prioresses and other sisters who had most actively opposed the measures of the vicar-general were deposed, and deprived for three years of both active and passive votes.

Anne of Jesus suffered most heavily. In addition to the above penalties she was ordered to remain a prisoner in her cell for three years, and might only receive Holy Communion once a year to fulfil the Paschal precept. At the entreaty of the Empress Maria and of the whole community of Madrid the severe ruling with regard to Holy Communion was afterwards modified, and the venerable religious was allowed to approach the Holy Table once a month. She was to have been sent away from Madrid, but through the influence of the Empress she was allowed to remain.

The nuns regarded the humiliations to which their late prioress was subjected as so many marks of God's favour, and Father Doria himself acknowledged that her action had not been sinful. She, on her part, submitted to everything in silent obedience.

The Empress, deeply edified by the way Anne of Jesus accepted her punishment, offered to procure a room for her

---

[52] St. John of the Cross retired to Peñuela, and died at Ubeda, 13th of December, 1591. Father Gracian was transferred by the Pope to the Calced Carmelites, and died at Brussels 21st September, 1614.

with the Franciscans, but the Servant of God would not even consider such a proposal, and answered when this and other favours were pressed upon her: "I need nothing except to love and serve Jesus Christ." This answer so delighted the Empress that she had it printed on parchment in large gold letters, and she used to declare that whenever she read it she experienced great consolation of spirit. During these years of seclusion Our Lord did not withdraw His favours from His faithful Servant. When she made her monthly communion the Sacred Host remained in her mouth all day, so that she was obliged to keep a strict fast. In a note written with her own hand she says that she asked her Divine Spouse the meaning of this favour, and that He replied: "I do this to convince thee that I am more closely united to thee than ever."

At the moment of his death St. John of the Cross appeared to his former friend and penitent and told her that he was going to Heaven. He appeared to her again later, brilliant with glory, and conversed with her for some time. Anne of Jesus never spoke of what passed between them, but one day, when pressed to do so by Mother Beatrix of the Conception, she answered: "I can tell you nothing; it would mean speaking in my own praise." St. Teresa, too, often visited her faithful coadjutrix during her time of trial, leaving in the venerable Mother's cell the sweet perfume of her presence. Sister Mary of the Incarnation having several times perceived this fragrance, said: "I know our Holy Mother has been here." Anne of Jesus did not answer, though her face lit up with a happy smile.

At the General Chapter of 1593, held in Rome, Father Doria proposed the total separation of the Discalced Carmelites from the rest of the Order. This was granted by a Bull of December 20th of the same year. He was nominated first general of the Discalced Carmelites in the following year, but died a few months later. He was succeeded by Father Elias of St. Martin, a mild and gentle superior, of whom Mother Mary of the Incarnation wrote: "This Father's government is of consolation for both friars and nuns. He rules the Order as it was ruled in the time of our Holy Mother, St. Teresa."

The Constitutions of Alcala were during the ensuing years presented by the friends of Anne of Jesus to each succeeding Pope for confirmation, and were carried by her into France and Flanders when she went thither to establish her Holy Mother's Reform.

The three years seclusion imposed on Anne of Jesus expired in 1594, and although Father Doria was now dead, she faithfully fulfilled the promise she had made him to leave Madrid, and obtained permission to return to Salamanca. Mother Mary of St. Jerome and Sister Anne of St. Bartholomew were to be her travelling companions.

The actual Carmel of Madrid founded by Anne of Jesus exists no longer. It was demolished early in the nineteenth century to make room for an open square, since known as the Plazuela de Santa Aña, perhaps so called from the former Carmel of St Anne. In 1829 a second convent was built with the same patroness, but that also was subsequently pulled down to make room for private houses in the street now called del Prado.

When Anne of Jesus went to France and Flanders she took with her the Constitutions (1581-88) for which she had endured so much. To secure their observance, when the Bull for the erection of the royal convent at Brussels was promulgated, she obtained from the Nuncio, Guido Bentivoglio, Archbishop of Rhodes, who was acting as legate *a latere* in the Netherlands, that the name of Gregory XIV should be omitted in passages where the Constitutions were referred to. The same omission was asked for and obtained when the nuns in the Flemish Carmels made their submission to the government of the Friars of the Italian Congregation in 1610.

Consistently with her previous conduct, Anne of Jesus withstood a change in these Constitutions proposed in 1613, and applied to the Archduke for support. The latter instructed his agent in Rome, Chevalier Mats, to plead for the maintenance of the Constitutions of Alcala.

When Father Thomas of Jesus, who had been in Rome for the General Chapter, returned in 1614 as Provincial in the Netherlands, a compromise was arranged, similar to that arrived at in Spain during the Generalship of Father Elias of St. Martin, and at once put into effect. Each prioress prepared a list of the confessors she desired for her community, and submitted it for approval to the Provincial of the Discalced Carmelites, their Ecclesiastical Superior, as appears from a document written and signed by Father Thomas of Jesus in 1617.

"Jesus, Maria!

"We, Father Thomas of Jesus, Superior of the Discalced Religious, men and women, of the Virgin Mary of Mount Carmel, in the Provinces of Flanders and Germany, give, by these presents, permission to hear the confessions of our Discalced nuns of Brussels, first to the Discalced friars of our Order, whom we shall nominate from among the religious in our priory at Brussels, as ordinary confessors; secondly, to M. Navet, chaplain to the above-named Sisters; to the Reverend Father-Confessors of their Highnesses, to the Rector of the Company [of Jesus], to Father Thomas and Father Roland,[53] so that they [the sisters] may confess to them in

---

[53] Fr. Roland Otrasius (van Overstraeten) S. J., under whose direction the engraving facing p. 146 was executed c. 1630.

cases of necessity.

"Given in our Convent of St. Joseph and St. Anne, in Brussels, January 28th, 1617.

"(signed) FRAY THOMAS OF JESUS."

There are several references to the dispute about the Constitutions among the historians of the Order and others, which show that it was, at the time, very acute, and that it was renewed after the death of Anne of Jesus. One ancient MS. preserved by the nuns of Flanders says, when referring to Anne of Jesus and the modified Constitutions:

> "She would never receive them, nor give up those of St. Teresa. Hence this courageous woman would not allow the least change to be made in the convent which she governed, nor in those of Flanders which sought her counsel, and she persevered in this determination until her happy death."

Speaking of these troubles one of her spiritual daughters wrote in 1625:

> "Many occasions presented themselves on which her superiors reproved her severely, though she was not in fault. Notwithstanding this, her soul was so calm that a few moments afterwards she would go up to receive Holy Communion in great peace and tranquillity, though the difference had not been adjusted."

Another sister gives practically the same testimony:

> "God purified our venerable Mother Anne of Jesus, and proved her constancy and patience by all sorts of trials, persecutions and sufferings up to the last moment of her life, just as gold is tried in the furnace. Although she had to bear many reproaches and much abuse and contempt in consequence of calumnies uttered against her in matters of spiritual import, she nevertheless showed throughout all these attacks a virile and uniformly generous spirit, so that nothing of all this

disturbed her in her pursuit of important undertakings, nor weakened her noble-minded decisions in anything which she judged would be for the greater glory and better service of God."

It need not be said that through all these years of trial the daily life of the nuns went on undisturbed. This is proved by the entries made in the Convent registers at each canonical visitation. In 1615 Father Ferdinand of St. Mary, then General, declares that he "found all the nuns faithful in the observance of their Rule and of the Constitutions." A like entry occurs under the date 1619, while in 1621, the year in which Anne of Jesus died, Father Matthias of St. Francis wrote:

> "Having examined, according to custom, the spiritual and temporal affairs as appointed by the Sacred Canons and our Constitutions, we have the consolation of finding the religious very faithful in observing their Rule and Constitutions. The government of this house is well regulated."

Often during these years Anne of Jesus would recall what she had suffered in Spain, and many a time, turning to her faithful nurse, Sister Margaret of the Mother of God, she used to say: "My daughter, you will enjoy in peace the results of all my sufferings, for if, by God's grace, I had not been so firm, our Order would not be in the flourishing state in which it is to-day."

With what was almost her last breath, the venerable prioress recommended to her nuns the faithful observance of the Constitutions, the preservation of which had cost her so dear. Over and over again she would repeat: "My daughters, the best devotion you can practise is to keep your Rule and Constitutions faithfully; that is sufficient to make you SAINTS."

S. TERESA vi Ordinem B. VIRGINIS primo vigori restituat
V. IOANNEM A CRVCE & V. ANNAM A IESV in coadiutores
eligit, quorum opera sacer ordo per vniuersum orbem propagatur

CHAPTER XIII

ST. TERESA'S DAUGHTERS ARE ASKED FOR IN FRANCE

1583-1604

IT had been one of St. Teresa's most cherished desires that her daughters should establish themselves in France, and about a year after her death God inspired John de Quintanaduenas, Seigneur de Brétigny, to commence negotiations to that effect. Born at Rouen, of a Spanish father and a French mother, the young man had spent the greater part of his youth at Seville. There, in 1583, he came into contact with Mother Mary of St. Joseph, who encouraged his project of founding a Carmel at Rouen. It took about two years before he obtained written authorisation from the Superiors of the Order and a promise of support from M. de Longlee, French Ambassador at the Spanish court. He then called at the Carmel at Madrid, and saw Anne of Jesus, who had arrived there just three weeks previous to his visit. She gave him great encouragement, and he, hearing that she was taking steps to have St. Teresa's works published gave her generous alms for that purpose. When he returned to Rouen, he took with him a copy of the Rules and Constitutions of the Discalced Carmelite nuns,[54] which he later on translated into French. The original in M. de Brétigny's handwriting still exists. Great enthusiasm was felt in many of the Spanish Carmels concerning the proposed foundation, and the Sisters' letters during the years of waiting often contain allusions to it. "I wish you could have seen the ship that came a-sailing in our convent the other day," writes one, "it bore a crimson ensign, and

---

[54] The Constitutions printed in 1581, since in 1585 no others existed.

had all its sails unfurled, while drums were beating—'Who will go to France ?' You would have seen a great number of the nuns embracing the cross, and declaring themselves willing to die for the Faith." The persecutions raging at that time in England, and the bitter religious war in France, made the nuns connect going to the latter country with certain martyrdom.

When Rouen, a stronghold of the Catholic League, was besieged by Henry IV in 1591, all thought of a Carmelite foundation there was set aside, and other places proposed, but without success. At last, yielding to the prolonged and earnest solicitations of his father, M. de Brétigny consented to enter the married state. One day while praying to find a suitable wife, he heard God saying to him interiorly: "My son, I have a Spouse to give thee, such as thou hast asked for, that is to say, one who both loves and fears me, and is of an old and noble family, the Order of Mount Carmel. Wilt Thou accept?"

From that moment the young man devoted himself entirely to the development of the Order, and, to escape the importunities of his father, he went again to Spain and visited many Carmelite convents, beginning with that of Madrid. Anne of Jesus told him that the time for the French foundation had not yet come, and foretold that he would visit Spain for a third time, when she hoped to accompany him back to France herself. M. de Brétigny, on his return to Rouen, studied for the priesthood, and after his ordination in 1598 occupied himself in translating St. Teresa's books into French. His work was published in 1601.[55]

Under the guidance of his saintly director, M. Gallement, parish priest of St. Aumale, M. de Brétigny kept up his

---

[55] The autograph copy of these translations is now in the possession of the Carmelites of the Convent of the Incarnation, Clamart, France.

interest in the Carmelites, not only by petitioning the Holy Father for a Bull sanctioning the erection of a Convent of the Reform in France, but also by instructing several young ladies who were desirous of becoming Carmelites "according to the Rule and Constitutions sent by the nuns from Spain."

In 1601 God drew together the various instruments He had chosen to bring about His designs. M. Gallement was preaching a course of sermons in the French capital, and there he met Mme Acarie, known to all her friends,[56] including St. Francis de Sales, as a very holy woman. Her advisers most concerned in this history were M. Andre du Val, a learned member of the Sorbonne, the intimate friend of St. Vincent de Paul, and Pierre de Bérulle, afterwards cardinal, the founder of the French Oratory, about whom St. Francis of Sales could say: "He is all that I should like to be myself." Somewhat unwillingly Mme Acarie had been persuaded to read the new French edition of St. Teresa's writings. The Saint afterwards appeared to her and told her that God would make use of her to introduce the Carmelite Reform into France. However, after her spiritual guides had consulted together about the matter she was told to dismiss the project from her thoughts. Seven months later St. Teresa visited her again, telling her that in spite of many difficulties to be encountered, the Carmelite Foundation would succeed. This time Mme Acarie assisted at the consultation, at which St. Francis de Sales was present, and her simplicity and faith won a favourable decision.

A letter written in 1603 by the saintly Bishop of Geneva urged these matters on the attention of the Holy Father, and represented that the permission to found at Rouen had been accorded in 1585, although the Discalced Friars were not yet

---

[56] Among these were several English Capuchins then living in Paris: more especially Father Benet Canfield and Fr. Archange de Pembroke.

established there. He also referred to the proposed ecclesiastical superiors—M. de Bérulle, M. du Val, and M. Gallement—as "men chosen for their learning, uprightness and ability."[57] The consent of the King of France, Henry of Navarre, was obtained through the Princesse de Longueville, whom God had named to Mme Acarie as future foundress. Matters had advanced thus far, when God raised up another lay promoter of the work. This was M. de Marillac, keeper of the royal seals, the uncle of Blessed Louise de Marillac, who, some years later, founded, with St. Vincent de Paul, the well-known Sisters of Charity, distinguished everywhere by their devoted service of others. One day M. de Marillac was in a bookshop and picked up casually "The Life and Miracles of St. Teresa." God spoke three distinct times to his soul, as he turned its pages, urging him to aid in founding a Carmel in France.[58] Through a mutual friend he was put in touch with Mme Acarie, and from that day devoted his time, influence and fortune to the business of the foundation, and remained the staunch supporter of the Carmelite nuns all his life.

---

[57] Owing to the prejudice in France against Spain at that time there was no possibility of the French Carmels being governed by Discalced Friars. Supreme jurisdiction was to remain in the hands of the reigning Pope who delegated his authority as indicated. A Canonical Visitor was appointed later.

[58] M. de Marillac recorded his experience in Latin thus:

	Reply
(1) *Id volo, fiat opus.*	*Fieri non poles! videtur.*
I wish it, set to work.	It seems impossible to accomplish.
(2) *Aggredire, ipse audeas.*	*Aditus mihi non patet ullus.*
Take courage, set thyself to work.	No way to do so is open to me.
(3) *Omnipotens jubeo.*	*Per me, Domino, Infer quod vis.*
I, the Almighty, command thee.	Do, through me, whatever Thou dost will, O Lord.

The letters-patent authorising the foundation were signed by Henry IV on 18th July 1602 and registered on 1st October of the same year by the French *Parlement*, after an endowment had been arranged for by Mme de Longueville. It seemed as if nothing remained to do except choose the site and commence building. Meanwhile, in Spain God had not left the Carmelites without indications of His Will. To some who were to accompany Anne of Jesus to France God gave a foreknowledge of their destiny. Mother Isabel of the Angels[59] was watching before the Blessed Sacrament one day, the rest of the community being at table. While rapt out of herself in prayer God showed her the kingdom of France, and told her she would live to found many convents there, in which He would be generously served. So great an impression did this vision make on her that she wrote at once to the Father General, asking to be allowed, when the time came, to go to France. In 1599 a holy lay-brother Francis of the Infant Jesus, said to Sister Eleanor of St. Bernard (Spinola), then recently professed at Loëches, that she would one day found a house in France. The young religious laughed gaily at the prophecy, and declared herself too young and insignificant even to think of such a thing, yet Brother Francis's words came true.

Again, the holy lay-sister Anne of St. Bartholomew had a vision of Our Lord in 1602, in which He appeared resplendent in glory and said that He was going to France to see His spouses. At the same moment He showed her a great number of Discalced Carmelite nuns, whose faces she recognised later on in postulants who presented themselves at Paris. Several of them were at the time members of a religious association of St. Genevieve, and were being

---

[59] Isabel de Messia, daughter of Don Juan de Marquez and Maria Ibagnez.

trained as future Carmelites by Mme Acarie, under the direction of M. de Bérulle and Père Coton, S. J.

By 1603 the building of the Paris Carmel was begun. The site was that of an old Benedictine priory, known as Notre Dame des Champs, in the Faubourg St. Jacques. Here tradition asserted that St. Denis first preached to the inhabitants of Paris,[60] and a very ancient picture of Our Lady, attributed to St. Luke, had been venerated there from time immemorial, together with relics of her veil. M. de Marillac offered himself as surety, and on 29th April 1603 the foundation stone was laid by the Duchess de Nemours acting for the Queen, Marie de Medici, Mme de Longueville and her sister laying a second stone. A few days later the first stone of the nun's choir was laid by M. de Bérulle, Mme Acarie and M. de Marillac. During the ceremony Mme Acarie saluted M. de Bérulle as spiritual founder, and M. de Marillac as founder in temporal matters. Her humility kept her silent about the part she herself was to take. St. Teresa had already shown her that she would become a lay sister in the Order, but that before that came to pass she would have much to endure before the Discalced Carmelites were safely established in France. In religion she was known as Sister Mary of the Incarnation. Pope Pius VI declared her Blessed in 1791, and she is universally honoured as the foundress of the Order of Mount Carmel in France.[61]

---

[60] The Crypt, where St. Denis baptised his Catechumens, together with an ancient shrine of St. Michael, were destroyed during the French Revolution. It was rebuilt on the old foundations in 1855. The ancient picture of Our Lady is still venerated there, and over the nun's choir was the antique statue of Our Lady which gave the Priory its name.

[61] It is interesting to note that Mme Acarie used to visit the young Benedictine Abbess of Montmartre, Elizabeth de Beauvilliers, when the latter was in difficulties about the Reform she was inaugurating.

Meanwhile, towards the end of October 1602, all the documents relating to the Paris foundation were taken to Rome by M. de Santeuil, for the purpose of obtaining the Papal Bull for the erection of the new convent. After some delays the Bull was issued, authorising not only a single Carmel, as requested, but also all that should, in future, be founded from it. The parchment bears the date 13th November 1603, and was signed by sixteen cardinals, in a meeting presided over by Clement VIII himself. While the Bull of Erection was being negotiated in Rome M. de Brétigny was busy trying to obtain for France Carmelite nuns who had been trained by St. Teresa herself. There were serious obstacles to overcome before the General of the Order could give his consent.

About 1588 it had been decided, for weighty reasons, that the Discalced Carmelites should not make foundations outside the Spanish Peninsula, and this principle was embodied in the constitutions of the friars. It is true a start had been made in Mexico, but that had occurred accidently through a missionary friar, who was preaching in the Canaries, being captured and carried off to Mexico, where he planted the Reform. Fr. Doria had also founded a house in Italy, as has been related. Having established Discalced Friars at Genoa, he wished to get a footing in Rome, chiefly in order to have access to the Holy See directly, and not through the Procurator-General of the Order, at that date undivided. Beyond this the Spanish Friars of the Reform would not go, so that when, in 1597, Clement VIII wanted to introduce the Discalced Friars into Rome, the General and his Definitors refused to make the Foundation, on the

---

Montmartre was the parent abbey of Mantargis, now represented by the Priory at Princethorpe, the first to be built in England after the Reformation.

ground that if the Reform spread outside Spain it would lose its primitive spirit and fervour. Thereupon His Holiness sent for fifteen out of the thirty friars at Genoa and erected a monastery of the Discalced at La Scala, Rome. He then absolved the friars of the two Italian monasteries from their obedience to the General of the Spanish provinces and erected them into an independent branch of the Reform, under the title of the "Congregation of St. Elias." He endowed the new Congregation with all the privileges enjoyed by the Spanish Discalced Friars, and gave them power to found houses "in all the cities of the Christian world except those subject to Spain"; but in accordance with the regulations of the Church at that time, forbade them to undertake the government of any religious women, even of their own Order.[62]

Thus it came about that when M. de Brétigny applied to the General of the Spanish Discalced Carmelites for leave to take some nuns into France the request was persistently refused; the General, without a direct authorisation from Rome, could not, even had he wished, act contrary to the constitutions. When it was suggested that religious could be asked to come from Italy, M. de Brétigny was counselled not to accept. Mother Mary of St. Joseph writing to him on 2nd May 1603, says: ". . . It seems to me that you would have small satisfaction in getting nuns from Italy, since your intention is to begin with disciples of our holy Mother. The religious at Rome began by themselves." Fr. Gracian, then at Rome, and still in touch with all that concerned the Reform, was of the same opinion, while Anne of Jesus wrote from Salamanca, 28th June 1603:

---

[62] According to the Code of Canon Law at that date the Holy See reserved to itself the appointment of Ecclesiastical Superiors to convents of nuns. It was not a question concerning only the Carmelite Order.

FRANCE ASKS FOR ST. TERESA'S DAUGHTERS

"Our Lord knows with what devotion I offered myself to my superiors on the receipt of your [M. de Brétigny's] first letter, begging them to name me amongst those to take the journey. I shall do all I can to obtain so happy an issue, though I do not merit it in the least . . . what you are asking for is so right and just that Our Lord will grant it."

Prayers and devotions were multiplied throughout the Spanish Carmels for the success of the French foundation. Even the Queen became interested, and cheered by this encouragement, M. de Brétigny wrote again to the Spanish Father General on 18th July, asking him to lend the nuns if he could not give them.

"I am not afraid, Reverend Father, of importuning you, for, as a servant of God, you will not regard as an importunity the fact that so just a demand is urged more than once. It is the opinion of devout and enlightened persons here that no success will attend the establishing of a Convent of the Daughters of Teresa of Jesus, unless several can come who have been initiated from the beginning into the Rule and Spirit of their state. You have under your authority some who have the happiness of having been instructed by the Foundress herself, and it is these who are best fitted to take part in founding the first convent of your Reform in France. As to what regards your jurisdiction, the gentlemen[63] who are seeing to the foundation are willing to follow your good pleasure in everything and to receive from your hands, with the necessary faculties, the Rule, Constitutions, Ceremonial, Manual and any other statute concerning the customs and government of the Reform. If you are unwilling to accept the jurisdiction, and the Holy Father ordains otherwise, that will not hinder the great good which is to

---

[63] M. de Bérulle and the other priests associated with him.

be expected. You could, all the same, as we beg you to do, and as the Princesse de Longueville hopes that you will, send the documents I have just asked for here, and especially three or four of your nuns, at least for a few years. We undertake to send back, at a date fixed by you, the religious who are actually under your jurisdiction..."

This idea of lending nuns to France did not commend itself to the Father General. That country was in a very disturbed state, and real risks would have been encountered by any party of Spaniards travelling to Paris. On the advice of some of the Discalced Friars who were favourable to the project, M. de Brétigny decided, after consulting his own colleagues, to obtain a Brief from the Pope which should waive the articles of the Constitutions regarding foundations outside Spain, and authorise the sending of nuns to France. In the meantime Mme Jourdain, a pious widow and one of the members of the Association of St. Genevieve, felt herself inspired by God to offer to go to Spain to fetch the Carmelites. Her proposal met with approval, and she set out with several companions, on 26th September. They went by water from Nantes to Laredo, and encountered such terrible storms that they made a vow, if they reached Spain in safety, to go barefoot on a pilgrimage to the miraculous crucifix of Burgos. M. de Brétigny had relatives in that city who received the travellers with every mark of kindness. They fulfilled their vow early the next morning, in spite of the ground being covered with frozen snow. At the Burgos Carmel the French ladies were allowed to spend the recreation hour with the nuns, to their mutual edification. After resting for a few days Mme Jourdain and her friends went to Valladolid, where they hoped to find the

Spanish King, who had, however, gone to Madrid.⁶⁴ As matters did not seem to M. de Brétigny to be moving fast enough he wrote to M. de Bérulle and begged him to come to Spain to superintend the negotiations. Coming via Burgos and Valencia, M. de Bérulle and his valet, Edmund de Messa, and M. Gaultier reached Valladolid by the end of February 1604. In a personal interview with Philip III he received permission to treat of the Carmelite affairs directly with the Nuncio, and applied for a Papal Brief authorising him to choose nuns from any convent in Spain. A previous Brief, dated 23rd September 1603, had given leave for nuns to be taken from Portugal, and M. de Brétigny had hoped to secure Mother Mary of St. Joseph, then at Lisbon. In the meantime Mother Mary of St. Joseph had been sent to Cuerva, near Toledo. The journey, made in the depths of winter, cost this holy Carmelite her life. Anne of Jesus while praying for her on 19th October heard interiorly the words: "The souls of the just are in the hands of the Lord, and the torments of death shall not touch them." And on the following morning: "They are in peace." When news of the death of Mother Mary of St. Joseph reached Salamanca, the Servant of God understood that St. Teresa's former friend and counsellor was already enjoying her heavenly reward.

On 24th February 1604 the Pope sent a Brief to the General of the Discalced, enjoining him to send "apt and capable sisters" to France, in consequence of which Mother Thomasina-Baptist, prioress at Burgos, was named as foundress for Paris, with power to choose her companions. But God had not destined this sister for the work, and a few days after her nomination He called her to Himself. The

---

⁶⁴ At the instance of Don Francisco de Rojas de Sandoval, Duke of Lerma, Philip II removed his Court to Valladolid in 1601. On April 13th, 1606, it returned to Madrid.

choice next fell, at M. de Bérulle's suggestion, on Mother Isabel of St. Dominic, but on the very day on which she received the document authorising her departure she suffered so bad a fall that she was rendered permanently unfit for so arduous an undertaking. Mme Jourdain and her companions, far from losing heart at these delays, redoubled their prayers and mortifications, while M. de Bérulle, in spite of the great heat of the Spanish summer, travelled hither and thither, trying to secure what he wanted, going twice to Alba to pray at St. Teresa's tomb. At Salamanca Mother Isabel of the Angels wrote again to the Father General, asking to go to France, while at the Carmel of Medina del Rio Seco, Mother Stephanie of the Apostles, whose virtue St. Teresa mentions so often in her letters, received a command from Our Lord to write to tell the Father General that it was God's will that Carmelite nuns should go to France. At the General Chapter held in 1604 at Pastrana, St. Francis of the Mother of God was reelected General of the Discalced, and knowing that many of the friars were opposed to the project, he forbore to press the French question, though he gave M. de Bérulle a written permit to visit six of the Spanish Carmels. It looked as if the French ladies would, after all, have to return to Paris alone. But, as so often happens, God came to their aid in an unexpected manner, using as His instrument the saintly Doña Luisa de Carvajal.[65] This heroic Spanish lady was living at Valladolid in 1604, and had been told interiorly by God that some strangers were coming to the city, whom she was to help. When she saw Mme Jourdain and her friends at Mass she realised that they were the strangers she was expecting, and she took

---

[65] Not long after 1604 Doña Luisa de Carvajal went to England to assist the Catholics persecuted under James I. She died in London in the odour of sanctity, and January 1614.

them into her own house as guests, where they remained for two months. She was conversing with them one day about the death of Mother Thomasina-Baptist, and said: "If you could manage to secure Mother Anne of Jesus to take to France, she would suit you very well. She is a very good religious of great talent, and was received by the Holy Mother Teresa of Jesus, who held her in high esteem. But it would be a very difficult matter to accomplish."

This advice was communicated to M. Bérulle, who acted on it at once, and wrote to the Father General, asking for Anne of Jesus, and also for Anne of St. Bartholomew, whom he had met at Avila, where she had conversed with him by a miraculous gift of tongues. M. de Bérulle knew very little Spanish (his negotiations were carried on in Latin), and Sister Anne of St. Bartholomew knew no French, but when they were together both spoke in their native tongue and understood each other perfectly.

It happened not unnaturally that Anne of Jesus was the last sister the General was willing to give, so he proposed that Anne of St. Bartholomew should receive the black veil of a choir nun, and be put at the head of the French convent. The imperfect education of the saintly lay-sister made her unsuitable for a post of such a grave responsibility, and in addition her temperament was timorous and sensitive, and M. de Bérulle and his friends, unsatisfied with this arrangement, determined to obtain the support of Fr. Bañez, and to go to Salamanca to obtain that of Fr. Antolinez and of others at the University there. Their hopes were not disappointed. Fr. Bañez gave them a written attestation, in which he declared that, in his opinion, Anne of Jesus was the most fitted to undertake the new foundation. It runs as follows:

> "Mother Anne of Jesus, Discalced Carmelite nun, was for many years the companion of Mother Teresa of Jesus

in the foundation of her convents. She was her well-beloved daughter, because Mother Teresa recognised in her great humility and prudence combined with a true religious spirit. Since the death of Mother Teresa she has advanced much in these virtues, so that if any religious at all ought to go to France to found and establish a convent of her Order, Anne of Jesus is, in my opinion, the one most suited for the work.

"I can give this testimony, for I knew Mother Teresa and heard her confessions for the space of twenty years, and since then I have kept up my intercourse with all the more noteworthy religious of her Order. On account of the intimacy I have had and still have with these sisters, and because this testimony may be of some importance in the service of God, I give it in writing and sign it with my own hand.

"Given at St. Andrew of Medina del Campo, 4th July, 1604.

"(signed) BROTHER DOMINIC BAÑEZ."

Other testimonies to the same effect were obtained, for, as Manriquez says, it was the general opinion throughout Spain that "Among all those who enjoyed close familiarity with the Saint none had the advantage of venerable Mother Anne of Jesus."

Cardinal Gymnasio, the recently appointed Nuncio in Spain, had so high an opinion of the saintly Mother that he called her "The one woman of her time," and he sent Fr. Peter of the Mother of God, one of the Discalced Friars favourable to the French foundation, to visit Anne of Jesus and tell her how reluctant the Father General was to let her go. Her only answer was, "I shall go, and shall make the foundation without incurring any harm, because the Lord, who commands it to be done, will give me the necessary strength." When the messengers urged the grave reasons for hesitation, that France was in the throes of civil war and religious strife in which Catholics received no mercy at the hands of the Huguenots, while anything Spanish was a special object of hatred, the holy Mother replied: "Oh, the plans of men! will your Reverence tell my Lord, the Nuncio, that His Divine Majesty will arrange this journey for His own good pleasure, by means of which His Lordship little dreams."

Then speaking of the Father General, she added: "He will gain great merit by the contradictions he will meet with, but his plans will not succeed. I shall go, and go with his blessing, in spite of all the objections he is making at present. His fear about sending us among heretics only animates my courage and makes my faith all the stronger."

To her sisters in religion Anne of Jesus spoke with even greater confidence, repeating over and over again: "Nothing will be done without me." The Father General sent strict orders that the venerable Mother was to hold no communication whatever with M. de Bérulle and his friends, and it was diligently circulated outside Carmel that she had an invincible repugnance to going to France. This was not true, but from time to time the devil did all he could to prevent her from undertaking the work, by causing her soul to experience great trouble and extreme desolation of spirit. Her faith triumphed over this painful trial, and on 12th July 1604 she wrote to Fr. Diego de Guevara:

> ". . . My cloud must not distress your Paternity, for God has thrown light upon it by the cries of which my Anne of Jesus has told me. Your Paternity would do me a charity if you would ask her whether they were uttered because I am going or because I am staying here. The difficulties will not stop at that, if it is the devil who is causing them."

Some time previous to this letter the lay-sister had been sent to Alcala, and there, on the day that the Father General felt the first interior movement inclining him to grant the petition that the two Annes might go to France she heard most terrible howls and cries, and was given to understand that they proceeded from the devils, who had raised a great part of the opposition to the French foundation, because of all they would lose by the establishment of St. Teresa's Reform in France.

Anne of St. Bartholomew suffered a great deal also. Opinions at Avila were divided about the holy lay-sister's vocation to go to France. To one who hoped to go in her stead, God replied: "She must go; you, on the contrary, must not"; and He sent her another consoling message: "Tell her she must go without any fear. I foretell to her, as I did to My disciples, that she will be persecuted and despised, but her suffering shall be turned into joy."

Finally, St. Michael, in the guise of a young prince in armour, appeared to Sister Anne of St. Bartholomew herself, saying: "Do not fail to go. Take courage." By these and other similar consolations the servant of God in her autobiography declares "the thorn that timorous people had planted in my heart was withdrawn."

M. Bérulle likewise was not left unconsoled. Whenever he was in Madrid he used to go to see the saintly lay-brother, Francis of the Infant Jesus. One day when he called as usual Brother Francis ran forward to meet him, and throwing his arms round the French priest's neck, exclaimed: 'You will get the mothers you want, and others besides—good ones." "Indeed! and who told you this?" "The Infant Jesus." From that moment M. de Bérulle never doubted again of his ultimate success. He had previously written to Mme Acarie, telling her to find some French lady to direct the Paris Carmel, as he despaired of obtaining sisters from Spain. Each time Mme Acarie approached the subject with M. du Val, her director, God intervened, and by seizing her soul in ecstasy prevented the matter from being discussed. Now M. de Bérulle made another effort, and representatives of the Augustinians, Franciscans and Jesuits all united with him in trying to obtain the consent of the General of the Discalced to let the nuns go. As the General Chapter of the Discalced had not dealt with the matter, the General felt himself obliged to refuse again. The Pope had not sent a command, but had expressed his hope that permission for the French foundation would be granted, which, in view of the constitutions, could not be. The Nuncio was at last obliged to issue a command sanctioned by canonical penalties to be enforced for default that permission should be given for the nuns to leave Spain. The General was thus obliged to obey, and promised to prepare the necessary documents. He has been much blamed for his delay, but there is no doubt that he acted prudently throughout the whole business. He was responsible to his Chapter, and it was essential that he should be able to show that he had done his duty, until he was compelled to yield.

Still, three weeks passed, and no written permission for the nuns to leave for France was forthcoming. Finally the Nuncio sent a confidential messenger to the Father General, with instructions that the "Obedience" for the nuns must be delivered to him within an hour, or the General would be put under major excommunication and be deprived of his office. This had the desired effect. The document was handed over at once, and as soon as the Nuncio received it he sent it on to M. de Bérulle. It reads:

"Jesus, Maria.

"Brother Francis of the Mother of God, General of the Discalced Order of Our Lady of Mount Carmel in the Kingdom of Spain: seeing that the Most Illustrious and Most Reverend Lord, Cardinal Gymnasio, Nuncio, and Apostolic Collector General of His Holiness in three kingdoms, has charged and commanded me, by a letter signed by His Most Illustrious Lordship and sealed with his seal, to give as foundresses of a monastery of Discalced nuns of our Order, which the Princesse de Longueville purposes, with the permission of His Holiness, to establish in Paris, in France, Mother Anne of Jesus, who is in our convent in Salamanca, Sister Anne of St. Bartholomew, who is in our convent in Avila, with two other religious whom the said Mother Anne of Jesus shall choose: Hence, obeying the good pleasure and command of his Illustrious Lordship, I give my consent and my permission, and I command in virtue of Holy Obedience, the said Anne of Jesus and Isabel of the Angels and the other[66] 1 whom she shall choose, and the said Anne of St. Bartholomew, so that all the four together may go to the said town of Paris and do, concerning the Foundation of the said Convent, whatever shall be ordained and commanded them by His Holiness: and I command, in virtue of Holy Obedience, that no religious sister, superior or subject shall prevent the said religious from leaving their convents; that they shall take leave of them with the accustomed affection of fraternal kindness; and I enjoin and command the prioresses and nuns of the convents through which they shall pass while on their journey to receive them with charity and give them hospitality.

"In testimony of which I give these presents, signed with my name and sealed with the seal of my office.
"Given in our monastery of Madrid, 4th August, 1604.
"(Signed) BROTHER FRANCIS
OF THE MOTHER OF GOD,
"General."
Place of the Seal of the Order.

---

[66] The name Beatrix of the Conception was in the original, but, on account of difficulties regarding her family, it was erased and replaced by the words "y otra."

CHAPTER XIV

SALAMANCA ONCE AGAIN

1594-1604

THE last chapters have digressed somewhat from the chronological record of the life of Anne of Jesus. To pick up its threads it will be necessary now to go back to 1594, when arrangements were made for the venerable Mother to return to Salamanca. On the way to that city lay Avila, and in that hallowed spot Anne of Jesus rested for a day or two before going on to Alba de Tormes, to which in 1586 the holy body of her beloved Mother had been restored. Faculties had been obtained for once more examining the sacred remains, and one of the two friars who accompanied Anne of Jesus from Madrid being a Definitor-General, he was to preside at the exhumation. As before, the Saint's body was found fresh and incorrupt and it exhaled a most delicious perfume. When taken out of the coffin, it was reverently set upright, and so perfect was its preservation that it seemed to the assembled community as if their holy Foundress were alive again and standing in their midst. While Anne of Jesus was reverently handling the body she noticed a stain of blood upon one of the shoulders. She applied a linen cloth to the spot, which instantly became soaked with bright red blood. A second cloth was applied with a like result, and at the same time Anne of Jesus heard her holy Mother's voice, telling her that she loved her so much she was giving her her very blood, and thanking her for all she had done.

It is well known that when Avila claimed St. Teresa's body the ecclesiastical authorities at Alba detached and retained her left arm. When the body was restored to the latter city the arm had been enclosed in the same case as the rest. Now, however, Anne of Jesus, had the arm placed in a silver reliquary in order that it might be ready for the veneration of the faithful, when the Cause of the Beatification should be completed.

Once Anne of Jesus reached Salamanca, her sole desire was to live as one of the community, unnoticed and unknown. Nevertheless, her reputation for wisdom and infused theological knowledge had preceded her, and many visitors came to consult her on all sorts of topics; while learned professors, clerical and lay, of the University of Salamanca came to ask her advice. Fr. Dominic Bañez, went so far as to say, in defence of a thesis he was propounding: "Even if there were nothing else in its favour, it is proof sufficient, in my opinion, that Anne of Jesus supports this view." The professor of Scripture, Fr. John Alphonsus Curiel, used to go over his lectures with the humble Carmelite nun as a means of ensuring their success, and he used to call her "One of the wonders of the world."

These men continued their correspondence with her after she had left Spain. It is not to be wondered at, therefore, that her sisters in religion often urged her to commit to writing the lights vouchsafed to her from heaven. But this she never consented to do. "All I want is that my name be written in heaven," she would reply. If her friends urged the glory her writings would give to God, she would smile gently, and say: "The glory of God must be in dire straits if it needs a pen like mine. And as for my neighbour, I should, in writing, do more harm by my ignorance and errors of judgment than I could ever do good."

Anne's virtue gave her great power over others. A lady of Salamanca, whose husband had been murdered, absolutely refused to forgive the perpetrator of the outrage.

SALAMANCA ONCE AGAIN

Anne of Jesus, hearing of this, sent for her, and after listening to her story, suggested that they should say an "Our Father" together. At the petition. "Forgive us our trespasses as we forgive them that trespass against us," the prioress stopped, and turning to her visitor said, "Do you really mean to ask God's pardon on that condition. "Of course I do," was the reply. "Then, surely, to obtain your own forgiveness you must forgive your husband's murderer." At these words God's grace triumphed and a complete reconciliation ensued.

In March 1596 Anne of Jesus was chosen prioress of Salamanca Carmel by a unanimous vote. Some of her novices left written records of her methods of training.

> "She had a gift for doing good to those confided to her care," writes one, "and of recognising the natural dispositions and virtues of each, and the path by which she should be led.... One day, soon after I had come, she asked me to tell her any faults I had noticed in her. 'Mother,' I replied, 'I certainly do not myself know any fault of which I can tell your Reverence, but since you oblige me, I must tell the truth. I have heard it said that you are very strict, and I think you are, too.' The saint replied: 'Now, my dear daughter, I shall not correct myself of that so long as I have daughters such as I have at present, animated with so good a spirit. For I would have you know that St. Bernard says that it is taking bread out of the mouths of children to deprive any souls of mortifications that they are able to bear.'"

The same sister relates that when Doña Felicia de Mendoza brought one of her daughters as a postulant and was grieved at the austere life she would have to lead, the holy prioress replied: "Do you think that God will be satisfied with this one pledge of your love? Come, offer Him generously your other two children, for you will give them both to Carmel." Four years later her second daughter entered at Salamanca, and her son, who had been married, lost his wife, became a priest, and later on joined the Friars of the Mitigated Observance.

On another occasion when a little daughter was born to Doña Aña de Castro the mother sent to Anne of Jesus, begging her prayers and a blessing for the child. When replying, the prioress foretold that the little girl would be a Carmelite. Twenty years went by, and the mother began to form plans for her daughter's marriage, as she herself desired to be free to enter Carmel. "Would to God," she exclaimed, "that Anne of Jesus were here to tell me what is God's Will." A night or two later, as Doña de Castro lay awake, she saw by her bedside a Discalced Carmelite nun, leaning on two sticks. At first she thought it was St. Teresa, who was thus showing her that her daughter ought to enter Carmel, but would become lame. Then she heard a voice saying: "Neither the one nor the other." Upon which the figure disappeared. For a few days the lady was in great perplexity, but at last she went to the Carmelites for advice, and their chaplain showed her a portrait of Anne of Jesus lately received from Brussels. What was her astonishment to behold the very nun whom she had seen at her bedside. This decided her to withdraw her opposition to her daughter becoming a nun, and she arranged for her to be received at Salamanca.

As early as 1599 Anne of Jesus was suffering from dropsy and other maladies, yet she kept her resolution of never fully satisfying any desire, especially in her bodily needs. Sometimes, by way of encouraging her, the nuns would speak to her of the sufferings of Our Lord. But to the tender and loving heart of His spouse this brought no relief.

SALAMANCA ONCE AGAIN

"It makes me smile," she once said, "to hear the sisters urging me in my sufferings to think of the Passion of Our Lord. For to think of what He endured hurts me much more than my own pain." In her cell the Servant of God had a wooden crucifix. More than once she had, when gazing at it, seen herself enshrined in the Heart of her Divine Saviour.

Yet with all this, perhaps because of it, Anne of Jesus was alert and capable in all the temporal affairs of her convent. Her free moments were spent making altar linen or lace. In 1602 there was question of her being sent to found a Carmel at Ciudad Rodrigo, but for some unknown reason the project came to nothing. That year the general elections among the friars were due, and the matter was earnestly recommended to her prayers. Two names in particular were spoken of as likely to receive votes. One day, speaking to the rector of the Carmelite college, she said: 'Father, you must find someone else for the post of General, for neither of the two friars about whom there is so much talk at present will fill the vacancy." The rector questioned her further and elicited the reply that she had seen both of them buried. Her words proved true. Both friars died before the elections took place, and the new General was Fr. Francis of the Mother of God. Another day while the holy prioress was going to confession she stopped in her accusation, and after a moment's pause, said: "Fr. Alphonsus of the Mother of God has just died; a wall has fallen on him and he is buried in the debris. Give thanks to God, Reverend Father, and be comforted, for he has had only a moment of purgatory." Her confessor, the rector just mentioned, put no faith in his penitent's story, but before he left the Carmel messengers arrived confirming what she had told him. He confidently hoped that her word about the sequel to the Father's death was equally true.

Nor was it only for members of her own Order that Anne of Jesus received supernatural enlightenment. Once, when both the Augustinians and Dominicans aspired to fill the chair of Scripture at the University, she declared unhesitatingly that it would be filled by Fray Antolinez, the Augustinian candidate. Again, Don Diego de Corral was, out of deference to Anne of Jesus, offered a high post in Lima. Before accepting it he asked her advice. "Do not take it," was the answer, "you will have far higher ones here." Words which were verified later.

A letter written by Anne of Jesus towards the end of 1602 contains these words: "God wants me to live where I shall serve Him best. Our Reverend Father is praying about it, for I desire nothing so much as to please God. His Divine Majesty conferred so great a favour on me lately that I hardly know how I bore it. Therefore I besought our Reverend Father General, who is asked to make a foundation in France, that if he sends any nuns, I may be among the number. And the foundations will probably take place, for all has been arranged for at Paris. Our loving Lord so overwhelms me with His favours that I would suffer myself to be torn in pieces, if by so doing I could advance His glory and find means of showing Him my gratitude."

Probably the favour thus referred to was a consoling vision granted to the holy prioress on the feast of St. Luke. She saw a great light entering the Church, and in its rays many Carmelite nuns.

In August 1604 M. de Bérulle and his companions set out for Salamanca, the very day they received from the Nuncio the "*Exeant*" for the nuns. All of them were full of joy at obtaining at last "The treasure for which they were seeking." On their arrival, however, there were fresh delays, Anne of Jesus was still kept "*arrinconada*," "in a corner," with express orders to hold no communication with the deputation from France. While waiting for matters to be arranged, Madame Jourdain and Mademoiselle de Pucheul spent much of their time praying in the church attached to the Carmel. It was furnished, as Carmelite churches at that date often were, with one or two small parlours, in one wall of which a small closed grate communicated with the enclosure. Such structures were popularly called "confessionals," and they were used by people seeking advice from the nuns. The two French ladies, hearing a gentleman's voice proceeding from one of these confessionals, begged him to let the sister know that others wished to speak to her when his interview was finished. In due time they went to the grate together, and were delighted to find themselves speaking to Mother Anne of Jesus. Mlle de Pucheul explained what had brought them to Salamanca, and how, after many disappointments, they had at last obtained leave from the Father General to take her to France. The venerable Mother then made known her willingness to go, contradicting all reports to the contrary, but added that she would not leave without bidding farewell to the friars and obtaining their blessing, for she wished two of them to accompany her as far as Paris.

This unexpected request caused further delays. M. de Bérulle and Mme Acarie, who had foreseen the difficulty, since the Spanish knew very little French and would need confessors, objected to the plan. But the venerable Mother held to her wish, and M. de Bérulle had to go back to Valladolid to arrange the matter and obtain the necessary authorisations. While he was away the French ladies were often at the Carmel. One day when the venerable Mother herself was in the speak-house, Isabel of the Angels, hearing that the French ladies were there, obtained leave to go and see them. It happened that M. de Bérulle had just returned, and being present, he asked the new-comer her name. "Isabel of the Angels." "Oh, then," was the reply, "you are one of those named in the obedience." God had answered her two seemingly unheeded letters to the Father General, and she was filled with consolation. Unknown to these two sisters, St. Teresa herself had indicated to Anne of Jesus those whom God had chosen. While she was praying during matins for the success of the journey to France, she one day saw St. Teresa tenderly embracing the sub-prioress, Mother Isabel of the Angels and Mother Beatrix of the Conception. It was on this account that their names had been inserted in the Father General's permit.

All documents being at last to hand, Anne of Jesus highly commended the zeal and despatch of M. Bérulle. "This little Don Pedro," she said, "has more vigour and determination than all the friars put together. Our holy Mother would have loved him much."

CHAPTER XV

THE JOURNEY TO PARIS

August 20th - October 15th 1604

WITHIN the Carmel at Salamanca preparations for the journey to France had been made with the utmost secrecy. On St. Bernard's feast, 20th August, the nuns and French ladies got into their respective coaches at one a.m., their escort of friars, priests and serving men being on horseback. M. du Val thought it a good omen that the journey should commence on the feast of one of France's most glorious saints, while Mme Jourdain wrote in her diary:

> "... What can be said of the happiness of the French travellers who, after so much pain and trouble, at last possessed the living stones of the edifice they wish to build, stones cut and polished by the hand of the Most High, and by that of His most dear friend, the blessed and holy Teresa of Jesus ..."

The first stop was at Peñarandu, where the priests said Mass very early. The same day Avila was reached, where the nuns lodged at St. Joseph's Convent. Here news arrived that there was a young nun at Löeches who knew French. Anne of Jesus thought she would be useful and as the General, Fr. Francis of the Mother of God, had come to Avila to meet the travellers, permission was given for M. de Brétigny to go and fetch her. It turned out to be none other than Sister Eleanor of St. Bernard, to whom five years previously Brother Francis of the Infant Jesus had foretold her mission to France.

During the delay thus caused the nuns received every kindness from the community of Avila. August 24th was the anniversary of the foundation of St. Joseph's Convent, and on that day Mme Jourdain and her companions were allowed to converse with the nuns with the grate open.

On 29th August the journey was resumed. The nuns had begged hard for a relic of their Holy Mother, but this was refused. The Father General went with them for five or six miles on the way to Burgos, and before finally taking leave of the nuns he appointed Anne of Jesus prioress, and Isabel of the Angels sub-prioress. It was the hottest part of the summer and the whole party had much to suffer. Two of the nuns contracted fever, while the prioress's habitual maladies caused her a great deal of discomfort. M. de Bérulle did all he could to make things easy, but some of the country people would not sell even a loaf of bread to a Frenchman, so that he determined, once Burgos was reached, to carry provisions with them. The friars, alarmed at this state of things, insisted on staying at Burgos until some arrangement had been made to secure their having enough money in hand to pay for their return to Salamanca, should that be necessary. M. de Brétigny was able to obtain a loan of 2,000 scudi, and during the delay thus caused the community at Burgos made the nuns very welcome. One of their number, Sister Isabel of St. Paul,[67] a distant connection of Mlle de Pucheul, had written to her higher superiors some months previously, urging them to allow the French foundation to be made, though she abstained, through humility, from offering to go herself. It happened that one of the sisters named for Paris could not go, and Anne of Jesus suggested to the Father Provincial that Isabel of St. Paul should take her place. The latter was sent for, and the Provincial, without more ado, told her to be ready to start for France the next morning. "Whatever your Reverence pleases," was

---

[67] Isabel de Chavaira. Her mother was Flemish, name unknown.

the reply, and though it was then eight p.m., Sister Isabel was ready by four a.m. the next day.

After leaving the Carmel the travellers went to venerate the miraculous crucifix in Burgos Cathedral. The journey was by no means a comfortable one. "I received many a good scolding," Mme Jourdain writes, "when anything went wrong." She was ill herself, and Sister Anne of St. Bartholomew consoled her by telling her that twenty years previously she had had a vision of the journey to France and had seen Mme Jourdain herself among the French Carmelites. The diary gives several quaint anecdotes quite in keeping with Teresian tradition.

At Irun the Provincial of Catalonia joined the party. He was to accompany the nuns to Paris instead of the Provincial of Castile. A relative of one of the friars had a large country house in the neighbourhood, where he invited the travellers to rest. All were eager to do so except Anne of Jesus. "If we delay for a single day," she said, "we shall find ourselves obliged to give up our enterprise and return to our convents." It was decided therefore to continue the journey. When the small river separating France from Spain was reached the nuns were taken across in rowing boats. As soon as she stepped on to French soil Anne of Jesus exclaimed "Agora yo soy Madre," "Now, indeed, I am a Mother!"

The Psalm *Laudate Dominum*[68] was intoned with the antiphon: "*The snare is broken and we are set free.*" There was more reason for rejoicing than they knew, but the day passed peacefully, and next morning they reached St Jean de Luz. As the travellers left the church after hearing Mass, Mme Jourdain suddenly perceived a delicious perfume and found herself rapt in profound recollection. When she told

---

[68] Praise the Lord, Psalm 116 (117). -Editor.

the Spanish Mothers they replied "It is our Holy Mother Teresa of Jesus, who is walking with us." The nuns had themselves been consoled by this assurance that their Foundress was welcoming them to France.

That evening a courier arrived from Spain bearing an order from Cardinal Gymnasio that the nuns were to return to their convents.[69] Anne of Jesus had been right, and when the two Provincials learnt the purport of the courier's message they crossed themselves devoutly, recognising in her refusal to delay the manifest intervention of God.

> "The venerable Mother herself," wrote Mother Beatrix of the Conception, "smiled at the wonder of those about her, and said that she had great hopes that God would be well served in the undertaking, since He had arranged everything so perfectly. She also added that it was their holy Mother Teresa who obtained these graces, and that she was watching over their journey with great joy."

No delay was made on account of this letter, for the nuns were already in France, where no Spanish authority could compel obedience, and the party pushed on to Bayonne. Delayed by a terrific thunderstorm, the nuns had to pass the night in their coach. Sister Anne of St. Bartholomew notes:

> "It was so dark that we could not see our own hands. The best inn we could get was to stay where we were. It was the vigil of St. Matthew the Apostle, and we were all fasting. God permitted that our provisions ran short, so that we had nothing to eat—no bread, no wine, no water except what was falling from the heavens so abundantly that it seemed to come down in bucketsful. The wind was furious enough to overturn everything, and the sea, which was quite near, roared to such a degree that at any

---

[69] Some accounts say that the despatch was not from the Nuncio, but from King Philip III.

other time I should have been very frightened."

The Father Provincial of Castile declared that "the nuns had been brought away to be killed, not to make a foundation."

Two days were spent at Bayonne, and when the travellers started again the Provincial of Castile returned to Spain. When crossing Les Landes, a low-lying sandy plain covered with pine forests, the nuns had to go on foot, Anne of Jesus leading the way and encouraging the others. When they were able to get into the coaches again, they were so anxious to court martyrdom (as they thought) by proclaiming themselves Catholics that they held their rosaries and crucifixes outside the windows to proclaim their readiness to die for their Faith. As they neared Guyenne six brilliant stars appeared in the heavens. They were stationary at first, but afterwards all except one disappeared in a northerly direction, thus symbolising that only one of the six Spanish Mothers would die in France.[70]

At Bordeaux the Spanish coaches were dismissed, and the nuns stayed four days in the house of a Spanish gentleman. M. de Bérulle, however, went straight to Paris, leaving M. de Brétigny in charge. This devoted friend purchased outright "a coach and four beautiful black horses." After stopping a night at Saintes, the travellers went on to Poitiers, where the nuns lodged in the royal abbey of the Holy Cross.

Meanwhile M. de Bérulle had been received at Fontainebleau by Henry IV, who sent the nuns a cordial message of welcome, and recommended himself to their

---

[70] This was Mother Isabel of the Angels. She was foundress and prioress at Amiens, Rouen, Bordeaux, Toulouse and Limoges, where she lived twenty-five years. She died there in the odour of sanctity, 14th October 1644, aged eighty-four.

prayers. Finally, on the twenty-second anniversary of St. Teresa's death, the nuns arrived at Paris. They drove past the new convent which was being built for them by Mme Acarie, and went to St. Denis, then a village outside the city, to venerate the proto-martyr of France. The Princesse de Longueville and her sister, with Mme Acarie and other illustrious ladies, met the nuns, who got out of their coach to be embraced and welcomed. That night they stayed at Montmartre with the Benedictines, and in the morning M. de Brétigny said Mass there and gave Holy Communion to the nuns. He spent several hours afterwards in prayer and thanksgiving for the accomplishment of the work for which he had been praying and suffering for twenty years.

Anne of Jesus wrote a letter describing the journey to France, and sent it to Spain in the spring of the following year. It mentions the first foundations she made as well as other matters, and so forestalls what will be related in future chapters.[71]

Jesus.

> "May God be blessed, Who has deigned to allow that I should receive a letter from your Lordship in the land of our exile where we are living in order to please His Divine Majesty. For that it was which made us leave Spain. Our departure was so hurried that we had not time to speak to our own Sisters in the convent, nor would they give permission for us to visit those we passed on the way, excepting at Avila, Burgos and Vittoria where a halt was indispensable. I do not know if this was due to some fear on the part of our Father General, or if it was

---

[71] The letter bears no address and no name. The abbreviation used in the Spanish original "V.S." (Vuestra Señoria) together with several of the phrases used make it seem probable that the addressee was some Bishop, very possibly her cousin, Christopher de Lobera, Bishop of Osma, to whom she was wont to sign herself "Your subject."

the wish of Fr. Provincial who accompanied us nearly half way, for he is a man of many contrary qualities.

"The incidents of the journey were full of difficulties and I may say it was a miracle that we came through alive. Of the three hundred leagues that we had to travel, we were certainly on foot for more than a hundred, and yet we walked with so much ease that the fatigue never lasted for long. My first real sorrow was when we crossed over into France, where I saw the Blessed Sacrament treated with great disrespect. I cannot describe how It is reserved in many places. To mention one place among others, we found the Sacred Host Itself covered with maggots; it was a year since It had been renewed. We could not touch It and were forced to leave It as It was. Judging by the reverence, love and sorrow we felt in seeing His Majesty in this state, I think there must have been a small portion left that was not corrupted. God allowed this, no doubt, in order that we might see accomplished that which He once said through His prophet of Himself 'I am a worm and the outcast of men.' The majority boast of being heretics. Some of them, of good standing, have by the mercy of God been converted since our coming into this country. We arrived here two days before St. Luke. The Princesse de Longueville, our foundress, came to meet us on the way, accompanied by several other ladies. We wanted to make our entry privately, in order to go to St. Denis before entering the convent. For this reason we crossed the whole of Paris, which is an extremely large town. St. Denis is two leagues away, and that is the distance the saint walked carrying his head in his hands. We went to the spot where he was beheaded, as well as others martyred at the same time. The way these holy places have been preserved is marvellous. They are kept up with great reverence, and are so richly ornamented, that all that one sees at the Escurial is a mere trifle in comparison to the rich treasury of relics here. They are enshrined in reliquaries adorned with precious stones, so numerous that it is impossible to count them. Among other relics a Nail, a very large fragment of the True Cross, a considerable portion of the Crown of Thorns, the Tunic worn by Our Saviour, which remains entire, and innumerable bodies of Saints. The church is so magnificent that it recalls the temple of Solomon, for not only the walls are inlaid with work in gold, but even the floor-space on which the people walk. All the shrines and reliquaries which contain the bodies of Saints were opened for us, which is only done for Kings; they are of inestimable value. I do not know how to describe all this so as to give you a true idea of it, nor yet the richness of the crowns and other antique objects which are preserved in that spot. There are even vases brought by the Queen of Sheba to Jerusalem as a gift to Solomon, and many other things which I cannot describe by letter. All this is entrusted to a monastery of Benedictine monks. There are many monks of that Order here, but they are not reformed, in spite of the fact that they spend most of the day chanting in choir. People say that the King intends to oblige them to adopt reform, and that if they do not, he will withdraw them from St. Denis: he has been here twice since my arrival.

"I will tell you now how we returned thence to Paris, after stopping on the way at a convent of Benedictine nuns, built on the very spot where the saints suffered martyrdom. They are saints themselves, for, thanks to the books of our holy Mother, they adopted the reform two years ago, so that in some ways they resemble the Discalced. Moreover they treated us altogether as sisters.

"Immediately after this, we went to our own house, which is one of those our holy Mother would have had pulled down, if it were not for the fact that it had been built in piety and ignorance by seculars for it is quite certain that they have spent more than 60,000 ducats upon it, and as yet it is not finished. If the church which adjoins it is finished, 200 ducats will not cover the expense.[72] As to this last, I may say that it awakens great devotion. Under the High altar, is the very grotto in which St. Denis lived when he was preaching Christianity in this kingdom, and where he said the first Mass [in France] and hid with his companions. From that time he dedicated the spot to Our Lady, and our glorious Father St. Joseph, and left their images there carved in stone: they are very devotional. The Church has ten very beautiful chapels, each of which seems like one of the most sumptuous oratories in Spain: it contains the tombs of many saints; of one especially the following story is told: So numerous were the miracles he worked that the peace of the monastery was disturbed. The Superior forbade the Saint to work any more, and he, though dead, obeyed the order. St. Martin of Tours came to this locality and founded a monastery of his Order here. There was also there up to the present time a Priory, which has been bought for us. It consists of a house and a very beautiful garden, with a revenue of 400 ducats. This money will be apportioned to the Church: it will be used to have Masses said, and for other purposes connected with Divine Service.

"While the new convent is being built, we are living in a house close by. The Blessed Sacrament was placed there on St. Luke's day, and the enclosure erected, which we have needs made more strict than in Spain. Thus we have withdrawn from the Princess[73] the Brief which allowed her, as foundress, to enter [the enclosure] accompanied by one of her ladies in waiting. She was

---

[72] This is the figure given but it should probably be 20,000. The fact was that forty-eight nuns' cells had been built instead of twenty, and the rest of the house was in proportion. Anne of Jesus was horrified when she discovered this, but it was too late to have it changed.

[73] Mme. de Longueville.

very sorry about it but submitted, for she is a very great servant of God, and I think that she will take our habit. She has conceived great affection for us, and a great reverence for our Order. We received three novices at once, and began to make arrangements for the return of our friars to Spain before the winter is too advanced. We remain with three learned priests to whom the Sovereign Pontiff has entrusted the government of this convent, and of others that will be founded in France, so far as temporal affairs are concerned. As Visitor, His Holiness has appointed the Prior of La Grande Chartreuse, so long as there are no religious of our Reform in France; for when there are some, His Holiness wishes them to be superiors. It is no use hoping that our General will allow friars to come from Spain, so I am trying to get the help of those in Italy. Will your Lordship recommend this matter to God and since you command me to tell you everything, will you, please, not be tired of so long a letter? I miss your Lordship very much indeed. The prior of the Carthusians has accepted the post of Visitor: I hope that God will not allow him actually to make a Visitation, but that it will be our friars who make it. In case the latter do not come, the Bull ordains that Bishops shall visit us,[74] but that would not be at all suitable, because they are not all Catholics.[75]

"As to the secular priests whom His Holiness has actually nominated as our Superiors, they are staunch Catholics; and although they have received power to add to or modify the constitutions, according to what may be necessary in this country, they nevertheless wish only for whatever has been left us by our holy Mother. I told them on my arrival that so long as they kept to that, they

---

[74] For the canonical visitation as Ecclesiastical Superiors.

[75] The errors of Gallicanism and Quietism affected some of the French Bishops at this time, especially near Paris.

should have us; but that if they broke away from this agreement, we should return to Spain. Withal they have acted with much moderation, taking care not to offend us in anything. They are much edified by our manner of life.

"We have received seventeen novices from the most Catholic and best families of this town. I would not accept anyone who was born or brought up in heresy, but it will be impossible to avoid this in this kingdom because they are all so mixed up. I held firm in withholding my consent, short of an order from the Sovereign Pontiff. He is to be consulted on this point, and I do not know what his ruling will be. I have moreover, begged Fr. Pedro [M. de Bérulle] to supply all information over there [i.e. at Rome].

"The reverend gentlemen named by the Bull as our Superiors have laid down no rules, hence we have complete liberty for all enjoined by the Order, and we act for the best according to circumstances. We have founded a second convent seven leagues from here, in a town called Pontoise. We could not avoid doing this, because the Archbishop of the locality, who is brother to the king,[76] desired it. He was going to start for Rome where he is to be a Cardinal and he wanted the thing done before his departure. We gave the black veil to Sr. Anne of St. Bartholomew here with all due solemnity, so that she might go there as Prioress. I went with her to make the foundation: we were accompanied by two other nuns from Spain. I found everything so well prepared that as soon as we arrived the Blessed Sacrament was brought, the enclosure erected and the habit given to four very promising novices. With several others from this Paris house, where we have already received seventeen, I left Mother Isabel of St. Paul (who is from Burgos) to be sub-

---

[76] Charles de Bourbon III, Archbishop of Rouen, was a near relation of Henry IV. First he was Bishop of Lectour, and was nominated Archbishop of Rouen, 26th March 1574.

prioress, so that I was able to go back to Paris at the end of the week.

"They were longing for my return, for the affection with which we are held is very great. It is truly a miracle, for the generality here have little sympathy with Spaniards. People are astonished to see such great friendship and close union amongst us: the French [novices] say that in the whole kingdom there are no daughters of the same father and mother who love one another as we do. They are much struck with the manner their souls advance in perfection from the first moment they take the habit, and their spirit becomes, as it were, renewed in a different manner of prayer. I take care that they meditate on Our Lord and imitate Him, for here people very seldom think of Him. All is done by a simple glance at God: I do not know how. Since the days of the glorious St. Denis, who wrote on mystical theology, everybody has striven to be united to God by suspension rather than by imitation. This is a strange way of acting. To tell the truth I do not understand it at all, no more than I do their way of talking. I cannot even read [French]. But God has given the grace that, without knowing their language and they being ignorant of ours, we understand one another perfectly and live in great peace, following with great exactitude all our community exercises. Since I left Spain His Divine Majesty has given me sufficient health to enable me to follow community life, but I do it with so little fervour that it seems as if God and my soul had stayed in Spain. May your Lordship have compassion on me and ask His Divine Majesty to exercise His Divine mercy in my regard, and give me grace to do His Holy Will in all things.

"The sovereigns of this country show us much good will. The queen came to see us as soon as she came back to Paris, for she was away when we arrived. She has taken such a fancy to us that she wants to come again. I sent to beg her to put this off till after Advent: up to this she has not been. Just now both she and the king say they want to come. I am taking measures to prevent their coming until we have got into our new house, which will be in about two months from now.

"They send me messages every day, and ask my prayers through Father Coton, of the Society of Jesus, who is confessor and preacher to their Majesties. As a matter of fact, we pray for them very much: may it please God that they benefit by it! The king is greatly in need of such help, although people assure me that he is a good Catholic, and that his needs are not occasioned by a want of faith. There is very little of this last in many districts in France, but here at Paris, which is truly a world in itself, evidences of religion are to be seen everywhere: the frequent reception of the Sacraments rivals that of the primitive church. As to that, people are astonished not to see us at Holy Communion more frequently: we keep to what is practised by the Order.

"Our superiors named by the Bull are themselves our confessors; for us Spaniards, a priest is appointed who knows our language. I have already begun to invite confessors of other Orders to come for all the nuns, so that they may enjoy what was taught us by our Mother; but as I do not know any personally, I act with due precautions. May the Almighty guide me in all things, and may He give your Lordship patience to read so long a letter. I should be very grateful if you would show it to your daughters, our sisters. I cannot write to them just now, nor send you the answers to what you asked me to say to Mother Anne of St. Bartholomew, for she is prioress at the second convent we have founded seven leagues from here, as I have said. It bears the name of our holy Father St. Joseph, and this Mother governs it as a saint. Your Lordship well knows that she is one. Moreover, her absence leaves a big void, although those who are with me are a great help, in particular the two from Salamanca. They are both brave souls, and are dying to be martyred. For the moment, however, I see no reason for thinking this will happen, unless it be a long time hence. May the Holy Spirit strengthen us.

"I implore your Lordship to ask this grace of Him for us: and to help us by sending some books containing printed sermons, for we did not bring any with us; also some other devotional books, the sort that suit your own taste. I should very much like, besides this, all that you possess in the way of the writings of our holy Mother, provided it is not what I sent your Lordship from Salamanca. Father Thomas of Jesus ought to have finished that. It is very easy to get parcels by way of Balbao and Barcelona; they come very safely by sea. I beg of you also to send us some perfumes for our church;[77] they have none here, and I have nearly used up all I brought. Your Lordship knows with what veneration the most Blessed Sacrament is surrounded among us, and in this country that is still more necessary than it is elsewhere.

"I should also like some pictures of the Nativity, for those made here do not satisfy me at all. We all beg your Lordship to do us these favours, and we pledge ourselves to assist you by our feeble prayers, which indeed is an obligation. Be so good as to ask our sisters to write to us and to deliver to them the enclosed letter. I have no news of the Lord Bishop of Cordova, nor of our other friends; their letters must have been lost. They come safely when they are addressed to the Spanish Ambassador here, whose name is Don Baltazar de Zuniga. It is not at all the same with the couriers, and this knight is quite willing to do us this act of kindness; he is the brother of the Count de Monterey. The Flemish Ambassador, named Philip de Ayala, does us a like favour. If the envelope bears the address of either of these two noble lords, the letters will be put into my own hands. I am sending this to our

---

[77] The custom of burning perfumes in church is still in use in certain localities.

Father Peter of the Mother of God in answer to his, though this will cause it to make a roundabout course.

"May His Divine Majesty preserve your Lordship for us, with all the sanctity we beg of Him to bestow on you.

"From Paris, at the Convent of the glorious St. Joseph of the Incarnation.[78]

"March 8th 1605.

"My Lord and my Father,
"I am your Lordship's unworthy daughter and subject,

ANNE OF JESUS,
Carmelite."

---

[78] It was perhaps a custom in Spain to add St. Joseph's name to that of any convent which did not already bear it. Anne of Jesus does that here; and Sr. Mary of the Incarnation, in speaking of the Carmel of Madrid, calls it "Our Convent of St. Anne and St. Joseph," though its official name was "St. Anne."

CHAPTER XVI

THE CARMEL OF THE INCARNATION, PARIS

1604

AFTER a day spent with the Benedictines of Montmartre, the six Carmelites were conducted in the evening of 15th October to their temporary Convent of Notre Dame des Champs. A great crowd gathered to witness their arrival. According to custom, Anne of Jesus intoned the *Laudate Dominum*, and after spending a short time in prayer visited the house. All was in order—even the domestic utensils were of the same pattern as those the nuns were accustomed to use in Spain, for the Princesse de Longueville had consulted M. de Brétigny on even the smallest detail. When the prioress came to read the Bull of Erection, however, she found that the convent in Paris was given jurisdiction over any others that might subsequently be founded from it. This was quite contrary to St. Teresa's Constitutions, as Anne of Jesus explained to the French superiors. They at once renounced any pretension of making Paris the headquarters of the Carmelite nuns in France, and gave most solemn pledges that they would do nothing contrary to the Constitutions of the holy Mother. Earlier in the day the bishop, regretting the permission he had given for the new foundation, sent word that no public ceremony might be held. The nuns were exempt from his jurisdiction, and this did not please him. With much tact M. de Gallement went at once to see him. "My lord," he said, "the nuns will most certainly be under your jurisdiction, for they are under mine, and I am entirely devoted to you." For answer the bishop sent his own chaplain to say Mass in the convent the next morning. A great crowd assembled, and the Blessed

Sacrament was exposed all day. Anne of Jesus wished to dedicate the first foundation to St. Joseph, but M. de Bérulle and Mme Acarie, to whom it owed so much, overruled her desire, and the convent was dedicated to the Mystery Of the Incarnation. Three days later the Queen of France, Marie de Medici, and the princesses, with all their suite, came to visit the nuns, bringing with them many rich presents. At the queen's request M. de Brétigny was presented to her, and she thanked him cordially for bringing the Spanish Mothers to France. In his reply he gave all the credit to M. Bérulle. "As for myself," he added, "I was only a hindrance by my lack of talent and virtue."

Almost at once many postulants presented themselves. Anne of Jesus knew no French, and Mothers Isabel of St. Paul and Eleanor of St. Bernard were not very proficient, so the task of selecting suitable subjects was left to the ecclesiastical superiors. These in their turn delegated the choice, to Mme Acarie. Three were accepted, who were to receive the habit on the feast of All Saints: Mme Jourdain to be presented by the Princesse de Longueville, Mlle Hannivel to be presented by the Princesse Estouteville, and Andree Levoix, lady's maid to Mme Acarie, presented by her late mistress. After welcoming them all at the door of the enclosure, Anne of Jesus stretched out both hands to Andree Levoix and drew her forward, so that she was the first to enter the cloister. The two princesses, far from taking offence, regarded this action as a proof of the prioress's virtue, and the other two postulants begged that Andrée might be clothed first. Thus it came about that the first novice of the Carmelite Reform in France was a girl of humble birth.

A few days later two more were received—Mlle de Fontaines and Mlle Deschamps—and on the feast of Our Lady's Presentation a young widow—Mme de Coudray (*Née*

Sevin)—was clothed, another one—Mme la Marquise de Breauté—having the same happiness on the feast of the Immaculate Conception, bringing the number up to seven. "These," say the MS. annals, "were the foundation stones whereon was built the edifice of the Reform in France, which, brought up and nourished in the spirit of St. Teresa by her first daughters, has since spread so many blessings throughout all the provinces of the kingdom."

God worked an habitual miracle for His chosen spouses, enabling Anne of Jesus speaking in Spanish to be perfectly understood by her French novices, while she on her side understood all they said to her in French. This miracle was not extended to the prioress's dealings with outsiders; for this she had to make use of an interpreter.

Contemporary manuscripts give an excellent idea of how the venerable Mother governed:

> "Mother Anne of Jesus exacted great simplicity from her daughters. The least evasion was an unpardonable fault in her eyes as well as in those of the other Mothers ... They thought a spirit of gaiety essential to the spirit of a good Carmelite and spared themselves no trouble in preparing little amusements in recreation time. They composed hymns as each festival came round, and had scenes enacted from the lives of the saints."

Two of these hymns, composed by Anne of Jesus, have been preserved. The longer one bears no title and consists of six stanzas, each ending with the same refrain. The first runs as follows:

> God of heaven's eternal height,
> Beauty beyond compare,
> Almighty One, our sole delight,
> Who three one Godhead share,
> Forgive me through Thy mercy sweet,
> I bring my sins to Thee:

> See me, dear Jesus, at Thy feet:
> What dost Thou ask of me?[79]

The other is interesting because it is a hymn to Christ the King:

Mirad al Rey de los reyes.	Behold the King of kings.
Que por hacernos seriores,	God made man He chose to be
Se sujeto a nuestras leyes	And on Himself took all our pain
y se cargo de dolores.	That we as lords with Him might reign.
	Who seeing what this brings
Quien abra que viendo esto	To His Creator, God, and Lord,
En su Dios y Criador	Will not deny his will
no se deshaga a si rnismo	Whene'er occasion doth afford,
y tome por occasion	
negar todas sus quereres	In order that he may fulfil
y da gusto a este Serior	The Will of God both day and night,
que siendo Rey de los reyes	And so return to Christ thus make,
se sujeto a nuestra amor.	Who King of kings by every right Was subject for our sake?
Sujetose de manera	To God, His Father, Jesus gave
en su nacer y morir,	Throughout His life obedience meek
	To Calvary's mount from
y en el modo de vivir	Bethlehem's cave;

---

[79] The above English version is taken from a French translation of the Spanish original.

que no se puede imitar	And though our strength is yet too weak
sino solo procurar	To follow His most perfect ways,
Cumplir con amor sus leges	We can at least with strong endeavour Fulfil his laws and give him praise;
Confesando que siempre El es	
El Rey de los reyes.	Confessing that He is for ever, The glorious King of kings.
Madre Aña de Jesus.	*Mother Anne of Jesus.*

So great was the attraction exercised over their souls by the Blessed Sacrament that the nuns used to carry their spindles into the choir between the hours for office and sit there spinning and singing hymns, or conversing with Our Lord by ejaculatory prayers, often uttered aloud.[80] One day when Anne of Jesus was, as prioress, intoning the Divine Office, the French novices, hearing what was to them a strange pronunciation of Latin, burst into a fit of uncontrollable laughter. The venerable Mother was so displeased at such behaviour in choir that afterwards she not only reprimanded them strongly, but imposed a severe punishment. M. de Bérulle, however, interceded on the novices' behalf, and the penance was withdrawn. Behaviour in the refectory was a point about which Mother Anne took particular care. It pleased her very much to see a novice partaking of what was served without any sign of repugnance, and she used to say that such a one would make a good nun. Undoubtedly the refectory afforded many a trial on both sides. One feast day, Sister Anne of St.

---

[80] After a time this practice was discontinued.

Bartholomew, who was cook, prepared what she thought would be a great banquet—steaks of cod, with highly-spiced stuffing and prune sauce. The poor novices, unaccustomed to this Spanish dish, could do little more than taste their portions. Later on Anne of Jesus said to them: "So, my dear sisters, every day we have to eat dishes prepared to your taste, yet even once in a way you cannot relish our style of cooking." The remark was made in all good faith, but the earliest French chronicles record that even the best food, when cooked by Anne of St. Bartholomew in the Spanish fashion, was more calculated to take away appetite than to promote it. However, the scribe takes care to add that "no evil results ensued, thanks to the saintliness of her who prepared the meals."

It seems beyond doubt that the government of Anne of Jesus leant to the rigorous side. One day Sister Mary of the Trinity (Mlle Hannivel) was in the speak-house with some members of her family who, in the presence of Anne of Jesus, inquired about her health. Quite simply the novice said she was suffering from some little indisposition. When the visit was over the venerable Mother reproved the novice for her frankness. After receiving the correction humbly, Sister Mary asked what she was to say if she were again asked a similar question. "You must say you are quite well according to the will of God," was the answer, "for all our well-being is in His good pleasure."

Sometimes Anne of Jesus made it her business to visit the different offices when she knew that the sister-in-charge was absent, and to try her virtue pulled some of the things out of their places. Then she would send for the sister and ask her if that was the way she looked after the things of God. On these occasions the nuns never excused themselves, but received both reprimand and penance with great humility; and this, as the chronicles relate, gave "great joy and consolation to their prioress." "I have seen such or such a thing done by our holy Mother Teresa of Jesus," Anne would say, "I do not teach you anything new, but only wish you to practise what she taught us." One day a young sister put a few stitches in her veil, to make it sit better. The fault was made an occasion for a public reprimand. "God deliver us from these novelties," said the venerable Mother. "We must not change a single stitch of what our holy Mother prescribed."

Anne of Jesus was often aware of the troubles of her spiritual daughters before they made them known, and her motherly care always endeavoured to relieve them. She used to say that the nuns, having given up everything, ought to find in their prioress both father and mother. Another Sister Mary of the Trinity (Sévin) wrote about her mistress of novices as follows:

> "I should have profited much if I had done all she pointed out to me with so much fervour. She was extremely zealous about my perfection and showed me much kindness. I hid nothing of my interior from her. She liked this confidence, and I benefited by it because I kept receiving fresh instructions how to walk towards God in safety, for He had called me to Himself in quite an unusual way."

This nun was favoured, while still a novice, with several visits from St. Teresa. The saint smiled upon her, and told her she had come to see her Order in France, and was pleased to be able to call the novices her daughters.

It was about this time that the saintly Jesuit, Père Coton, declared that no one in France did more to break the power of Satan than Anne of Jesus.

CHAPTER XVII

FOUNDATIONS AT PONTOISE AND DIJON

1605-1606

DURING the first few months after the arrival of the Carmelites in Paris, so many presented themselves to be received that Mme Acarie proposed making a second foundation. Both M. de Brétigny and M. de Marillac offered their services; and contributed generously to the expense. With the consent of the superiors and of the Cardinal Archbishop of Rouen, Françoise de Joyeuse,[81] some property was bought in Pontoise; it only remained to choose the community. M. de Bérulle and his colleagues proposed to give the black veil of a choir nun to Sister Anne of St. Bartholomew, and appoint her prioress, but the other Spanish Mothers, except Eleanor of St. Bernard, strongly opposed this measure. Both Anne of Jesus and Anne of St. Bartholomew went through a period of suffering, but in the end Anne of Jesus withdrew her opposition, and after Anne of St. Bartholomew had received the black veil, the two went together to Pontoise, accompanied by Beatrix of the Conception, Isabel of St. Paul, and some French novices. On 15th January, 1605, a great concourse of people came out from Pontoise—Our Lady's city, as it was called—to meet the nuns and conduct them in triumph to their new home. The convent was dedicated to St. Joseph, and as soon as the clergy had conducted the community to the choir, Anne of Jesus intoned the *Laudate Dominum*. Monastic enclosure was erected the next day, and that same evening four ladies

---

[81] Charles de Bourbon III was Archbishop of Rouen from 1574 to 1st December 1604, when he resigned. It was probably with him that the negotiations were carried on. He died on 15th June 1610.

were accepted as novices. One of them had been ill in bed for some time, but Mme Acarie asked her if she would be brave enough to get up and be clothed with the others. "Certainly," was the answer, and the next morning she found herself cured, and was the first to receive Our Lady's habit.

During recreation that evening Anne of Jesus kept the novices near her, and told them about St. Teresa and the first beginnings of the Reform. "You are now members of so holy an Order," she said, "that if you keep its Rules and Constitutions perfectly you will go straight to heaven when you die." At Pontoise, as at Paris, Mother and daughters understood one another in spite of being ignorant of French and Spanish respectively. It was the prioress, Mother Anne of St. Bartholomew, who took the novices up to their cells. They slept two together in two small rooms, but no sooner were they alone than they perceived a heavenly perfume. The next morning they eagerly questioned the prioress, who joyfully explained that it must have been St. Teresa who had come to visit them and to give them her blessing.

So well had everything been planned and carried out that Anne of Jesus found that she could return to Paris within a week. She left behind her besides the prioress, Mother Isabel of St. Paul, sub-prioress, Mother Beatrix of the Conception, and Sister Louise of Jesus (Mme Jourdain), still a novice, taking as her companion for the return journey another novice, Sister Aimee of Jesus.

For about eight months M. de Bérulle remained at Pontoise, in order to help Mother Anne of St. Bartholomew in her new and unaccustomed duties. She suffered much in spite of the consolations lavished on her by Our Lord, but she did not break off relations with Anne of Jesus on whose experience she relied.

Before the month of January was out, Anne of Jesus

found it was impossible to get on at Paris without her constant helper and companion, Mother Beatrix of the Conception. She writes:

"Jesus!

"May Our Lord strengthen you with His grace, my dear daughter. Make haste and set all in order regarding the Divine Office,[82] for I want you to come back for Candlemas Day. We cannot have the blessing of the candles without your Charity. Your absence leaves me very lonely; all our sisters miss you, too, and send their love.

"Toribio[83] will tell you the news I have from Spain. Ask him about it, and be quite sure that it is God who arranges all these things, so that our desire to suffer without consolation may be fulfilled.

"Let that be our only consolation, my dear daughter, that and the thought that God seeks to glorify Himself in us. How happy we ought to be, to be able to render His Divine Majesty this service. I beg your Charity to pray for this grace and to abide in His love. I cannot tell you any more just now, except that M. Gallement assures me that very good laysisters will be sent to you without delay to replace Frances.

"I am, my dear daughter,
'The servant of your Charity,
"ANNE OF JESUS."

Mother Beatrix answered the call, and the ceremonies of Candlemas were kept at the Convent of the Incarnation as

---

[82] Anne of St. Bartholomew did not know the rubrics of the Church, and had to learn how to conduct the chanting of the Divine Office.

[83] Toribio Mancanas was nephew to Anne of St. Bartholomew. Her prayers had instantly restored him after he had been almost crushed to death between a wheel of the coach and a stone wall during the journey from Madrid.

desired.

During the Lent of 1605 the first French Carmelite winged her way to heaven. This was Andree Levoix, in religion, Sister Andrew of the Saints. Fervent prayers for her recovery were offered both at Paris and Pontoise. From the latter Carmel, Anne of St. Bartholomew wrote to Anne of Jesus.

> ". . . I am very distressed about the illness of Sister Andrew. We pray much for her here. I feel her sufferings keenly, as well as the pain you must be feeling, you and Madame Acarie, my dear Mother. Your trouble and hers is also mine, on account of the deep affection I bear you both in Jesus Christ. . . ."

It was not God's will to spare the sick novice. After receiving Holy Viaticum, and pronouncing her vows on Good Friday, she died in the arms of Anne of Jesus. On Easter Sunday morning while Mme Acarie was at Matins in the church of St. Gervase, Sister Andrew appeared to her in glory, and thanked her for all she had done for her. This vision was told to the novices, in order to encourage them in the practice of even the least customs of the Order.

It was during this time that Anne of Jesus had a great deal of trouble about receiving as novices Huguenot converts, or the children of such.[84] The difficulty first occurred at Pontoise, with regard to Mlle Abra de Raconis, formerly governess to Mme Acarie's children. Mother Anne of St. Bartholomew thought herself justified in receiving such postulants, as the French superiors assured her that they had faculties to omit the clause: "Are you born of free

---

[84] Besides being mentioned in the Carmelite Ceremonial for Clothing at that time, the point was, at that date, a question of Canon Law. One of the conditions for admission to any Religious Order being birth of Catholic parents.

and Catholic parents?" in the ceremony of Reception. Mother Anne of Jesus, while fully recognising the fact that it would be impossible to refuse all convert heretics into the Carmels of France, nevertheless considered the question of so much importance that it ought to be settled by the Holy See. Supported by Mothers Isabel of the Angels and Beatrix of the Conception, she withheld her consent to the reception of Mlle Abra de Raconis, and in March, 1605, wrote to Rome for a pronouncement on the question.

Many letters were exchanged between Paris and Pontoise, but it will suffice to quote only one which throws light on the painful question of the differences between the two prioresses, and makes it evident that in this, as in other similar matters, Anne of Jesus judged Anne of St. Bartholomew, not from the standpoint of her sanctity, of which she never doubted, but simply from that of her lack of the experience necessary in conducting important affairs. The letter is addressed to M. de Bérulle and bears no date, but it was probably written about Whitsuntide, 1605.

"Jesus, Maria.

"May the Holy Ghost shower all His gifts on your Reverence, together with good health and the strength His grace alone can give. I desire this same divine grace for myself in order to accomplish my duty perfectly, but I do not know whether the Divine Majesty wishes this to be in France, since your Reverence and Doctor du Val find me of so little use here. I have come to think that it is a point of duty for me to do what Our Lord Jesus Christ ordains, which is to stay where we are well received but not where we are not. His Divine Majesty well knew that difficulties like this would befall us.

"For my part, I hold that an account of this innovation[85] should be rendered to the sovereign pontiff,

---

[85] The reception of convert heretics as novices.

since in France it is a necessity. It was no want of [there is a passage here which is illegible in the autograph original] ... At the very beginning of March I wrote that to Rome, and received from there a reply saying that the question would be examined and decided if we were still in this kingdom [France]. If the Pope had not died, the matter would have been settled, but he who is at present Pope will arrange it shortly.

"As for Mother Anne of St. Bartholomew, she has had no occasion up to the present of knowing what it means to make or abrogate a point of Rule or of the Constitutions. If our holy Mother, four or five years before her death, had her constantly with her, it was not to help in business, but only to dress and undress her and to help her to write letters, for her Reverence had broken her arm and the choir nuns could not be always with her. Mother Subprioress herself, although trained by a very holy prioress,[86] has never been called upon to decide anything of importance.

"As for myself—for my sins—I have had to do this from the very first, even before my profession. Since then I have never been able to avoid it, and for more than thirty years I have been in charge of different foundations. As to these, it is fitting, doubtless, that I should concern myself only with their commencement. May God guide them to their perfection, and may He preserve your Reverence, as we all pray that He may ...
"ANNE OF JESUS."

Again to M. de Brétigny, who begged her through charity to receive Mlle de Raconis, the venerable Mother wrote:

"... Blessed be He who has given you such charity towards me. Assuredly it implies much that you should

---

[86] Mother Isabel of St. Paul, trained at Burgos by Mother Thomasina-Baptist.

show any to me, who, you say, have so little. That must
make you constantly ask God to bestow this virtue upon
me, and to make me humble, for I desire that very much.
I think that to be here in France only as a guest, as these
gentlemen put it, is very calculated to give me humility."

Meanwhile no decision came from Rome, so Mother Anne of St. Bartholomew, with the superiors' approval, decided to give the habit to Mlle de Raconis, calling her Sister Clare of the Blessed Sacrament.

Mother Anne of Jesus, in her position as Foundress of the Reform in France, was endeavouring to establish its rules and customs in their integrity. At the beginning of the controversy she had declared that, rather than consent to modifications and changes, she would return to Spain taking the Spanish Mothers with her. When she heard what had been done at Pontoise, before any sanction had been received from Rome, she thought at first of putting her threat into execution. Eventually she gave her consent to the reception of Sister Clare. In her letter to M. de Brétigny quoted above, she concludes with these words:

". . . I pray God to bless Sister Clare of the Blessed
Sacrament. It is a matter of much regret to me that Sister
Eleanor of St. Bernard should have replied, when she
asked for a word from me, that I could not speak French
and that a message was quite unnecessary. I am not
writing to dear Mother Prioress [Anne of St.
Bartholomew] because I count on you to tell her how we
all are, and to recommend me to her prayers and to those
of her saintly daughters. All of us in the convent look
upon ourselves as belonging to you, and we beg the
Divine Majesty to safeguard you by giving you all the
sanctity I desire for you."

Sister Clare of the Blessed Sacrament lived to the advanced age of a hundred. She became Prioress of Tours, and founded the Carmels of Dieppe and Caen, returning to

Pontoise to die.

In reading of these early days of Carmel in France it must never be forgotten that the French had insisted on having nuns who had lived with and been trained by St. Teresa herself, and that if, having obtained what they desired, they then wanted to impose their own ideas on the Spanish Mothers, Anne of Jesus was only doing her duty in protesting that, if she were not allowed to do what she had come to do, it would be better for her to return to Spain.

On St. Bartholomew's Day, 1605, the forty-third anniversary of the Foundation of St. Teresa's Reform, the Paris Carmelites took solemn possession of the convent which had been newly built for them under Mme Acarie's directions. Everything had been provided with the greatest care, and the establishment, though Anne of Jesus never ceased to deplore its great extent, was admirably conducive to all the exercises of contemplative religious.

Soon after this installation, Anne of Jesus received a visit from Beatrix Zamudio, one of her former friends, who had known and loved St. Teresa. Beatrix had begged the holy Foundress to receive her into the Order, but after praying to know God's will, St. Teresa had told her to remain in the world. The saint's advice was accepted, but the pious lady took the name of Magdalen of St. Jerome, and devoted herself entirely to good works. She was held in high esteem at the Spanish Court, and in 1599, when the Archdukes Albert and Isabella took over the government of the Netherlands, she followed them to Brussels. In 1605 she had to visit Spain on business, and it was on her return journey that she called at the Paris Carmel. Delighted with everything she saw, she made up her mind to introduce St. Teresa's Reform into Flanders. Before any steps had been taken to secure this, however, a third foundation was projected at Dijon. It was proposed to Anne of Jesus by the

Rector of the Jesuits, and made possible by the generosity of a pious widow, who offered the nuns her house and all she possessed. As a matter of fact, the house was very small, and the income on the same scale as the house, but the venerable prioress, inwardly fretting against the size and convenience of the houses at Paris and Pontoise, was delighted at the prospect of founding in real poverty.

> "Out of deference to her feelings," says the chronicle, "all necessary permissions and documents were obtained, not without some difficulty, and only after M. de Bérulle had pledged himself to provide subsistence for the nuns until the new convent became self-supporting."

Anne of St. Bartholomew supported the undertaking, and urged M. de Bérulle to send to Dijon the three Mothers from Salamanca, telling him that one of her novices had had a vision, in which she had been told that Our Lady would take the new foundation under her special protection, and that it would do much for the glory of God. Anne of Jesus was named prioress at Dijon, but the superiors arranged that she should also retain that office at Paris, leaving a sister to govern there in her name, and under her advice. The other sisters were Mary of the Trinity (Hannivel), who acted as interpreter and secretary to Anne of Jesus, Frances of the Cross from Pontoise, a lay-sister Mary of St. Albert, and two postulants who could not be received at Paris, the number of the community being complete. The departure was fixed for 9th September. At the last moment Sister Mary of St. Albert was taken dangerously ill, and the doctor refused to let her travel. After praying earnestly for her, Anne of Jesus, confident in Him whose name signifies "Healer," went to the sister's bedside. "After all, Sister," she said, "the doctor is not God. Get up, for we must start after dinner." The young novice obeyed. Weak and trembling, she dressed herself and crawled downstairs, but no sooner had she been helped into the coach than she was perfectly and permanently cured.

The first night the nuns slept at Troyes, where they were welcomed at the celebrated Abbey of Our Lady. Through her interpreter, Anne of Jesus spoke of Our Lord with such burning love that her words remained indelibly impressed on the young niece of the Lady Abbess, who later on used her influence to reform the community, which had fallen into lax ways. On learning that a slight detour the next day would take them to Clairvaux, the holy Prioress decided to go there, in order to venerate the body of St. Bernard. Dijon was reached on 20th September, and the nuns found the house "poor and mean." However, the pious donor had prepared a small oratory on the ground floor, and there Anne of Jesus joyfully intoned the *Laudate Dominum*. The Bishop of Langres sent his Vicar-General that very evening to welcome the sisters, and the next morning Mass was said, and the enclosure established.

At that time anti-Spanish feeling ran high in Burgundy, and especially in Dijon, so that when the people realised that nuns from an enemy country were actually established in their midst, they determined to drive them away. An incident, petty in itself, helped to increase the ill-feeling.

Anne of Jesus had ordered the usual grate for the choir, and the man who made it ornamented it with fleurs-de-lys. The venerable prioress, finding such ornamentation superfluous, seized the offending lilies, and, although they were made of iron, wrenched them off, and cast them on the ground. News spread through the town that the king's emblem had been defaced, and the agitation against the nuns grew fiercer than ever. Another version of the story has it that there was but a single fleurs-de-lys on the central support of the grate, and that when the prioress desired the workman to remove it, he fell into such a passion of anger that he broke the bar together with the emblem, and then spread the report that the "Lilies of France" had been insulted.

Whatever the fact, a tremendous disturbance ensued, so that the municipal authorities came in a body to expel the nuns. Happily the wife of their president had taken the Carmel under her formal protection; and when she heard what was going on, she hastened to the convent, and pointed out to the enraged gentlemen that, far from insulting the fleurs-de-lys, the nuns had used it as an ornament surrounding their tabernacle. With some difficulty the crowd was thereupon dispersed, and the nuns were left in peace. Anne of Jesus showed her usual broad mindedness in continuing to employ the same workman, who, touched by her trust and generosity, served the nuns faithfully for many years.

There was much to be done to make the house into a convent, and, in all that the nuns could do themselves, Anne of Jesus worked first and last. But the strain weakened her, and she was attacked by a sort of pestilence which was ravaging the neighbourhood. Reduced to extremity she had no fear of death: "I have no regret except that I am dying in my bed," she said. "I have greatly desired, and often prayed, to die on the scaffold, cut into pieces for the love of God."[87]

The doctor at Dijon insisted that the prioress should be isolated. This was not easy, for the sisters were for the time being sleeping together in a room divided by curtains. Anne of Jesus sent for the novices to carry away their beds; then, seeing the Spanish Mothers preparing to do the same, she stopped them, saying: "Do not go, my daughters, but give me that toque belonging to our holy Mother. She has cured

---

[87] Perhaps the venerable Mother had in mind the martyrs, whom Luisa de Carvajal was at that date assisting in England, and of whose sufferings Luisa's letters to her were full.

me of several illnesses, and I hope, by the goodness of God, that she will cure me of this also." As soon as the relic was applied, St. Teresa, radiant with glory, appeared to her faithful daughter. Forgetting all about being cured, the sight of St. Teresa only reminded the prioress of her Mother's promise to come for her when she was dying, and she cried out, "Oh welcome, dear Mother!" But the saint, looking graciously down upon her, replied: "It is not time yet; these sisters would be too lonely." Then, approaching the bed, she cured her completely, assuring her that no one would take the disease, and that the novices might bring back their beds. Later on Anne of Jesus confided to Sister Mary of the Trinity that St. Teresa had told her on that occasion that she would found and develop the Order of Our Lady of Mount Carmel in a third kingdom in honour of the Blessed Trinity. The young sister, distressed at the prospect of losing the venerable Mother, asked what kingdom was meant. "Perhaps it will be Flanders," was the reply, though at that date the foundation at Brussels had not been asked for.

The miraculous cure of the Carmelite prioress opened the eyes of the people of Dijon to the treasure their city possessed, and alms of all kinds came pouring in. By 28th October, the feast of SS. Simon and Jude, the alterations in the church were so far completed that it was possible to hold the ceremony of a clothing. Three novices were received, two of whom afterwards died in the odour of sanctity in the Carmels of Beaune and Besançon respectively. It was at this "poor Bethlehem" at Dijon that Sister Mary of the Trinity (Hannivel) made her profession on 1st November, 1605. An exception, was made in her regard, so that she pronounced her vows in the choir, not in the chapter room as St. Teresa had prescribed.[88]

Sister Mary of the Trinity was one of God's chosen souls. Even before the coming of the Spanish Mothers, Our Lord had told her that He wanted her "in the Order that has My Mother for Mother, and St. Joseph for Father," and from that day the young girl had never looked back. Anne of Jesus treated her as her "eldest daughter," and so deeply did she drink of the spirit of the Reform that she afterwards helped much to pass it on to others. Indeed, the happiest relations existed between the Spanish Mothers and all their French daughters, so that the former often used to say: "If our holy Mother could see you, sisters, how much she would love you. We might be in Spain during the first days of the Reform." What praise could be higher than that?

At Dijon Anne of Jesus once again experienced the spiritual consolations to which she had been a stranger since leaving Spain. One day, one of her novices was so absorbed in prayer that she failed to go to the grate to receive Holy Communion. Our Lord made known to the prioress during her own thanksgiving how much He desired to be present in the heart of the fervent sister, whose state of soul He revealed to her. When Mass was over, Anne of Jesus asked

---

[88] The Formula is as follows: "I, Sister Mary of the Trinity, novice of the Convent of Paris, having come, in obedience to my Superiors, with Mother Anne of Jesus, Prioress of the said convent, to found that of Dijon, make my profession for that same Convent of Paris, and promise Obedience, Chastity and Poverty, to God, Our Lord, to the Blessed Virgin Mary of Mount Carmel, and to you, our Reverend Father Master, James Gallement, and to the other Superiors appointed in France by the Bull of Our Holy Father Clement VIII, and to their successors, according to the Primitive Rule of the said Order of Our Lady of the Carmelites, which is without mitigation, until death.

"(Signed) SISTER MARY OF THE TRINITY"

November 1st, 1605.

the priest to come back to give the novice Holy Communion, much to the astonishment of the community, who had had experience of her firmness in not allowing the grate to be opened at unusual hours. Another day during recreation, a novice, who had a very beautiful voice, sang some couplets, in which occurred the refrain:

> "Angels of glory,
> Come, seek my soul,
> Lift it to heaven above!"

The words so strongly affected the prioress that she could not contain her ardour, and led the whole community to the chapel. There, like David before the ark, the venerable Mother executed a kind of religious dance, singing and clapping her hands in Spanish fashion, but with so much dignity and devotion that all present were deeply edified.

Many outsiders sought counsel and advice from the holy prioress. Her interpreter was usually Sister Mary of the Trinity, but Sister Teresa of Jesus (Mercier), who had learnt Spanish in a way that was almost miraculous, sometimes took her place. Anne of Jesus took great pains in training Sister Teresa, and used to say: "I will teach this young sister everything, because she will instruct others."

One day the Servant of God was talking to a gentleman who was a member of a French *Parlement*. Finding her visitor in good dispositions, she presented him with a bracelet made of steel points, exhorting him to wear it whenever he signed a death-warrant, as a reminder that he would one day have to render an account of his administration of justice.

During 1606 an offer was made to open a Carmel at Amiens. Anne of Jesus accepted the foundation, but did not go in person to superintend it, sending Mother Isabel of the Angels in her stead. Mother Beatrix of the Conception took the latter's place as sub-prioress at Dijon, and this gave occasion for the appointment of a new mistress of novices. Sister Louise of Jesus (Jourdain) was chosen for this important post, and came from Pontoise for that purpose. By the summer of that year it became apparent that Anne of Jesus would have to go to Flanders, and so great was her confidence in Sister Louise that she named her prioress at Dijon. The two religious always remained closely united, and letters often passed between them. Anne of Jesus left to Dijon the stick which St. Teresa had used during her many journeys, as well as other precious relics. To Amiens was reserved the blessing of Mme Acarie's entrance there as a lay-sister in 1614. Her husband died in November, 1613, her three daughters were already Carmelites, and she chose Amiens as the place where she could best give herself to God in seclusion and humble toil.

There is one other enterprise undertaken by Anne of Jesus while she was at Dijon which must not be passed over. This is an application she made to Rome, for permission to exceed, at the Convent of the Incarnation in Paris (and there alone), the number appointed by St. Teresa as the limit of Carmelite communities. The document itself gives her reasons, and though it is probable that as it stands it was not sent to Rome, since the concession was granted later on different grounds, a MS. copy preserved at Brussels is in the handwriting of the Servant of God, and is signed by her and by the other sisters at Dijon.

Anne of Jesus had also for some time been doing all she could to persuade the Carmelite friars to found in France, but she met with persistent refusals. Nevertheless she confidently affirmed that the project would be successful, and that through the very person who, in 1605, was most opposed to it, a statement which was verified later.[89]

Another important event, which took place while the Servant of God was at Dijon, was the nomination of M. Gallement as Ecclesiastical Visitor to the Carmelite nuns in France "Until the Holy See should ordain otherwise... even if the Discalced friars obtain a house in Paris in the meantime or in the future." He was succeeded by M. de Bérulle in 1614.

The Carmel in France soon became one of the most flourishing branches of Saint Teresa's Reform, not only by the number of its Convents but above all by the spirit of fervour and perfect regularity of its nuns. Like other Religious Houses, the Convent of the Incarnation was confiscated during the French Revolution, the nuns being turned out and obliged to wear secular dress. This happened on the 29th of September 1792.[90] For the most part the nuns lived together in little groups observing their vows, practising the Rule as well as they could, and keeping in touch with their prioress, Mere Louise de Gonzague. By 1802 they were able to recover the ruins of their Convent and part of their former property, and went back there on the 18th of October 1802, the 198th anniversary of the day on which Venerable Anne of Jesus had the joy of having the Blessed Sacrament reserved in the convent chapel for the first time. The community remained there till 1855, when they removed to the rue d'Enfer. It was from this convent that at the request of Cardinal Manning a foundation was made at Notting Hill, London, in 1878. From there

---

[89] Chief among these was a M. Vivian, Counsellor to King Henry IV and Comptroller of his accounts. In 1610 he gave large sums to the friars who came to make a foundation in Paris.

[90] The summons dated "l'an IVe de la liberté et le Ier de l'égalité" is preserved at Clamart.

foundations have gone out to all parts of Great Britain, no fewer than twenty-seven having been opened since 1903, each becoming a centre of prayer and penance for the needs of the country.

Under the iniquitous laws passed in France at the beginning of this century the Convent of the Incarnation was again seized by the State, and the Community in 1901 found a refuge at Anderlecht-lez-Bruxelles. In 1920 the nuns were allowed to return to France, and are now (1931) at Clamart (Seine).

La Venerable M.ᵉ Ana de IESVS compañera de Sᵗᵃ Teresa, y muy parecida en sus heroicas Virtudes, Fundadora de Francia, y Flandes: tubo singular prudencia, y don de profecia. Viua Fe, firma esperança, encendida caridad, tubo visitationes diuinas en la oracion, y obro Dios por su medio muchos milagros en su vida, y aora despues de su dichoso transito los obra muy insignes. Viuio en la Religion 51. años, paso desta vida ala eterna de 76. en Bruselas a 4. de Março. Año 1621.

CHAPTER XVIII

FROM FRANCE TO FLANDERS

1606-1607

THE first step towards the establishment of the Reform in Flanders was most certainly the visit paid to Anne of Jesus in Paris by Magdalen of St. Jerome, who on her return to the Court of Brussels, entertained the Infanta with a detailed account of the Spanish Carmelites, and of all the services rendered by M. de Brétigny. As a result she was commissioned to write to M. de Brétigny in the name of Her Serene Highness, and ask him to visit her with a view to entrusting him with a similar service towards Flanders. He at once complied and threw himself wholeheartedly into the Infanta's plans, "for the love and service of Jesus Christ his Master." Within a short time he was entrusted with a letter for Anne of Jesus, written by Isabella's own hand:

> "To Mother Anne of Jesus, Prioress of the Discalced Carmelites of Paris.
>
> "Although some time has elapsed since I greeted you, and wished to see the daughters of Mother Teresa of Jesus in these States, up to the present it has not been God's good pleasure to grant my wish. But I hope you will not refuse to come and found a convent here, as Quintanaduenas[91] will explain more in detail, for I have lately consulted him about the matter. I hope he will be able to overcome all the difficulties that may arise, so that you will be able to leave with those who must necessarily accompany you for what I have just stated. I beg of you to choose yourself the most suited for the purpose I have

---

[91] M. de Brétigny.

in view, namely, the glory of God, the greater exaltation of the faith, and the advancement of His service. I hope Mother Teresa will obtain us all this in return for the service we are doing her. Pray that this may be so, as I also do. I think that because I was, and still am, devoted to her, she will not refuse me this.

"I am delighted to think that I shall often see you, since, as Quintanaduenas will tell you, the site I have chosen for the convent adjoins our palace, a thing I have always wanted, so that we may share a little in the happiness which is yours.

"Let me know in great detail all that ought to be prepared, with everything as Mother Teresa prescribed, for I do not wish to exceed her wishes in the least point, no matter how small. This will not be displeasing to God, I think, and even less to the titular patrons of the house, for it is our intention that these shall be St. Anne and St. Joseph: the mother and son-in-law will get on together.

"As Quintanaduenas will give you all details, I will not write more, except to ask you to recommend me to God, so that He may always guide me in what relates to His service. May He keep me as I wish He may.

"St. Dominic's Day, 1606.
"From Brussels.   "A. ISABEL"

Warned as she had been from heaven about God's will in the matter, Anne of Jesus made no difficulty about granting the Infanta's request. The necessary permissions were obtained from the superiors of the Order in France, who, though grieved to lose so many of the Spanish Mothers, dared not oppose an extension of the Order which seemed calculated to bring so much glory to God. The Infanta had asked particularly for Mother Isabel of St. Paul, because she knew Flemish, but this permission was not granted till later. The new foundation was not to take place for six months, and Anne of Jesus spent the interval quietly at Dijon, where she instilled into the young professed and novices the true spirit of the Reform. At Brussels the Archdukes, after obtaining all necessary authorisations through the Nuncio, and the appointment of M. de Brétigny as Ecclesiastical Superior of the Carmelites in Flanders, entrusted the building of the new convent to Anne de Quesada. Until it was ready, a house adjoining the palace was to serve as a temporary Carmel.

In the depths of a continental winter, 3oth December, 1606, Anne of Jesus left Dijon for Paris, on her way to Flanders. She was accompanied by Mother Beatrix of the Conception, and Sister Mary of St. Albert (lay-sister). The former was to be sub-prioress at Brussels, and when she heard this she begged to be left at Dijon. With her usual vigour Anne of Jesus replied, "If you will not come with me, I shall not go at all," and Mother Beatrix took this as an indication of God's will, and resisted no longer. At Paris Mother Anne of St. Bartholomew was acting as prioress, though Anne of Jesus nominally held that post, and when Sister Teresa's coadjutrix arrived from Dijon, all the community went in procession to meet her at the door of the enclosure, chanting the *Te Deum.* Mother Anne of St. Bartholomew offered her the keys of the house, but these the Servant of God refused to take until it was explained that it was the express wish of the superiors that she should do so. Just before her arrival at the Convent of the Incarnation, she had been met by M. de Bérulle, who, with suitable retinue, had ridden out of Paris to welcome her. When Anne of Jesus recognised who it was who had thus come to do honour to St. Teresa's daughters, she stopped the coach, and getting out knelt in the snow with the other sisters for her superior's blessing. "No circumstance whatever should hinder us from showing respect to our superiors," she said. For a week the Paris Carmel enjoyed the presence of its venerable foundress. Then two coaches arrived from Brussels bringing Magdalen of St. Jerome, two Maids of Honour, and the Infanta's chaplain, who were to escort the nuns to Flanders. Anne of Jesus wanted very much to take Anne of St. Bartholomew with her, but that holy Mother answered, "It is not yet time for me to come down from my cross." She did eventually leave France, but for the moment Mother Eleanor of St. Bernard went in her stead. Among the French Carmelites Anne of Jesus badly wanted Sister Magdalen of St. Joseph and Sister Mary of Jesus, the first two professed at the Convent of the Incarnation, but neither Anne of St. Bartholomew nor the superiors would let them go. "It would be taking away the heart and head of the house," the former declared, and Anne of Jesus had to give way. She left Paris on 7th January, 1607, and proceeded with her three companions to Pontoise, where she again received a royal welcome, and added to her party Sr. Claudine of the Holy Ghost. The last stop on French soil was at Amiens, the only Carmel in France which she had not founded herself. Mother Isabel and her community were delighted to see their venerable Mother, and, as had been done at Paris and at Pontoise, all the nuns were left free to visit and converse with her. Anne of Jesus afterwards declared that the interior sanctity of the religious in all the French Carmels had given her much consolation, and that they were true daughters of her holy Mother Teresa. Both the Servant of God and Mother Beatrix of the Conception did their best to persuade the Prioress of Amiens to accompany them to Flanders. Torn between her love for them and an inward attraction to pray and suffer for France, Mother Isabel while at prayer heard Our Lord say: "Dost thou wish to flee from the cross thou wilt find in making foundations in France?" At another time when she was tempted to join Anne of Jesus, Our Lord again consoled her. Thus strengthened, she resisted all persuasions, saying, "God has given me France for my inheritance, and I will never leave this country." However, she gave two of her community for Flanders, Sister Aimee of Jesus, and another Anne of Jesus, thus bringing the number for Brussels up to seven.

The travellers reached the capital of the Netherlands on 22nd January. The Archdukes sent their Major Domo, Jerome Walter Zapata, to meet the nuns' coaches at Notre Dame de Hal, the famous shrine of Our Lady about six miles out of Brussels. His instructions were to bid the Carmelites welcome, and to conduct them in state to the Royal Palace. Anne of Jesus begged to be excused this honour, so the nuns were driven quietly to the palace gates, where a royal escort awaited them. With all the ceremonial demanded by Court etiquette they were conducted to the apartments of the Infanta. The premier Maid of Honour, Mme de Jacincourt, led Anne of Jesus by the hand, and presented her to the Infanta. As the venerable Mother stooped to kiss the hand of her royal benefactress, Isabella bade her raise her veil, and ask the other nuns to do the same. After giving their names, and being welcomed each one individually, the nuns lowered their veils again, and were entertained by the ladies present, while the Infanta took Anne of Jesus aside and conversed with her for about an hour. Then the Archduke came in, and after a short interval Isabella broke up the interview, and herself led the prioress and her nuns back to M. de Brétigny, who was waiting for them. Among the many ladies struck by the sanctity which radiated from Anne of Jesus was Yolande de Croy, then only a girl of thirteen. She made up her mind there and then that she would become a Carmelite, and entered as soon as she had reached the age required by Canon Law. Another was Doña Maria Aña de Vega, who had been struggling for some time against a manifest call to religion. No sooner had she caught sight of

Anne of Jesus than her repugnance vanished, and a few months later she entered the noviceship and became an excellent Carmelite.

Towards evening the seven religious were conducted to their convent by a retinue of knights and gentlemen. On entering the church attached to the new foundation Anne of Jesus intoned, as usual, the *Laudate Dominum*; and after a few minutes spent in prayer, the nuns passed into the community quarters. There several ladies were awaiting them, notably Anne de Quesada and her two daughters. Transported with joy at seeing Carmelites in Brussels, the pious lady exclaimed: "Oh, Reverend Mother, if only I might have one of my daughters a nun, since I cannot be one myself!" At this, Anne of Jesus looked steadily at the elder daughter, Margaret Manrique, and giving her a little tap on the arm said: "This one will be the first to whom I shall give the habit." But Margaret at that time had no intention of being a nun, much less a Carmelite. "If this saint cannot prophesy better than that," she thought, "she will find that this time she has made a mistake. But aloud she turned off the unwelcome words with a joke. "Will your Reverence be pleased to clothe some other novices first," she said, "so that I can see whether the habit is becoming, and watch all the ceremonies."

Nevertheless the holy prioress's word came true, and this daughter of Henry Manrique and Anne de Quesada, who was cousin of M. de Brétigny, was the first professed Carmelite of Flanders, even as another of his cousins, Mme Hannivel, had been the first to be professed in France.

During three days the new Carmel was open to visitors. Many ladies visited every part of the house, some prompted merely by curiosity, others drawn by the reputation for sanctity which had preceded Anne of Jesus. Among the latter was a Mlle de Taxis Van de Noot. Coming up to the prioress, she begged her to raise her veil. As a rule the Servant of God refused this favour, but on this occasion she made no difficulty, and throwing it back embraced the young girl very affectionately, saying, "Know that God wants you for this convent." Nothing was further from her visitor's thoughts: yet sixteen months later, the prediction was fulfilled and Mlle Van der Noot was received as a novice. Another incident shows that the foundation was foretold long before it took place. A virtuous girl of humble parentage was in the service of one of the ladies of the Infanta's Court. Many years previously the Mother of God had appeared to this girl, Margaret Van Hoort, and told her that some day she would be a daughter of her Order and showed her two nuns in the Carmelite habit. When her mistress went to visit Anne of Jesus, she took her trusted servant with her. Margaret was present when the nuns raised their veils. Instantly she recognised in the prioress and Mother Beatrix of the Conception the two Carmelites in the vision, and telling her story begged to be received. Needless to say, she was accepted as a lay-sister, though she did not enter till later. In religion she was known as Margaret of the Mother of God.

On the feast of the Conversion of St. Paul, 25th January, 1607, Mass was said for the first time in the Carmelite Chapel. The Archdukes attended in person, and the celebrant was Mgr. Caraffa, Papal Nuncio at Brussels. After the Holy Sacrifice, Albert and Isabella were received by the religious at the enclosure door, and conducted in procession to the choir. Anne of Jesus was radiant with joy, at seeing yet another sanctuary opened for the Blessed Sacrament. Then the ceremony of enclosure was performed, the grates closed and curtained, and regular observance began.

On 25th March of the same year the Foundation Stone of the new convent was laid with the usual ceremonies.

Meanwhile, like the true apostle that she was, Anne of Jesus was already dreaming of fresh conquests for Our Lord. In a letter to Father Diego de Guevara, she writes:

> "May Our Lord be ever with your Paternity, and may He reward you for the pleasure your letter gave me. It is the first I have received from you since I left Spain. I can assure you I had been longing for it, as well as for the papers you took away from me to Alcala, together with the declaration about our holy Mother. You have given me great pleasure by sending the treatise written in her defence, although it is not necessary in this country, where she is held in high esteem. I am at present having her books translated into Flemish, for though everybody here *speaks* French, they cannot *read* that language.
>
> "I hear that Father Antolinez is still Provincial. I should very much like to know how he is making use of your Paternity. I am distressed to see you so discouraged about your work, for love cannot bear to be idle. See, dear Father, what a life I lead, and I feel as if I had not yet begun. As to my companions, they are dying to undergo greater labours. None of us will rest till we have given our lives for Him, who gave us life by His death. Ask him, Father, to grant us this grace. Nevertheless, I doubt whether that will happen in these States, for the very day of our arrival the enemy made overtures for peace, and in order to settle its conditions, a truce of six months has already been proclaimed, during which time there will be no fighting. May God in His mercy grant that this peace may become permanent. The affair is of greater moment than they think down there [i.e., in Spain], because it appears that the Catholics have the upper hand, and the heretics are losing ground.[92] Many of the latter are in

---

[92] After the religious troubles in the Netherlands under Margaret of Parma and her famous general, the Duke of Alva, the Province, although independent of Spain, had up to 1607 a good deal of trouble with

Provinces [i.e., Holland] not under the sway of our princes. These last are so good and exemplary that they make themselves loved and respected everywhere. As to ourselves, I cannot tell you all we owe them, nor all the favours they heap upon us, nor yet the devotedness and generosity with which they supply all our wants. Be well assured, Father, that this foundation is equal to that of the Discalced Franciscans at Madrid,[93] and if I had had nuns enough to help me two other convents would have been founded as well. In the best towns in these States they want them—at Antwerp, Louvain and Ghent. If our Discalced Friars would come into these parts, they also could make a number of foundations. I have written to tell them so hundreds of times, but they never answer me. I think that at the next General Chapter God will bring it about that they decide to come. May He arrange all this according to what shall best promote His glory, and may He take us soon to England. The Father Guardian Fray Augustine (I mean Father Ignatius of St. Augustine) has written several times from that country.[94]

"As it is only a short time since I wrote to Father Master Curiel, I am not doing so now. May I ask you Father, to let him know what is in this letter, and to tell him we are all very well and so busy that we have not a free moment, no leisure at all. May His Divine Majesty give us time in which to serve Him, and may He support your Paternity with the grace of His Holy Spirit, as we all

---

heretics. Subsequent to that date peace reigned, education was fostered and many Religious Orders were introduced, among them refugees from England who, with the consent of the Archdukes, established convents and monasteries where they continued their religious life in Flanders.

[93] This convent was also a Royal Foundation.

[94] Some illegible words follow in the original. So far it has not been possible to trace the identity of Fray Augustine.

pray that He may, especially Mother Sub-Prioress, Beatrix of the Conception.

"From the Convent of the glorious St. Anne and St. Joseph, at Brussels. 1st April, 1607.

"My dear Father, your Paternity's unworthy daughter and servant,

"ANNE OF JESUS."

As the above letter says, the venerable Mother was busy about a Flemish translation of the writings of St. Teresa, made at her request by the Jesuit Fathers of Brussels. In a letter to Father de Guevara in 1608 she tells him that the volumes are published. She also superintended the publication, in Spanish, of St. Teresa's "Book of the Foundations," containing her own account of the foundation of Granada, written in obedience to Father Gracian. Besides all this, more than one attempt was made by this faithful daughter of St. Teresa to get her holy Mother's writings translated into Latin. For this purpose, she corresponded with Father Master Basil de Leon, nephew of Father Luis de Leon, but his translation, although completed, was never published. The Life of the Saint, written by herself, was translated into Latin from an Italian version in 1603. It was not until 1610 that St. Teresa's writings as a whole were published in Latin by Matthias Martinez, at Cologne. It was also about this time that Anne of Jesus had a picture life of her Holy Mother prepared and published, so that the many who could not read might yet learn to know and love her. Finally, a French version of the Rules and Constitutions brought from Spain was published under the supervision of Anne of Jesus in 1607, the printing being done "At Brussels, by Rutger Velpius," as extant copies attest. The translation is practically the same as that made by M. de Brétigny.[95]

For six months no postulants were received at Brussels, and all the temporalities of the convent were administered by officials directly responsible to the Archdukes. Although the foundation was made in January, the first account kept by the nuns bears the date of 23rd September, 1607.[96]

At the clothing of the first novice, on 22nd July, the Archdukes and their Court were present. Within the year nine had been received, as the Act of Foundation, signed on 15th October, attests. The document is too long to quote

---

[95] The word "Provincial" used in the earlier translation is replaced by that of "General of the Discalced" and some minor points concerning the novice-ship of lay-sisters are made clear. Anne of Jesus was well acquainted with St. Teresa's practice in the matter.

[96] The convent ledger has the following entry:
JESUS, MARY, JOSEPH.
Book of the expenses and receipts of the convent of the glorious St. Anne and St. Joseph, founded by their Serene Highnesses, the Archduke Albert, our Sovereign, and the Infanta Isabella-Clara-Eugenia, our Sovereign, in the year, 1607, the 25th January, the feast of the Conversion of St. Paul.
The receipts of the Convent of Brussels began on the 23rd September of this year, 1607, because from the time of our arrival up to this date, all that was necessary for us was supplied from the palace in great abundance, and because, at the aforesaid date, their Highnesses left for Binche, and they ordained that a sum of money should be sent to us for our current expenses. The Treasurer accordingly, sent us a hundred phillippics. (A philippic equals about £1 3s. 5d. in present money.)† This sum constitutes what has been received in silver up to today, 20th October of the same year. We bear witness to this by our signature.
ANNE OF JESUS, PRIORESS.
BEATRIX OF THE CONCEPTION
ELEANOR OF ST. BERNARD.
†Editor's note: The sum represented in 2015 money would be approximately, adjusted for inflation, £ 7,745, or $11,148.

here, but one paragraph is of special interest, as it gives the names of the original community.

> "Mother Anne of Jesus is the first prioress of this convent:
>
> "Mother Beatrix of the Conception, sub-prioress; Mother Eleanor of St. Bernard, novice mistress; Sister Aimee of Jesus, sacristan; Sister Anne of Jesus, portress; Sister Claudine of the Holy Ghost, vestier; Sister Mary of St. Albert, cook. Such are the seven religious who came from France."

The nuns did not get into their new convent for another three years and a half, but within three weeks of the signing of this Act, the venerable prioress set out from Brussels to make a second foundation at Louvain.

CHAPTER XIX

FOUNDATIONS AT LOUVAIN AND MONS

1607-1608

AMONG the many towns of the Spanish Netherlands which made requests for St. Teresa's daughters, Anne of Jesus chose the University city of Louvain for the second foundation. Many English refugees were living there, and this may possibly have influenced her decision. The temporal foundress was Constance Hellemans, who visited the venerable Mother at Brussels and offered her whole fortune for the building of a Carmel in her native city.

There was, at the time, a holy anchoress in Louvain, who used to spend her nights praying, and making reparation for the many sins committed in the city, especially by the University students. One night she saw a large and unusual star shining over the quarter of the town known as the Parish of St. Michael. For several nights the prodigy was repeated, and God gave the anchoress to understand that help would come from that district. Soon after, Doña Nuña Perez, one of the Infanta's personal friends, whom she was wont to call "The Saint of Louvain," together with Constance Hellemans, found a suitable house in that very quarter, in the rue des Orphelins. The erection of the Carmel was sanctioned by the municipal authorities on 14th September, 1607. St. Teresa appeared to Nuña Perez one day when she was depressed about the work of preparing for the nuns, and told her that God would be well and faithfully served in the Louvain Convent. Another supernatural manifestation regarding it was given to James Jansenius, a doctor of theology, and Dean of the Collegiate Church of St. Peter, who tried to stop the Carmelites from coming to

Louvain. The Dean was a very holy man, and used to spend a great part of the night praying before a miraculous statue of Our Lady, in what was called the Flemish Chapel.[97] One night some souls in purgatory appeared to him there, and warned him in God's name "To beware of opposing the foundation of a Convent of Discalced Carmelites because great glory to God would result from it, and that it would also bring relief to the Souls in Purgatory." From that time onward Doctor Jansenius became one of the nuns' staunchest friends.

While these things were happening at Louvain, Anne of Jesus, not having enough sisters to spare at Brussels, asked M. de Brétigny to go to France to fetch Mother Isabel of St. Paul from Pontoise. This holy prioress, according to her promise, made no difficulty about obeying, and the French superiors generously allowed her to take three French sisters with her, one from her own community, and two from Paris. The little party reached Brussels towards the end of October, 1607, after calling at Mariemont, by the express desire of the Archdukes, who gave them a cordial welcome. So quickly were matters pushed forward at Louvain that, by 1st November, Anne of Jesus set out with Mother Eleanor of St. Bernard, the newly-arrived nuns from France, and a lay-novice. M. de Brétigny accompanied them to Louvain, together with Mme de la Chaux and one of her nieces. Constance Hellemans and a great number of ladies came out to meet the nuns, and escorted them to the rue des Orphelins. There were a few difficulties to be overcome, but on 4th November, High Mass was celebrated in the convent chapel, and the Blessed Sacrament placed in the tabernacle,

---

[97] A chapel added to the Collegiate Church in 1601 as a shrine for a miraculous statue of Our Lady, which had previously stood in a hollow of a tree and had been honoured by the faithful from time immemorial.

FOUNDATIONS AT LOUVAIN AND MONS

in the presence of a numerous and distinguished congregation. The new Carmel was dedicated to St. Joseph. A crowd of postulants at once presented themselves, among whom Anne of Jesus chose the most promising, and to these she gave the Carmelite habit at once, as was then the custom. Before the end of November the venerable prioress was back in her own convent at Brussels. Mother Eleanor of St. Bernard and a French nun, Sister Mary of St. Joseph, returned with her. The Carmel at Louvain prospered exceedingly under Mother Isabel of St. Paul and her successors. An old MS. preserved among the archives reads:

> "It seems that when God gave this convent in Louvain the grace of being founded by our venerable Mother Anne of Jesus, He willed at the same time to bestow on it her spirit, which is the spirit of our holy Mother, Teresa of Jesus. To this source must be traced the pure and holy observance which, by the grace of God, has been kept up in this house from its commencement to the present day,[98] her daughters believing that they could in no better way satisfy the everlasting debt they owe their illustrious and worthy Foundress than by preserving inviolably the principles she instilled into them."

While these events were taking place, another foundation was being prepared at Mons. It had been accepted as early as the previous June, and the authorization of the Bishop of Cambrai was dated 30th June, 1607. In a document dated 18th July, the town authorities declared unanimously that the Carmelites "Might take up their residence at Mons, to exercise there the rules of their Order and Profession."

---

[98] No date is given—from the context it would seem probable that the MS. was written after the death of Anne of Jesus probably between 1621 and 1630, when her life, in Spanish, was being prepared.

The foundation has a particular interest, as it was the last made by Anne of Jesus in person, a fact of which she herself seems to have been aware. Moreover, it was made in great poverty, and only after many difficulties had been overcome. The Carmelites had been asked for by the Baroness de Roisin, who promised to help the foundation as much as she could, and the venerable prioress entrusted her with all the arrangements. God permitted that the Baroness's talent for domestic affairs was not equal to her good will; and her fortune, which she had made over entirely to the nuns, was not very large. Hence the nuns had much to suffer. Whether Anne of Jesus foresaw this or not is uncertain, but she had no sooner returned from Louvain than she set about preparing to go to Mons. In vain did all her friends—more especially the Infanta—try to dissuade her from her purpose, or at least to persuade her to wait till the spring. Once her mind was made up she was inflexible, and her letters at this time show that she was still "hungry for suffering." Writing on 2nd December, 1607, to Father Diego de Guevara, she says:

> ". . . We know by experience that His Majesty sends us troubles in proportion to the talents He confides to our keeping. . . the meek possess the land, and the soul by patience possesses itself. Thus are the saints fashioned: if we would be such, let us imitate them. They are constantly persecuted and overwhelmed; they lived as if they were already dead, and now that they are actually dead they have risen again before the general Resurrection. But I do not know, Father, why I write to you what you know better than I do. One day you heard me say how unhappy those people were who suffered nothing in this world for love of God. Every hour I grow more hungry for suffering, but my troubles are so small that, far from satiating me, they do not even serve to break my fast! I do not know the meaning of that word

about Our Lord, '*He was saturated with reproaches,*' since I see His members still athirst for humiliations. Contempt of ourselves involves a great many: so long as we do not firmly embrace this truth we shall not find peace, for peace can only be enjoyed when we have learnt how to conquer, or to be conquered, and can say, 'Now is your hour.' We ought to consider life as even less [than an hour], for eternity and happiness that can have no end depend but on a moment, while anything that comes to an end is not really an evil. . . . Since the holy Duchess of Gandia affirms that her troubles are due to my prayers, no doubt her Excellency will bear patiently those that have fallen upon her recently. She has managed to give me a good share in them."

On 9th December, 1607, the venerable Mother set out from Brussels with Mother Eleanor of St. Bernard, four professed sisters from France, and two novices. They had much to endure. The roads were bad, the season very severe; in some places their coach was axle-deep in water, and every moment the nuns expected their prioress to succumb to her infirmities. Instead of this, says an eye-witness, "she made fun of all the inconveniences of the journey, and showed a courage which astonished everyone." The first halt was at Enghien, where they were received for the night with great hospitality by the Duke of Arenberg. In private conversation with Anne of Jesus he opened his heart to her, and received much spiritual consolation. December 10th brought the nuns within sight of Mons, which they entered, not by the high road of to-day, but through the little village of Nimy. Here a characteristic incident took place. Outside the wayside inn Anne of Jesus noticed a group of soldiers idling away their time. Distressed at this, she cast about in her mind for some way of helping them to something more worthy, and at length remembered that she had with her a book treating of the Sacraments, and especially of the

Sacrament of Penance. She begged M. de Brétigny to give the book to the idlers. "Aha, Mother," the good priest replied, "they will only laugh at us." But Anne of Jesus insisted, and finally her superior complied with her request. To his surprise they received the book quite respectfully, and coming up to the coach thanked the venerable Mother for her present. Nor was this all. The same soldiers came to Mons again some weeks later, and went out of their way to call at the Carmel to see the holy prioress, and insisted on her receiving as alms a good part of their pay.

As Anne of Jesus drove into Mons, a fit of deep depression came upon her, which developed almost into consternation when she found that the Baroness de Roisin had not been able to procure a house where the Carmelites could pass the night. Tenants were still in possession of the one she had rented, so the seven religious had to be taken in by the baroness herself, at great inconvenience on both sides. "She was very vexed about it," say the annals; and small wonder, for she had to find herself another home, at least for a time, besides having to placate her landlord, who was not at all anxious to see his property "transformed into a convent." To crown all, for nearly two months Mme de Roisin could not find a house, so the nuns had to live with her without enclosure, choir, or chapel, and in very small and inconvenient rooms. Almost every day, the Servant of God wrote to Mother Beatrix of the Conception, whom she had left in charge at Brussels, and to whom she was deeply attached. The first letter is dated 13th December, 1607:

> "May God give you His grace, dear Mother.
> "No doubt you are thinking that I am enjoying a good rest. God knows all about it, and how much I want to see myself settled at last in this house. Don Luis and Don Juan de Torres will tell you how we are situated with regard to this matter, and all that has happened. Ask the latter to come back at once with the letters from their

FOUNDATIONS AT LOUVAIN AND MONS 253

> Highnesses, those of the father confessors, of the president and of the auditor-general.... Oh, I wish you could have seen what an ecstasy Don John[99] was in, and what sort of beds he prepared for us! It was the same with the house. I would not go to see it, and shall stay where I am, unless one of the priests' houses can be obtained. Madame de Roisin is at our service for everything and in everything, and Doña Claudia's[100] amiability astonishes us... she waits upon us, sweeps the room and acts as our messenger... Send me some serge, for they tell me there are many ladies of good family who want to enter...."

On 28th December she writes:

> "... Oh, if you could see, dear Mother, all that the demon is doing to hinder this Foundation, and amidst what difficulties it is being established. I hope from the goodness of our great God that the house will be one where He will be well served. I think His Majesty will grant this grace in return for all I suffer by being deprived of your presence, my dear Mother, and well-beloved daughter. The very thought of this separation is agony to me, and I say to myself: 'What shall I do without my Beatrix?' I wish I had not made the experiment! Your want of health makes me suffer more than all that I have to put up with here, for I should reckon all that as little if I knew you were well. Have compassion on me for that reason, do what I tell you. Do not fail, either, to write to me, for I cannot bear such silence. As for myself, I write to you every day: I only hope my letters have reached you...."

Another letter followed a few days later:

---

[99] M. de Brétigny.

[100] Mme. de Roisin's niece.

> "May Jesus be ever with your Reverence, dear Mother, and true daughter of my heart.
>
> "How much and what much-needed consolation your letter of Holy Innocents' Day gave me. That same day I had written to ask you not to let me die because of your silence, and I complained that my daughters told me nothing. But they were compelled to keep silence through their numberless duties of the last few days. It appears, moreover, that everything was so well done that outsiders assure me that it seemed as if none of those who have come here were missing from the choir. . . .
>
> "Your absence costs me dear during my sleep, and is a constant pain to me when I am awake. What I am experiencing seems to me to be a kind of temptation. If your affection has like effects, I am truly sorry for you. Don John was much upset to-day when he saw the state I was in. He even wanted to send Navet[101] to you when your messenger arrived. It was Sunday evening. Everyone tells me it is foolish to be in such a state of distress. I told them it was not in my power to be any different. . . .
>
> "Take great care of my daughters, for I carry them all written in my heart. . . . I think that Madame de Roisin will find us a house to-morrow, and that will enable us to leave hers. She takes very affectionate care of me. . . ."

With regard to the house the venerable Mother's hopes were disappointed. On 4th January she writes again to Brussels:

> ". . . To tell the truth I have not yet received a single subject, and I shall not receive any until the convent is properly established. When that will be I do not know, for a house cannot be found for Madame de Roisin. . . . Everyone shows us much affection. We should enjoy it if your Reverence were with us, but not while we are deprived of the Blessed Sacrament. Ask Our Lord to grant

---

[101] M. de Brétigny's valet.

FOUNDATIONS AT LOUVAIN AND MONS 255

us the favour of possessing Him here....

"Oh, if you could see how Don John's severity vexes me! When I told him how upset I was at being in such a predicament, he answered, 'Do not say that, Mother; we shall die together here.' He does nothing, except act as porter. He puts me into a bad temper for, having told me that his powers[102] extended no further than Brussels, he now informs me that he has finished reading his papers of authorisation in which he is given jurisdiction to found throughout the State and Provinces. What sort of peace is this, Mother, and in a matter so essential as obedience? ..."

Ten days later another letter was on its way to Brussels:

"...I am still very sad without my true daughter," she writes, "and I am resolved, before God, never again to separate myself from your Reverence, unless I am told to do so by obedience. I see clearly that it is not good for us to be alone, one without the other in a foreign country. This is indeed a strange land. One must see it to believe it. I could never have believed that people could be so cold and hesitating. These qualities are killing me. They leave me gasping...

"On our arrival[103] she offered us her house and all its belongings: now she will not go away, and cannot find anywhere to go. Every day she tells me that she hopes for an answer. In consequence, nothing is done. Yet nothing comes of all that she has announced, except a beautiful bell which has been presented to us.[104] Truly, what King

---

[102] As Ecclesiastical Superior of the Carmelites in Flanders.

[103] Mme de Roisin.

[104] This bell was given to the Carmelites by the Canonesses of St. Waudru. A passage in the state archives at Mons reads: "On 12th January 1608 came M. de Brétigny, Superior of the Carmelites residing in the

Ferdinand said when he took Granada can be said of us, 'You have got the bell, but as yet you have not got the cow.'

"It was very foolish not to have taken the house of Berlaimont for the three months for which it was offered to us after the sale. Once installed there, we should have remained.... This foundation is costing me a great deal of fatigue. So much so that, even when I am asleep, it is still in my mind, and I am always dreaming that the troubles are beginning all over again.... It costs me much to see what a predicament I am in, even though I receive His Divine Majesty every day, and assist at two or three Masses..."

There were other troubles also, more difficult to deal with than the finding of a house. Mother Eleanor of St. Bernard, whom Anne of Jesus had hoped to make prioress at Mons, proved unfitted for the post, for the letter just quoted continues:

"Torres writes now that he will come to see Eleanor ... Tell him that he will see her over there [i.e., at Brussels]. For here people do not take to her. We shall have to make St. Bartholomew come, since the foundation at Tours—where they say it was hoped to take her—has not, it seems, come to pass.[105] Until the house here is well-established I shall not undertake any other...."

---

house of the late M. de Chocquetian, rented by Mme de Roisin, who through charity has given up her house to them. He saw Mesdames de Harchie, Hoogsttaete, Noyelle, and d'Essenghien in order to ask for, and obtain leave to take away a bell that they donated to him, the said day and year: to this I witness, having been present.

"(Signed) NICHOLAS LELEU"

[105] Mother Anne of St. Bartholomew founded the Carmel at Tours on 18th May, 1608, therefore she could not come to Flanders till later, but Anne of Jesus had not yet received news that the date was fixed.

FOUNDATIONS AT LOUVAIN AND MONS

About the middle of January affairs at Mons seemed a little more hopeful, and the venerable prioress writes:

". . . The business concerning this house has overwhelmed me, but at last Madame de Roisin is going, and the Blessed Sacrament will most certainly be reserved on the day of St. Paul's Conversion if Our Lord allows no further difficulties to occur. There have been some very big ones, and the good lady has taken so small a house that everybody is astonished to see her in so tiny a corner. Her niece and the domestic servants raise no difficulty about it, for which we must thank His Divine Majesty, as well as for their kindly feelings towards us. . . . Truly, I owe a great deal to Madame de Roisin."

After telling her friend of the privations which the nuns at Mons have to suffer, and of the abnormal severity of the weather, the letter continues:

"[The nuns] have never experienced such facility in prayer, and so much consolation. It is prayer that sustains me, for just now everything is lacking. Let Margaret of the Mother of God speak to Catherine and tell her, as if of her own accord, what she gave for her clothing in order that, if she has any money, she may give it to us. They are very close with their money here, and you cannot get anything done without paying cash down. I really do not know what we should have done amidst such people if Madame de Roisin had not been with us, for though she is undecided and reserved she acts like a lady nobly born. From her manner one can easily see what she really is."

In spite of her hopes, however, Anne of Jesus was again disappointed. The feast of St. Paul's Conversion came and went, and still difficulties multiplied about the new foundation. There was such deep sympathy between the Servant of God and Mother Beatrix that they each knew intuitively what was happening to the other, as the following letter shows. It is dated 24th January, 1608:

"... You tell me that while you were at Matins you understood that I was overwhelmed with trouble. It is indeed true. I have a thousand annoyances to put up with. ... As to our John,[106] he is delighted with everything. I told him to-day that his was no father's heart. He bathes in rose water while watching us suffer. He and Navet are comfortable with the priests who asked me for the privilege of putting them up. They have a good table, comfortable beds and large fires, the last being more necessary here than food. You cannot imagine what the cold is like here. Even the deepest wells are frozen, and all the cisterns. It is impossible for any labourer to do his work. In consequence, we have not been able to reserve the Blessed Sacrament, or establish the enclosure, but have to wait until the frost breaks. Truly heaven and earth combine to try us. ... Oh, if you could see how disgusted I am with it all. I eat all kinds of messes. But I endure all in the thought that never again will I separate myself from my dear Beatrix ... I am quite well, though tired of seeing that nothing can be done. I know that it is God who raises these hindrances, and who allows this severe frost. I am writing beside our little fire, and every minute I have to stop in order to take the icicles from my pen."

After explaining about a projected visit to Brussels on the part of M. de Brétigny, she adds jokingly:

"Do not see to this beforehand. We will let him experience a little inconvenience!"

A few days later news reached Mons that Mother Beatrix was not well. Anne of Jesus was quite distressed about her. She even thought of going over to Brussels herself, and on 4th February writes:

---

[106] M. de Brétigny.

FOUNDATIONS AT LOUVAIN AND MONS 259

"... If the Blessed Sacrament were in the chapel here, I should start off with Don Luis, so much does it grieve me to think of your being ill without anyone to act as your infirmarian.[107] If anyone comes to fetch me, see that a letter is brought from the archduke's confessor telling Don Juan that I ought to go, even if I have to return here at once. I think that will not be necessary if I leave Eleanor[108] here, for the house is convenient enough until another can be found, and there does not seem any likelihood of admitting postulants. Those who are going to enter have business to settle which will not be finally arranged until Easter, and I want to see you before then. If you were quite well, however, we could wait until we see whether we could get the Mother from Paris [Anne of St. Bartholomew], or the one at Louvain [Isabel of St. Paul] ... You could not believe all the trouble and worry I have had over this house. I hold it certain that God will be well served here, since it has cost me so dear.... There is no possibility, for another week, of reserving the Blessed Sacrament. The foundation is being laid in patience, for Our Lord has willed that we should have to practise it in everything."

This is the last letter from Mons. On 7th February, the feast of St. Romuald, the Blessed Sacrament was placed in a temporary chapel, fitted up at the last moment, and after the opening ceremony the convent was dedicated to St. Joseph. Notwithstanding her many troubles, Anne of Jesus experienced great consolations during her time at Mons. One day Mme de Roisin surprised her on her knees: "What is your Reverence doing?" she asked. "I am recommending this foundation to God," replied the prioress. "He has shown

---

[107] It must be remembered that the Spanish Mothers were in a foreign country and looked on French and Flemish methods with some distrust.

[108] Mother Eleanor of St. Bernard.

me that He will be faithfully served here." The Carmel at Mons was long famous for the sanctity of its inmates.

> "Its good odour was spread abroad," says Father Gracian,[109] "and made its influence felt on seculars as well as in religious communities. This was particularly the case with the canonesses of St. Waudru."

The inhabitants of the town used to come to ask for the venerable Mother's blessing, and accounted it a singular favour to have in their midst one whom they looked on as a saint. More than one young heart was touched with grace, the most remarkable case being, perhaps, that of Anne d'Espieres. This young girl of noble birth was a canoness of St. Gertrude at Nivelles,[110] and, accompanied by other canonesses, she visited the Carmel at Mons while Anne of Jesus was there. The holy prioress looked at her visitors closely, then, as the conventual Mass was about to be celebrated, she took Anne d'Espieres by the hand, and told her to go up with the Carmelites to Holy Communion. (It was before the enclosure had been erected.) The young girl was taken by surprise, and urged that not having been to Confession, she was unprepared. "That does not matter," was the reply, "follow me." Anne obeyed, and during her thanksgiving God spoke to her heart, and she gave herself wholly to Him. Six years later she entered at Mons, taking the name of Teresa Angelica of Jesus. While still a novice she was sent with Mother Isabel of St. Paul to Tournai.

Sister Madeleine Florence of the Cross declared on oath that many notabilities of Mons avoided going to see Anne of

---

[109] *Peregrinacion de Anastasio*, p. 153.

[110] Canonesses were often pious ladies living together under a rule of life but without religious vows. See *Flemish Mystics and English Martyrs*, Darrant, p. 125, Burns Oates and Washbourne.

Jesus, lest she should discover their sins.

> "My own meeting with her produced an extraordinary impression," she adds. "As a girl I had wanted to be a religious, and had had a taste for the things of God. But at the time I am speaking of I was in very different dispositions, and immersed in the vanities of the world. While I was looking at the reverend Mother I entered into myself, and became conscious of my errors. From that moment I esteemed her a saint. Later on, when I became a religious, I had the good fortune to attend her in her infirmities, and to mend her clothes. Such was the respect I felt for her that, if I had to unpick any part of her garments, I took care not to throw away the little threads, because I venerated her as a saint."

At Mons as elsewhere, knowledge of what was happening at a distance was often granted to Anne of Jesus. A lady of high position in Brussels had become very intimate with her. It happened that the lady's husband was a man of hasty and uncontrolled temper, but under the influence of the Servant of God, his wife bore with him meekly and never opposed his will. However, a dispute arose one day, and the angry husband gave his wife a blow on the face. At the same instant, Anne of Jesus, then at Mons, saw what was done and exclaimed, "May God forgive you! Have I not often warned you never to excite your husband's anger." The injured lady also had a vision of the venerable Mother, and heard her say the above words. Some days later she called at the Brussels Carmel, and told Mother Beatrix all that had taken place. When Anne of Jesus returned from Mons, the sub-prioress questioned her about this incident, and the prioress confessed that the story was correct.

A member of the first community at Mons writes:

> "Our venerable Mother, Anne of Jesus, was endowed

with so much natural talent that she merits the title Phoenix of our age.'" Then after a long eulogy of her virtues she continues, "I have often heard people tell our venerable Mother Anne of St. Bartholomew that, in Spain, Anne of Jesus was looked upon as the most charitable religious of the Order, and she used to say, 'My daughter, God will shower His favours on Mother Anne of Jesus because of her great charity.' As for prayer, I will only say that our venerable Mother had reached a very high state. Many a time I have noticed, as she came from prayer, that her face was aglow and a sweet perfume exhaled from her hands. I never looked at her without feelings of love and respect, as someone more than human and incomparably holier than others."

As soon as the enclosure was erected at Mons, Anne of Jesus hastened back to Brussels. She had been absent three months, and in spite of previous misgivings, left, Mother Eleanor of St. Bernard behind as prioress. The following October found her at Mons for a second time. The young prioress had out of pure charity sympathized and defended a lady who was in serious domestic trouble, and who had previously been a benefactor to the Carmel. Complaints of what had been done found their way to Brussels, and with her usual energy, Anne of Jesus arrived at Mons to investigate the case. When all had been made clear, she assembled the community and declared her approval of all that Mother Eleanor had done. Not only she herself, but even their holy Mother Teresa, she said, would have done the same in similar circumstances.

Surprised and touched at this vindication of her conduct, the young prioress threw herself at once on her knees, and begged to be relieved of her charge. At first Anne of Jesus would not accept her resignation, but afterwards she sent a messenger to Louvain, asking Mother Isabel of St. Paul to set out for Mons without delay. On her arrival the community was again assembled, and Mother Isabel was installed as prioress. Eleanor of St. Bernard returned with Anne of Jesus to Brussels, where she remained until 1612, when she accompanied Mother Anne of St. Bartholomew to Antwerp.

A letter to Father Diego de Guevara, dated 1st June, 1608, gives an insight into the thoughts of Anne of Jesus during these months, she writes:

> "... The three convents which have been founded in this country, and the five in France, are prospering to such a degree that one marvels at the way God hastens to make Himself known there. We are being urged to found in all the principal cities of the State, but I cannot do this because I have as yet no sisters trained according to our Order.[111] It is really necessary that the Discalced Fathers should come and govern us, and that we should have nuns from Spain. It is very sad to be so much alone...."

---

[111] As the first Flemish novice did not make her vows till 22nd July, 1608, and only young sisters had been brought from France, it was impossible for them to become Prioresses.

CHAPTER XX

DISCALCED FRIARS COME TO FLANDERS. THE OPENING OF THE ROYAL CONVENT

1610-1612

HOWEVER much Anne of Jesus longed for peace and quiet in the retirement of her community in Brussels, it was not in God's design to grant it to her. M. de Brétigny, as Ecclesiastical Superior of the three Carmels in the Netherlands, had many details to settle, and he referred everything to the venerable Mother. This was how it came about that she had acted with so much authority at Mons. As Teresa of Jesus had during her lifetime interested herself in, and decided all matters of importance concerning the Reform in Spain, so did Anne of Jesus in Flanders.

The civil troubles which had devastated the United Provinces for so long were brought to a halt by an armistice in 1607, which in 1609 was prolonged into a truce for twelve years. This cessation of hostilities was regarded by many as miraculous, and due to the coming of the Carmelites, or rather, to that of Anne of Jesus herself. The Archdukes had, in consequence, more leisure to bestow upon the internal government of their territory, and they often consulted the Carmelite prioress concerning their arrangements. So much so, indeed, that in a letter to the Prioress of Salamanca, written on 14th February, 1610, Anne of Jesus complains of the little time she has to herself:

> "Just think! I am absolutely worn out, and I have so much to do, and so many letters to write, that I do not know how I live. They do not leave me a minute in which I can commune with God, or have a little talk with those I love in Spain. . . ."

On the other hand the Servant of God was able to do much good through her influence over her royal patrons. Soon after her arrival in Brussels, she set on foot an inquiry into the state of prisoners throughout the Archduke's dominions. Learning that these unfortunate men never assisted at Mass, even on the greatest festivals, she represented the matter so strongly that an endowment was at once set apart to secure the services of a prison chaplain at least in Brussels. Anne of Jesus herself provided the sacred vessels, vestments and altar linen,[112] and undertook that her community should see to the washing and mending of the latter.

During her first years in Flanders Anne of Jesus cherished the hope that Spanish friars would follow the nuns to France and Flanders. She even went so far as to arrange that the novices received at Brussels, Louvain and Mons should, at their profession, promise obedience to the General of the Congregation of Spain, as the book of professions attests.

Again and again, the venerable Mother tried to persuade the Spanish friars to found a house in the Netherlands, entrusting her requests to the Archdukes' confessor, Father Iñigo de Bricuela, but all to no purpose. Finally she applied to Italy for friars, addressing her letter to the vicar-general, Father Ferdinand of St. Mary.[113]

---

[112] A receipt signed by the director of the prison of Trevrenhere, Brussels, 23rd December 1608, enumerates the different objects received from Anne of Jesus. It is still kept in the Carmelite archives of Brussels.

[113] The General of the Discalced died in the year of his election, 1608. Fr. Ferdinand acted as Vicar-General till April 1611.

"Jesus, Maria.

"Our Father, May the Holy Ghost increase His divine grace in the soul of your Paternity.

"On St. Luke's Day, five years ago, we founded the first convent in Paris, and since then, both in France and in these Provinces of Belgium, God has been pleased that foundations should proceed so fast that we have already ten convents.

"Such distinguished subjects have been received in them that it can be clearly seen that His Divine Majesty has chosen them Himself, and has given them in a short time what He accords to others after long years. One thing is wanting to them—the government of our Order. So long as they have not that, I shall look upon all that has been done as nothing. This is what I have told their Highnesses, and what I say to those who still keep asking for foundations: for I shall make no more until our Fathers are here. You are much desired in these States, and, in order that the Fathers may have proof of this, the Archduke is writing to the Auditor, his agent, telling him to see about the matter.

"I beseech your Paternity, for the love of God, so to manage that nothing can hinder the coming of some of the Fathers, and that they may be chosen from among the most fervent and learned: men suitable in every way, for that is very necessary in this part of the world. The Nuncio who is here assures us that you have excellent subjects in Italy, and that it will be easy to send men who will give every satisfaction.

"If your Paternity finds some who are willing to come to this country they will, as far as temporalities are concerned, meet with every convenience for a foundation, for many people have offered to help them, some have even promised in writing to do so. But his Highness, the Archduke, thinks it well not to accept anything until the Fathers see for themselves how things are. I confine myself, therefore, to assuring them that they will find here obedient and submissive daughters.

"With regard to the journey of the reverend Fathers, a sum of two hundred ducats is promised. If you need more, it will be paid on your arrival. Although the weather is not such as I should wish for your voyage, I hope that God will come to the aid of the Fathers, so that they may be here very soon. We shall not cease to beg this of His Divine Majesty, until we actually see them here. May He deign to protect your Paternity for us, and grant all the good things we ask of Him for you.

"Brussels,   "ANNE OF JESUS."
"8th October, 1609."

This request was warmly seconded by a letter from the Archduke, dated two days later. The venerable Mother also wrote to the Pope, then Paul V. After reading her letter, and in the presence of the Carmelite friar who brought it, the Holy Father exclaimed three times "O beata Mulier!" "O thrice happy woman!" It is probable that these letters only confirmed the decision already made by the Sovereign Pontiff to send some Carmelites to the Netherlands, for Anne of Jesus on 5th January, 1610, wrote to Father Diego de Guevara:

"... This spring we shall have our Discalced religious from Rome, who have been invited by their Highnesses and are so much desired in this country. Even before they were asked for, His Holiness had requested them to found both here and in France...."

The friars reached Brussels on 20th August, 1610, and the regular exercises of community life began on Michaelmas Day, but even before this the Royal Convent of Brussels had made its formal act of submission to the

Government of the Order. The Archdukes' notary drew up an account of the proceedings in duplicate, one copy being kept in the National Archives of Brussels, the other in those of the Carmelite nuns. The document is dated 18th September, 1610,[114] and expressly provides for the return of the Spanish Mothers to their native country whenever they wished to go.

This event was duly notified to the Holy See in a letter to Cardinal Borghese from the Nuncio, Guido de Bentivoglio, preserved in the Vatican Archives. After asking permission for the Carmelite friars to reserve the Blessed Sacrament in their oratory, the letter continues:

> ". . . The same Fathers will now set their minds to taking on themselves the care and government of the nuns of the same Order, who have convents in these provinces. And, as a matter of fact, this morning a start has been made with this convent of Brussels. But before coming to the act of giving obedience, Mother Anne of Jesus, a Spaniard, and prioress of the same convent, wished to make a declaration juridically through a notary, by the which statement she made it plain that she did not intend by the obedience which she was to give to Father Thomas of Jesus, appointed to this end by the General of Italy, to prejudice the condition upon which she and her companions came here: the which [condition] was that of being able to return to Spain, when the occasion should demand it. In accordance with the which [condition] an undertaking was made first

---

[114] Manriquez gives 14th September but the copies in the archives bear the date given above.

in France, and then here by these A.A.[115] to provide conveniently for their return, should the time come. This declaration having been made beforehand, and separately, by the same Mother Anne, next came the act of giving obedience to the said Father Thomas,- and to the Congregation of Italy. To the same declaration the same Father gave full consent, and thereafter he received her under his care and government. At both the aforesaid acts I was present to please the parties, who desired it.

"For the rest, I hope that this good work will go on ever increasing to the greater glory both of God and the Catholic religion in these parts: and in conclusion I most humbly kiss the hands of your Most Illustrious Lordship.

"From Brussels, the 18th of September, 1610.
"Of your Most Illustrious and Most Reverend Lordship,
"The most humble and devoted servant,
"GUIDO, ARCHBISHOP OF RHODES."

From fragments of letters written by Anne of Jesus about this time to her friends in Spain, it is clear that she sought advice constantly from John Alphonsus de Curiel, Rector of the University of Salamanca. The Father Master was so devoted to the holy prioress that he wrote to tell her that, as soon as he was free, he would come to Brussels in order to be able to enjoy her conversation and advice. She, however, dissuaded him from this project:

> "I put him off" she writes, "thinking I should soon be in Spain. May He who has bestowed on us such close friendship here, unite us for ever in heaven."

---

[115] The abbreviation A.A. used in the original Italian has more than one meaning. Here it probably stands for "Autorita," "Authorites," or for "Altessa," "Their Highnesses," i.e. the Archdukes.

DISCALCED FRIARS COME TO FLANDERS

God called Father Curiel to Himself on 28th September, 1610, so that Anne of Jesus was deprived of his wise counsels. She at once became anxious that her letters to him should be either returned to her or destroyed.[116] Writing to Father Diego de Guevara, she says:

> ". . . I am greatly distressed that your Paternity was not present at the death of good Master Curiel, for it was of great importance that you should have been there for several reasons, and on account of certain papers, which perhaps those who took charge of his would have given you. I beg your Paternity to try to recover them in my name, since they can be of no possible use to them, and here they would be very useful for the affairs of our Order."

Among the papers which this letter names as particularly important is "one very long letter" in which the venerable prioress says she gave the Father Master a detailed account of what had taken place in the Netherlands concerning the coming of the Discalced friars. In another letter to Father Augustine Antolinez, who succeeded Father de Curiel as Rector of the University occur these words:

> "It is all right about the letter which your Paternity says you have burnt. I think that good Master Curiel will have torn up those which were important."

And again after she had been assured by God that her

---

[116] The process for the beatification of Anne of Jesus speaks of "Very important documents" having been concealed or destroyed. Manriquez writes to the same effect. About seventy-two of the letters of the Servant of God are preserved in the present Carmel at Brussels but it has not been possible to consult them. Those quoted are taken either from Manriquez or the Memoire.

friend was already in heaven, Anne of Jesus, still under the influence of her previous anxiety, writes:

> "How much the holy Master Curiel would have found himself deceived, if he had not worked for God, who is now rewarding him with such glory."

And a few days later:

> "I am very pleased that no one has seen any of the papers that holy Master Curiel had. May the Divine Majesty increase his glory."

On 27th September, 1610, the Carmelites of Louvain made their act of submission to the Order, the elections of the previous year, under M. de Brétigny, being confirmed by Father Thomas of Jesus. M. de Brétigny, like the true man of God that he was, gladly yielded up his authority to the father provincial. He was appointed chaplain to the Brussels Carmel, and later on took an active part in the foundations of Dole, Besancon, and Beaune, becoming temporal founder of the last. He also endeavoured, though without success, to establish Discalced Carmelite nuns in the Congo.[117] In 1627 he became very infirm and retired to Rouen, where he died peacefully on 8th July, 1634. M. de Bérulle assisted him in his last moments on earth, during which he was consoled by the visible presence of St. Teresa, and Mothers Anne of Jesus and Anne of St. Bartholomew, for whom he had done so much. He was seen in glory after his death by the Prioress of Brussels, then Mother Margaret of the Mother of God.

While the matters related above were in progress, the Archdukes were pushing forward the building of the Royal Convent. All contemporary writers describe it as a

---

[117] At that date a small territory on the west coast of Africa.

magnificent establishment, "One of the best in the country." No expense was spared in its construction. Anne of Jesus would have much preferred a more modest dwelling, according to the wishes of her holy Mother; but though the Infanta yielded to her representations regarding the number of cells, the whole building was so spacious and convenient that the Servant of God was anxious and distressed, rather than pleased, at seeing herself and her daughters in such commodious quarters. Writing to Salamanca in 1615, she says with a touch of humour, in reference to the portress:

> "This charge is a trying one here on account of the size of the house. As it is a royal foundation we have a great deal of walking to do! I often say that we lose the merit of being cloistered by living amidst such a vast extent of gardens, with fountains, and ponds full of fish."

The Brussels Relation, or Chronicle, gives the following account of the convent:

> "Their Serene Highnesses made it their particular care that everything should be arranged very religiously, so that the nuns might take their recreation amid fountains and beautiful gardens, of which there are two, a kitchen garden and one for flowers with which to adorn the church. Beside one of these, the Infanta has had a number of trees planted in order to form a little wood. She herself planted several with her own hands, for having read in our Constitutions that there should be a place where hermitages could be built, to which the nuns could go to pray, she wished everything to be done in order."

Not satisfied with the extent of this wood, however, the Archduke made the nuns a present of an adjoining portion of his own royal gardens, where there was also a pond and a fountain. Here three hermitages were built, one dedicated to Our Lord was close to the fountain, which sprang from a rockery,

> "...formed with consummate art," says the chronicle, "with dazzlingly white stones. The water fell with a gentle murmur on another rockery below, as if it had been brought to this spot by a special Providence of God, in order to dispose and move our hearts to contemplation, love, and the singing of His Divine Praises."

The building of the convent, exclusive of the church, was completed by 1611 and it was decided that the nuns should remove there for St. Joseph's feast. After the first vespers of his Office, therefore, the Nuncio went to the temporary Carmel and carried the Blessed Sacrament thence in solemn procession to the chapel of the Royal Convent. The canopy was carried by the Archduke himself, with three of the highest nobles of the court. At the head of the procession were the royal musicians, followed by the clergy, including Father Thomas of Jesus and other Discalced friars. When the cortege reached the door of the enclosure, the nuns joined the procession coming out two and two, with their veils lowered and lighted candles in their hands. Anne of Jesus, as prioress, came last. The Infanta immediately took her disengaged hand, and, knowing her infirmities, whispered considerately, "Lean on me."

The crowd in the street was so great that halberdiers were on duty to keep the passage clear. When the new chapel was reached, the Blessed Sacrament was placed on the altar while the Te Deum was chanted. The nuns were conducted straight to the choir, where a grate had been already fixed. The ceremony concluded with the solemn singing of Compline. Afterwards the Infanta led Anne of

Jesus to the chapter room, and there begged her to solicit some favour in honour of the occasion. The venerable prioress first thanked her benefactress "For so royal a gift," and then begged that every year, on St. Joseph's feast, three prisoners in Brussels might receive pardon and liberty. The request was granted, and until the Infanta's death in 1633, three prisoners were released each year.

The Infanta herself conducted the prioress to every room in the convent until at last it grew so late that she felt the nuns would want to retire to their cells. "How glad I should be," she said, "to stay and help you to make your beds."

As soon as all the guests were departed, the convent and gardens were declared "enclosed."

The next day Pontifical High Mass was celebrated in thanksgiving. Father Thomas of Jesus preached an eloquent sermon. All documents relating to the temporalities of the new foundation, as well as those required by canon law, had been duly signed and attested by the Archdukes and the Carmelite Nuns and Friars, as well as by the Archbishop of Mechlin, and the civil Treasurers.

Nevertheless, the Bull of Erection granted in 1609 was not considered satisfactory on certain points which the royal patrons of the convent wished to secure permanently; while that of 1610, though giving permission for the nuns to be governed by the Fathers of the Carmelite Congregation of Italy, did not annul the jurisdiction previously granted to the Ordinaries.

The question was referred to Father de Briçuela, who advised that a request should be made to the Holy See for the insertion of a clause securing the government of the nuns by the friars of their Order. A long correspondence ensued between the Sovereigns of the Netherlands and their agent, Chevalier Maas, at Rome. The former did nothing without consulting Father de Briçuela and Anne of Jesus. Notwithstanding this, some of the Archdukes' wishes were of such a nature that the Sacred Congregation of Regulars caused them to be modified before presenting them to the Pope for confirmation. One clause, for instance, required that no one should be admitted as a postulant, or allowed to make her vows, without the "approbation" of the Archduke or the Infanta. Finally the word "consent" was substituted here, as savouring less of spiritual authority. This and other difficulties having been adjusted, a new Bull of Erection was signed on 3rd November, 1611. The Nuncio, Guido de Bentivoglio, promulgated it, and delivered it to the Archdukes, on 25 th September, 1612.

Among other points, this Bull appointed three chaplains and a sacristan who were to live together in a house provided for them. A fixed revenue is assigned to the royal convent, and the nuns are forbidden, under pain of excommunication, to alienate any part of the gift made to them, or give away any of the relics, crucifixes, church ornaments or vestments bestowed by their royal patrons.

One feels that Anne of Jesus must have prompted the tenor of article xix of the petition sent before the Bull was granted, to secure her nuns from possible future interference from the Archdukes or others. It reads:

> "We exact that in future no innovation or mitigation of the life of the aforesaid religious shall be made, but that they shall always observe the Rule and Constitutions that they practise today, and of which they have made profession; and that this article be faithfully kept without the least deviation, innovation or modification being introduced, for any reason, or by any authority whatsoever.
>
> "We implore His Holiness, and the sovereign pontiffs

who succeed him, not to sanction this in any manner whatever, and to grant no dispensation on any pretext."

The above request was incorporated in the Bull, which also secured prayers and suffrages from the nuns for the Archdukes, and reserved to the latter the right of altering what they had arranged, though the power was not to be transmitted to their successors. Finally the Bull secured to the new foundation all the spiritual privileges enjoyed by other convents of the Order. On accepting so much from their royal benefactors, Anne of Jesus drew up a solemn promise of the spiritual engagements entered into by the community on behalf of the Archdukes. Copies of this, engraved on brass tablets, were hung in the choir and chapter room. The inscription was as follows:

"Jesus, Maria.

"Table of obligations binding on the Carmelite Nuns of the Reform of the holy Mother Teresa, who are in the Royal Convent of Brussels, dedicated to St. Anne and St. Joseph, founded by the great munificence of their Serene Highnesses, Albert and Isabella-Clara-Eugenia, Archduke and Archduchess of Austria, and Prince and Princess of the Netherlands, in order that in this religious community there may be a perpetual remembrance of the most pious founders of this house, and that their holy generosity may be repaid by spiritual suffrages.

"All the prayers, penances and exercises conformable to the institute of this holy Order of religion, which this community shall perform during the lifetime of their Serene Highnesses, Albert and Isabella-Clara-Eugenia, shall be offered to God in order to obtain that His Divine Majesty may, for the universal good of Christianity, maintain them in health, give them abundance of grace to live in true and perfect charity, and end their lives happily, so that they may receive, after death, the immense treasure of glory acquired by their merits.

"All the above are likewise offered to God for the happy increase of the house of Austria, particularly for their August and Imperial Majesties, the Emperor and Empress, and for His Catholic Majesty, Philip, King of Spain, so that, of His Divine Goodness He may grant them long and unclouded prosperity during life, and after death the reward of abundant happiness.

"Their Serene Highnesses, Founders of this convent, request and exact that after their death there shall be offered every year in perpetuity a Solemn Requiem Mass, and that on the day preceding this annual solemnity, the entire Office of the Dead be chanted, with double rite.

"In order that posterity may have knowledge and perpetual remembrance of the above obligations, they have been engraved on two tablets of brass, of which one will always remain in the Choir, the other in the Chapter room."

The Archdukes, on their side, ever proved themselves loyal to their engagements. There is no instance in any record that either Duke Albert, or the Infanta, used the great concessions and privileges accorded to them by the Holy See otherwise than for the benefit of the nuns, nor is there any evidence to show that the Carmelites regretted the trust they had placed in their generous Sovereigns.

CHAPTER XXI

LIFE IN THE ROYAL CONVENT

1611-1615

AFTER the arrival of the Discalced friars the Infanta had often said to Anne of Jesus: "I do not recognise the Court since your Fathers have been here; it is quite reformed." But the devil, angry at so much good being done, wreaked his vengeance on the holy prioress. Whenever a new novice was received by the friars, Satan used to appear to her in visible form, abusing and tormenting her in various ways. This continued for eight years, and her confessor, Father Hilary of St. Augustine, and Sister Margaret of the Mother of God, who acted as her infirmarian, both left an account in writing of what used to take place. The latter asserts that the devil tormented the venerable Mother "in mind and body." "The terrifying noises he made during the night," she writes, "used to awaken us with a start.[118] Our Mother, broken with illness, used to say, 'My daughter, do you hear what is going on?' 'Yes, dear Mother,' I would answer. 'And I am very frightened.' Then she would add, 'I am on fire! My sufferings are indescribable: I feel as if I were at the point of death.'" Then she would ask to have the room sprinkled with holy water, for she was unable to raise her hand even to make the Sign of the Cross. After this had been done she was left in peace for the time being.

The number of Discalced friars increased so rapidly that

---

[118] Sr. Margaret slept at that time in the cell of Anne of Jesus because of the latter's many infirmities.

in the autumn of 1611 they were able to make a second foundation at Louvain. From 1608 to 1611, while the Order was governed by a vicar-general, no further foundations of Carmelite nuns were authorised, though many Flemish towns were anxious to have them. Writing to Father Diego de Guevara in October, 1611, Anne of Jesus says:

> "Here they are very desirous that we should make several foundations, but I do not know what the new General of the Congregation of Italy[119] will decide about it. He sets to work with so much prudence that I have written to tell him that if we may not make any more foundations, there is nothing further for us to do in this country."

It is clear that the thoughts of the venerable Mother were turning lovingly to her native land, and the only consideration that kept her in Flanders was the knowledge that her presence would be necessary, in the event of new foundations being allowed. In 1609 Mother Isabel of the Angels had founded a Carmel at Rouen and in the following year Anne of Jesus, who was always kept informed of the progress of the Order in France, wrote to Salamanca:

> "Our dear Mother Isabel of the Angels has already received five novices [at Rouen]. There is much to suffer in these foundations, but it is all easy to bear when one sees the fruit they produce, and the fervour of the sisters here, which increases every day. Truly they serve Our Lord with great fidelity."

Indeed, the holy prioress had only one regret: she herself received too much credit for all this progress. In 1611 she writes:

> "It is a matter of great confusion to me to be called

---

[119] Fr. John of Jesus Maria.

Foundress in France and Flanders, seeing that it is our holy Mother alone who is Foundress of all our convents."

About this time Poland was asking for the daughters of St. Teresa, and the superiors of the Order proposed that Anne of Jesus, in spite of her increasing infirmities, should make the foundation in person. The Servant of God would gladly have braved sufferings and difficulties, but she felt that her presence was necessary in Brussels, and wrote to the father-general to that effect. In the letter to Father Diego already quoted she says:

> "He [Father John of Jesus Mary] would like us to go to Cracow, but I excused myself on the plea of not separating myself from my superiors in Spain, and also because I find that our sisters in Genoa are nearer. It is twenty-six years since their first profession, and they have had great success in the two convents they have founded in Naples and in Rome, since our coming here. Other matters which I now pass over in silence also hold me back.... It seems to me that we have already travelled about enough. It is sufficient for the time being to busy ourselves in this country maintaining what is begun, as you yourself said, reverend Father. Mother Sub-prioress, with her usual fervour, would like to go far away, but God will not allow us to be separated until He calls me to Himself."

Mother Beatrix was not sent to Cracow, but the father-general was determined to have, at least, religious trained by Anne of Jesus, or by one of the other Spanish Mothers, so he authorised Father Thomas of Jesus to settle with her who should be sent. Those chosen were Mother Mary of the Trinity (Bleterswick), professed at Brussels in November, 1608, Sisters Margaret of Jesus and Teresa of Jesus from Mons, and Sister Christina of St. Michael from Louvain. The last-named was the only one who died in Poland. Her incorrupt body was reverently preserved at Cracow. It rested in the nuns' choir robed in a mantle of white velvet, covering a brown habit of the same material, the headdress and veil being of white silk.

Sister Teresa of Jesus was English, the younger sister of Mary Ward, the heroic and saintly Foundress of the Institute of the Blessed Virgin Mary, originally known as "The English Ladies." Sister Teresa was sub-prioress at Cracow, but returned to Mons after six years, and was sent from there to the English Carmel at Antwerp in 1619.

The little band left Brussels on 26th April, 1612, accompanied by a Carmelite friar, a secular priest, and a postulant. The Archduke gave them letters of introduction to the German princes through whose territories they had to pass. At Nuremberg in Bavaria, a cavalcade of Polish knights met the two coaches with their escort, and rode with them to Cracow, which was reached on 2nd June. This foundation subsequently sent out others, but the Cracow Carmel itself is noted for the great holiness of its religious. Besides Mother Christina of St. Michael, two other sisters died in the odour of sanctity, and their bodies remained intact and incorrupt. All these were still exposed to public veneration in 1878, clothed alike and lying in open coffins, which had then only recently been provided with glass lids.

Meanwhile preparations were begun by Anne of Jesus for the opening of a Carmel in Antwerp. A year previously, Mother Anne of St. Bartholomew, who was to be prioress there, had left France at her own request. While acting as prioress at Tours she had a vision in which her holy Mother, St. Teresa, had taken her by the hand, and led her along a road leading out of France. Though M. de Bérulle and the other French superiors strongly opposed her request to be allowed to follow the pointing of the vision, and insisted on her making a retreat in order to learn God's will in the matter, the holy religious persisted in her desire. Very reluctantly the necessary authorisation was at last granted, and, going first to Paris, she left the Convent of the Incarnation for Mons on 6th October, 1611. Her travelling companion was Sister Florentine of the Mother of God, a member of the Paris community.

A most cordial welcome was given to the holy Mother at Mons, where, for a whole year, prayers had been offered to obtain her presence in that Carmel. When her appointment as Prioress of Antwerp was made known, the nuns were grieved at losing their saintly guest. Mother Anne of St. Bartholomew herself was deeply troubled until Our Lord appeared to her, and comforted her with these words: "Take courage and go, for this foundation will be as a lighted torch illuminating the whole country."

The nuns named for the Antwerp community left Mons on 17th October, 1612—Mother Anne of St. Bartholomew; Sisters Florentine of the Mother of God, Anne of the Ascension (Worsley), and Mary of the Holy Ghost. At the express desire of the Archdukes they stopped the first night at Mariemont. On 19th October they slept at Nivelles, and from there visited the shrine of Notre Dame de Hal, on their way to Brussels, which they reached the next day. At the Royal Convent Anne of Jesus and her community, all carrying lighted candles, met the newly-arrived sisters at the door of the enclosure, and conducted them in procession to the choir, where the *Te Deum* was chanted. For six days the venerable co-adjutrix of St. Teresa lavished marks of respect and every possible kindness on her guests. The two former companions of St. Teresa had much to discuss together, and Anne of Jesus encouraged her sisters to open their hearts to Mother Anne of St. Bartholomew, whose simple faith and deep piety were well known to her.

The travellers left for Antwerp on 27th October, taking

with them as sub-prioress Mother Eleanor of St. Bernard, for whom Anne of St. Bartholomew had a tender affection. Before the latter took her departure Anne of Jesus questioned her upon the spiritual state of the Brussels community. "They are worthy daughters of their Mother," was the answer. To crown her hospitality Anne of Jesus lent the Antwerp nuns fifty flors, the only money they took with them.

For a few days Don Iñigo de Borja, Governor of Antwerp, gave the nuns a lodging in his own house, but by 6th November a temporary convent was obtained, and regular life began. Alms poured in so abundantly that Mother Anne of St. Bartholomew was soon able to purchase property suitable as a site for a permanent convent. The new church attached to the Carmel was the first dedicated to St. Teresa. This Antwerp convent is still the home of Carmelites, who, though turned out of Flanders in 1783, under the decrees of Joseph II, succeeded later in recovering their property.

Other foundations quickly followed, in all of which Anne of Jesus took a lively interest: Tournai welcomed St. Teresa's daughters in 1614, Mechlin in 1617, Valenciennes in 1618. The first and last of these had for their first prioress Mother Isabel of St. Paul, Mechlin was founded by Mother Eleanor of St. Bernard.

Shortly after the departure of the nuns for Antwerp the Royal Convent became the scene of a great ecclesiastical pageant. The Archdukes, as a signal mark. of their affection and esteem for St. Teresa's Reform, had obtained permission to transfer the relics of St. Albert—the martyred Cardinal and Bishop of Liege—from Rheims to the choir of the Carmelite nuns. The whole route along which the Sacred Relics were carried was splendidly decorated, and the occasion served for a great religious display. The cortege left

Rheims on 22nd November, 1612, but the progress was so slow that the great church of St. Gudule, in Brussels, was not reached until 12th December. There the Sovereigns went in state to implore the intercession of their sainted ancestor, for St. Albert called "Of Louvain," was the second son of Godfrey, Duke of Brabant, from whom Archduke Albert was descended.

At Mons the relics reposed for the night in the church of the Canonesses of St. Waudru. Among these ladies was Florence de Merode, to whom Anne of Jesus had foretold that she would be a Carmelite. Florence, then seventeen, went to venerate the relics of St. Albert, praying beside them about her desire to enter the Carmel at Mons, when she heard interiorly the words: "Where I am going you will come." She did not attach much importance to this experience, and delayed asking her parents' consent until the following year. Her mother then spoke of the matter to the Infanta, who immediately replied that she would like Florence to enter the Royal Convent at Brussels. Arrangements were accordingly made for this, and on 25th February, 1613, Anne of Jesus gave her the Carmelite habit. As the young novice, now Sister Madeleine Florence of the Cross, entered the nuns' choir, she recognised the splendid casket in which the relics of St. Albert were enshrined, and recalling the mysterious locution, felt greatly consoled.

On 16th December the yet unfinished church of the Carmelites was prepared for the ceremony of the authentification of the relics, the table on which they reposed being placed close to the grate of the nuns' choir, so that they could see all that was done. The Nuncio and his attendants, the Archdukes and their suites, together with a numerous and illustrious gathering of laity from all parts of the Netherlands, conveyed the casket in state from St. Gudule. When the ceremony was over, and the relics had been transferred to a new casket covered, with rich draperies, the procession formed again to proceed to the choir. Anne of Jesus and her community, in their white mantles, with veils lowered and each carrying a lighted candle, waited at the enclosure door. There Don Pedro de Toledo read aloud the act by which the Archdukes confided the care of the body of St. Albert to the Carmelites of the Royal Convent. Several nuns named as bearers then came forward, and received the casket, which they carried to the choir, the Infanta and her Maids of Honour forming the rear of the procession.

Finally, Anne of Jesus signed a formal document, in which she undertook, for herself and her successors, to guard the relics faithfully, and to yield them up again to the Archdukes, should they desire it.

Three years later the Infanta, with similar ceremonies and guarantees, confided to the care of Anne of Jesus and her community two large relics of her patroness, St. Elizabeth of Hungary.[120] These were placed before the grate below the relics of St. Albert, and Anne of Jesus signed a document concerning these new treasures of like purport to the one she had signed concerning the body of St. Albert. It is dated 19th November, 1615.

The conditional character of the gifts was cancelled by the Infanta before her death, both in her own name and that of the Archduke, who had died in 1621; and the precious relics, together with many others, including a thorn from Our Lord's crown and the body of St. Lidwine, became the property of the Brussels Carmelites.

The year 1614 brought Anne of Jesus the supreme consolation of the Beatification of her holy Mother. The decree bears the date of 24th April, 1614, and the completion

---

[120] One of the Saint's arms, and a portion of her lower jaw.

of the church attached to the Royal Convent was eagerly pushed forward, so that the solemnities in thanksgiving might be held within its walls. Both decoration and equipment were finished by September, and the festival was fixed for 5th October, the thirty-second anniversary of Teresa's holy death. On 28th September the church was solemnly consecrated by Matthias Hovius, Archbishop of Mechlin. Behind the high altar was a large painting of St. Anne and St. Joseph, the patrons of the convent, and above this was a statue of Blessed Teresa, in painted wood. The church was a very fine building with a double row of pillars and thirteen large windows, and it was furnished with everything necessary for carrying out becomingly the Services of the Church. The Archdukes had even carried their generosity so far as to provide everything in duplicate, one set being in silver, the other in less precious metal.

The Infanta and her Maids of Honour made the draperies used to decorate the interior for the first feast of the Foundress of the Carmelite Reform, the most striking feature being a magnificent dais hung with cloth of silver on which her statue was enthroned. After solemn High Mass this image of Blessed Teresa was carried in procession through the streets of Brussels, the Archdukes and all their Court assisting. Every day during the octave, Mass was sung in the church by different prelates, and the faithful heart of Anne of Jesus was overflowing with consolation at seeing the honour paid to the Mother she loved so well.

That same year (1614) saw the death of Father Jerome Gracian of the Mother of God. In 1596, by an order of Pope Clement VIII, he was attached to the Mitigated Order of

Carmelites, and since 1606[121] had been in Brussels, devoting himself to all kinds of good works. He was frequently in touch with Anne of Jesus, finding in her a living likeness of St. Teresa, whom, with Our Lady, he was wont to call "The Lady of his thoughts." In 1613 he preached the Lenten sermons at Antwerp, where he often visited Mother Anne of St. Bartholomew.

On 20th September, 1614, Father Jerome was working in the neighbourhood of Brussels, when he was taken suddenly ill. After the last sacraments had been administered, he declared with his dying breath that he forgave all who might have injured him. He then asked that the few poor treasures that he carried in his habit might be taken from him—small pictures of Our Lady and of Teresa of Jesus, together with the Foundress's little finger, which he himself had detached from her dead body. When this had been done he kept repeating feebly but over and over again the *Gloria Patri*, and the prayer for the feast of Blessed Teresa. Just before he died his friend and patroness appeared to him, and with the words "Blessed Teresa has been speaking to me; I am going to celebrate her Beatification in heaven," he gave up his soul to God on 21st September. The relic of the holy Foundress was taken from his cold fingers by Father Thomas of Jesus. Father Gracian had asked that it might be sent to his Carmelite sister at Seville, but the provincial of the Mitigated friars claimed it, on the ground that he was the religious superior of the deceased priest. However, the Marquis of Guadalista, who was present, begged the loan of the relic for his wife, who was about to become a mother.

---

[121] The "Memoire des Carmelites Dechaussees" gives 1604, but Fr. Benedict Zimmerman on p. 206 of his edition of "The Book of Foundations" (London, 1913) says that Father Gracian was called to Brussels by Archduke Albert in 1606.

LIFE IN THE ROYAL CONVENT 289

The story of what had happened soon reached the Archdukes, who, with somewhat unwarranted devotion, immediately applied to Rome for a brief authorising them to retain the relic, and present it to the Royal Convent. Paul V saw fit to grant this favour, and the brief was signed, 15th February, 1615.

After all the formalities had been complied with, including an act of renunciation and donation signed by the Provincial of the Mitigated friars, the relic, with all the documents setting forth its authenticity, etc., was delivered into the hands of Anne of Jesus on 13th October, 1615. The messenger of the Archdukes on this occasion was Joachim Dewzenhear, Keeper of the Crown Jewels. He carried back with him an acknowledgment written in Spanish and signed by the venerable Mother. It ran as follows:

> "Acknowledgment of the gift which by order of their Serene Highnesses, Joachim Dewzenhear, Keeper of the Jewels of His Serene Highness, Archduke Albert, made to Mother Anne of Jesus, Prioress of the Convent of Discalced Carmelite nuns of the town of Brussels, in presence of Mother Beatrix of the Conception, sub-prioress, and of several other sisters, of the relic of a finger of Blessed Teresa of Jesus, with the proofs of its authenticity, etc., recognised and legally admitted by his Holiness, our Father, Pope Paul V, and by the Most Illustrious and Most Reverend Archbishop of Rhodes, his Nuncio in these provinces; also a casket which encloses the said relic, of which full details are given below. For their Highnesses have ordained that we should receive all these things to keep them in perpetuity in this Convent, and it is on this condition that we accept them. . . ."

[Here follows a detailed list of everything received and of the documents referring to each.]

> ". . . For holding the aforesaid relic, a small ebony casket inlaid with ivory and mother of pearl, with lock

and key in gold. . . ."

The document concludes:

> "I, Anne of Jesus, Prioress of the Discalced Carmelites of this town of Brussels, have personally inspected everything mentioned in the six articles of this declaration. I have received them such as they are described, from the hands of Joachim Dewzenhear, Keeper of the Jewels of His Serene Highness, Archduke Albert, in presence of Mother Beatrix of the Conception, and of several other religious, and I undertake to retain and keep them as long as the charge of prioress, which I hold, imposes the responsibility upon me.
>
> "They will pass into the hands of the prioress who succeeds me, with the obligation of conforming, in all that concerns them, to the wishes of their Serene Highnesses, who forbid that the said relic, or any particle of it, be alienated in any way.
>
> "I oblige myself to this by this document, which I have signed with my name and sealed with the seal of our convent, after having caused it to be read aloud in the presence of the whole community in order that all may keep it in perpetual remembrance.
>
> "Given at Brussels, in our Convent, 13th October, 1615. "ANNE OF JESUS.
> "L ✠ S"

After this account of the treasures of the Royal Convent, with its magnificent appointments, and of those of its adjoining church, it may be well to note that Anne of Jesus, who, faithful to her holy Mother's wishes, had protested in vain against the sumptuous scale on which everything had been done by her illustrious benefactors, had a strange premonition of what would happen in future years. The nuns were one day extolling in her presence the extent and admirable proportions of their convent, when the venerable prioress interrupted them, saying: "However durable and solid these buildings appear to you now, the day will come when there will not be left of them a stone upon a stone."

This prophecy was literally fulfilled. Under the disastrous government of Joseph II of Austria, nicknamed "The Sacristan" from his persistent interference in ecclesiastical affairs, the Carmelites, in common with other religious, were expelled from the Netherlands in 1783, only the English Carmels at Antwerp, Lierre and Hoogstraet being excepted.[122] Two years later the Royal Convent in Brussels was totally demolished, its stones being used to build a new church, afterwards known as St. Jacques-sur-Caudenberg.

---

[122] Lierre and Hoogstraet were founded from Antwerp in 1649 and 1678 respectively.

CHAPTER XXII

SOME CHARACTERISTICS OF ANNE OF JESUS

WHILE Anne of Jesus was busy about many things concerning God's glory, and the good of her Order, God did not leave her without the gift of physical suffering. She had long been a martyr to gout and rheumatism, but in 1613 other ailments supervened. Soon after the nuns had taken possession of their newly-built convent, several of them became seriously ill, and the Infanta took their sufferings much to heart. A letter from her to the saintly prioress contains the following allusion to the state of affairs:

> "I would have come to see you, if I had not thought that I should have been in the way while you have so many invalids. I do not know why Our Lord wants to give the house such a bad reputation, unless it is that He wishes to mortify us all."

Anne of Jesus also grieved over the sufferings of her nuns, until St. John of the Cross appeared to her and said: "Why are you troubled? God loves them so much that He is fain to treat them as His own."

It was about this time that a young sister, Jeanne du St. Esprit, who had been an invalid for some years, came to the cell of the Servant of God, and while there was seized with some kind of nervous attack, which caused her whole body to tremble violently. The prioress took the poor sister in her arms, and, in spite of the remonstrances of the infirmarian, held her close to herself until the crisis had passed. When at length it was possible to carry Sister Jeanne back to her own cell, the strange trembling had taken hold of her venerable Mother, and from that day to the end of her life, Anne of

Jesus knew no rest.

Trembling-paralysis, sciatica, an internal growth and disease of the chest, all declared themselves, as well as a painful swelling of the throat, which threatened to choke her. The doctors who were called in all maintained that any single one of these maladies was sufficient to cause the prioress's death, yet she lived on for eight years. Her intellect remained, however, unimpaired, and the letters she dictated to her intimate friends, especially those in Spain, give us glimpses of what she had to endure.

To Father Diego de Guevara she says:

> "It would be a much greater consolation to speak to your Reverence than to write, for I cannot say all I wish, nor what the sequel is to the devotion I have had all my life to Holy Job. It is impossible to understand properly the difference there is between desiring to suffer and actual suffering. Job complained that God showed His power by pursuing a dry straw.[123] I am so completely reduced to this, my dear Father, that I cannot express it. In fact it is impossible to explain the state in which God keeps me. I used to call Him 'The Concealer of my sins,' but just at present I can say that He is making them known by the chastisement He is applying to them—a chastisement so lamentable, and which makes me so restless, that I hide myself from those around me. Day and night my limbs are trembling. I get not an instant's repose. Nevertheless I am allowed to hear Mass every day and receive His Divine Majesty. For this they carry me to the little grate. There the trembling is so great, that it seems as if my very bones would be dislocated...."

That was in 1615. On 2nd March, 1616, she writes again:

> "Every day I am in greater need of God's help, and of that of His servants. I am very pleased that our dear good

---

[123] Job xiii, 25.

Father Master Antolinez has compassion on me; if he could see me I am quite sure he would be more sorry for me than Job's friends were for him, for Job, at least, could clean his sores with a potsherd, while I am unable to move hand and foot. ."

In a letter to Salamanca, dictated in November of the same year, she says:

"See to what a state your poor mother is reduced, for she cannot even raise her hand to bless you. It is three years since I made the sign of the Cross. I can only bless you from my heart."

Other letters say that she could not herself wipe away the tears forced from her eyes by her weakness and terrible sufferings, nor restrain the groans of agony, when an acute attack of pain came on. Sometimes she would express a wish to go to purgatory to expiate her sins there, instead of on earth. "Not to escape her sufferings," she was careful to add, "but because it distressed her sisters to see her in such a state, and on account of the trouble waiting upon her caused them. One of her prayers made at this time was certainly granted. She had asked that none of those who attended her might suffer any harm from their devoted and unceasing ministrations.

As her maladies increased, Anne of Jesus experienced terrible night-sweats, so much so, that in a single night her garments and bedclothes had to be changed two or three times, those removed being wrung out as if they had been taken from a bucket of water. Both the door and window of the invalid's cell used to be set wide open even in the depths of a continental winter, so intolerable was the heat of the fever which consumed her. All this deprived the infirmarian of her sleep: she could barely get two hours of broken rest. One day as she was changing the venerable Mother's clothing for Mass, this devoted sister felt herself overcome with impatience, which she concealed with great difficulty. When all was finished, Anne of Jesus thanked her, adding: "Sister, you have been very patient with me. I will pray for you." When Mass was over, and the prioress had been carried back to her cell, she again referred to the temptation, saying: "I have asked God that as long as you nurse me you may never again feel impatient," a grace which Sister Margaret declared she experienced up to the time of the venerable Mother's death.

Other sisters who helped to take care of the Servant of God often declared that in waiting upon her they felt as recollected and close to God as if they were at prayer in the chapel. This helped the nuns to realise a truth of which Anne of Jesus constantly reminded them in her instructions. "God's true adorers," she used to say, "do not worship Him only when they are in church, but wherever they may happen to be: therefore, although you may not actually be in the choir, you can pray and adore God in spirit and in truth, always and everywhere."

It was probably in 1617 that Our Lord revealed to His faithful servant something of the torments of His Sacred Passion. She gave an account of the vision to her confessor, Father Hilary of St. Augustine. "All that is preached about the Passion," she said, "or written about it in books, however dreadful and exaggerated it may seem, all that the very gospels tell of it, or that the prophets predicted about it, would not all together give even an idea of what I learnt in this revelation." Besides showing her His physical sufferings, Our Lord made known to her the desolation that filled His Sacred Heart. He allowed her to share something of His Chalice with Him by withdrawing from her all consolation.

Writing to her cousin, then Bishop of Badajos, in October, 1617, she says:

> "At present, my Lord, all I can do is to endure these trials and excessive sufferings. It is a marvel that I am alive at all. For four years I have not been able to lie down even for an hour, and I only sleep for a few minutes at a time. I can only get about by dragging myself along the floor like a serpent; and in spite of the severe frost, I am consumed with such burning heat that I can scarcely bear the weight of my habit. My limbs are contracting, and I have lost the use of them all. . . . Sometimes my tongue is so swollen I can hardly speak."

And to the same correspondent two months later:

> "Do me the favour of having said at once the fifty Masses you promised to have said for me after my death, for indeed I am already dead I do not know why God wants me to go on living like this at the expense of the sisters, who have to do everything for me, as though I were a babe newborn. People say a great deal about Purgatory, but the Purgatory I am suffering in my body is such, that I am praying to go there to expiate the rest of what is due to me."

But if the holy prioress suffered in body, as she says, the mental anguish she endured was much greater. To Father de Guevara she wrote:

> "My interior is so distracted, that it is only because holy people counsel me to do so, that I receive Holy Communion. But the manner in which I do it seems to me almost an irreverence. I tell you this, Father, in order that you may obtain for me from His Divine Majesty mercy and forgiveness, for I have great need of both. May the holy will of God be done in me."

And to her cousin:

> "All I can do is to hear Mass, and go to Holy Communion, but with so little devotion that it seems as if I had no soul at all."

Again to the same a few weeks later:

> "Everything has been taken from me, for I can no longer even go to Confession. They take me to receive Holy Communion every day, but I approach the Holy Table almost like a brute beast."

Amid this aridity of spirit, the venerable Mother had the further trial of active persecution from the devil. She spoke now and again of this to Mother Beatrix of the Conception. "My daughter," she would haltingly say, "I am being tormented. He who made me is now destroying me, and He has given power to my enemies to do it. I could not suffer more if I were in hell. But though He should slay me, yet will I trust in Him."

Someone sent her a picture of Job. It appealed to her greatly. "How well he is depicted," she wrote in reply,[124] "with his wife and his comforters! I can almost hear them speaking."

In one of her letters occurs the following:

> "It seems to me that by living in the state I am in, I am being made an example of what Almighty God can do. It is past belief, I am constantly resisting a temptation, for such it seems, to think that no one has ever had sufferings equal to mine."

It is related that, in these times of trial and depression, the venerable Mother's one consolation was to speak of death. When she could find no rest and comfort in her cell, the nuns used to carry her in a low chair, which they set down on the spot where she was going to be buried. "Would to God," she sometimes said, "that I could without sin have myself placed under this stone. There at least I should find

---

[124] All her letters at this time were of course dictated. When she could she used to sign her name in shaky characters at the end.

rest."

God had not, of course, abandoned His servant and at times He refreshed her with some unusual grace.

Thus, when William, Prince of Orange, was dying in 1618, and the nuns at Brussels were all praying for him, God revealed to Anne of Jesus the moment of his death, and the fact that he was saved. She was also supernaturally enlightened about the death of her brother, Christopher de Lobera, S. J., and of that of one of her cousins, Gomez de Torres, brother of the Bishop of Badajos. Of the latter she wrote, in 1617, to the bishop, who was anxious about his salvation:

> "Do not worry about our dear Gomez de Torres, for he has very little to suffer for his youth."

As the meaning of these words was not very clear, the bishop evidently wrote for further information, for in another letter, dated 1618, Anne of Jesus says:

> "I certainly believe that our Gomez de Torres is enjoying the vision of God. But we must not on that account leave off doing all we can for the departed, since what we do contributes to the honour of God and their glory. But, although this may give some little satisfaction, it is not a thing to write about, or even to speak of. One should not easily mention matters like this, nor even believe them."

Writing to a newly appointed superior, about 1616, Anne of Jesus said:

> "Your Paternity should begin by doing yourself what you wish others to do. This is a rule which I have always followed, doing first myself whatever I wanted others to do, and sometimes, without my uttering a single word, I got what I wanted, and the work was done. All the same it is easy to see how imperfect my own practice was, since Our Lord has reduced me to a state in which I can

do nothing but give trouble to the Sisters."

It was because she could no longer follow this golden rule that the venerable Mother besought her superiors to relieve her of the office of prioress. With the Father General of Italy she very nearly succeeded in gaining her point, but the Archdukes insisted on her maintaining her position, according to an exemption already granted by the Nuncio that she was to remain prioress for life. This was a great trial, and a real disappointment as her letters tell:

"I am broken with pain and with constant trembling," she writes, "nevertheless they want me to be prioress, and force me to comply. May God forgive their Highnesses."

And again:

"These sisters are so foolish, they want a Prioress whom they have to carry about in their arms."

Anne of Jesus knew well whom chiefly she had to thank for this prolongation of office, for with a touch of her old spirit she wrote to Salamanca:

"Mother Sub-prioress is so fond of me that she distresses me by the way she grieves over my sufferings. She shows her grief so much that I have to scold her, and send her out of my cell, for she weeps so copiously, that I am filled with pity for her. In this I am, in a manner, revenged for the way in which she refused to be Prioress in order that I might remain in office, for I had actually persuaded Father General to set me free. But both young and old banded together against me—mere lump of clay that I am—and insisted that I should still crawl about."

In spite of these regrets, however, Anne of Jesus continued to prove herself an efficient prioress, helping her community as much by what she was, as by what she said and did. Sometimes while sitting in her low chair in the enclosure garden she would pull up all the weeds around her, as far as she could reach. When asked why she thus needlessly exerted herself, she replied "My daughters I must do what I can, and kill two birds with one stone by showing you at the same time how to take care of the garden of your souls by rooting out all your imperfections."

Sister Margaret of Jesus, the first novice received at Brussels, who was afterwards prioress there for fifteen years, left an eloquent testimony to the virtues and capability of her first religious Mother. She writes:

"During the fourteen years that venerable Mother Anne of Jesus was prioress at the Royal Convent, we always saw in her the living portrait of our Mother, St. Teresa,[125] and a faithful mirror of all her virtues. As for myself I always felt the highest esteem for her. The rare endowments I noticed in her, and the celestial graces with which God enriched her soul, made me often think that she was without a peer. What struck me most was her nobility of character, and the peace and calm with which she did everything. Nothing seemed capable of troubling her, and one would have said, on watching her evenness of temper, that she had no passions.

> "Her talent for government was quite unique, and she used so much tact, that she was loved and respected by all. Never put out, she performed each duty as if she had nothing else to do. Indeed, she used to say that she never worried about anything, but kept her mind directed to God. Her dealings with others were always cordial, for she had a very tender heart. Nevertheless she practised perfect detachment, her strong principles over-riding all. No one ever came in contact with her without being penetrated with respect, and as for us religious it was sufficient for her to appear at the door of the room where the community was assembled, for us to feel instantly

---

[125] The MS. is dated 1656.

recollected, so great was the impression made upon us by the almost superhuman dignity which emanated from her person."

Nor was it only in the seclusion of her own community that Anne of Jesus was loved and revered. Every day many splendid equipages drew up at the enclosure door bringing great ladies who wished to consult her, or ask her prayers. Many of the most enlightened and learned ecclesiastics of the Netherlands also sought her counsel. One of these, Father Andrew de Soto, confessor of the Infanta, was talking one day to the sacristan about the treasures of grace manifest in the holy prioress. "Let be, Don Utena," he exclaimed. "Let be. Much is said about Teresa of Jesus, much also will be said of Mother Anne of Jesus, for she is a woman of great and rare virtue."

"I have personally experienced," said one of the nuns, "that our venerable Mother had marvellous gifts. Many a time has she told me my thoughts. Now unless she had received light from heaven, that would have been impossible, for she told me of things about which I had never spoken, not even to my confessor."

One of the novices was resisting some persistent temptation, when the devil made a new and almost overwhelming attack. The poor victim fled for protection to the cell of her prioress. Anne of Jesus was busy at the moment discussing some matter of importance with several of the older religious, and her young visitor turned back without saying what was the matter. But the venerable Mother called her to her side. "Come here, dear child," she said, and tenderly putting her arm around her, she added "Go to matins and have great trust in God." At the same instant the novice's trouble gave place to a sweet calm, and she was never again tried by the same temptation.

One Wednesday in Holy Week, while the altar of Repose was being erected, the venerable Mother sent the nuns to make their prayer in their cells. One of them, tired with the heavy work of that penitential season, was more inclined to sleep than to pray, and instead of kneeling, sat down upon her bed. Presently she heard her name called, thrice several times, and recognised the voice as that of Anne of Jesus, who was at that time unable to move. To the first and second call the weary religious paid no heed, but at the third she saw her venerable Mother standing beside her, and saying something which she failed to understand. At once she knelt down and made her prayer as well as she could. At the end of the hour she went straight to the prioress's cell. Looking at her gravely Anne of Jesus said, "I am very sorry that I sent you to pray." The young sister asked pardon at once, and then told her venerable Mother what had happened, begging her to repeat again the words she had used. "I told you to take a becoming posture during your prayer," was the reply, and the lesson thus given was never forgotten. Another time this same sister begged the Servant of God to instruct her on certain points about which she needed help in her spiritual life. It was during the time when Anne of Jesus had great difficulty in articulating. After some moments, she managed to stammer, "My child, I cannot speak but I will ask Almighty God to make you understand what I am unable to explain." With that the young religious had to be content. But even as she was leaving her holy Mother's cell she was inundated with supernatural light, which continued without interruption, for three whole days, leaving her fully satisfied and at peace.

Sister Madeleine Florence of the Cross relates an even more striking instance of the gift of counsel as possessed by Anne of Jesus. A few days after she had received the Carmelite habit, Sister Madeleine Florence, alone in her cell, became a prey to a violent temptation against her vocation. To her great surprise the prioress entered (Anne of Jesus could at that date walk only with difficulty), clothed in part of her religious habit, and leaning on a stick. "My child," she said, "I am come to see you because you are in distress." Then she sprinkled the room with Holy Water, and after a few comforting words to the young sister, went back to her own cell.[126] On another occasion about five o'clock in the evening, Sister Madeleine Florence was at prayer when she saw hell open before her, and two places prepared there, which, so she was given to understand, were for herself and the gentleman, a German Lutheran, whom her parents had wished her to marry. The terrified novice thought it was her fault that his soul was lost, for the devil represented to her that he would have become a Catholic, had she married him, and so would have saved his soul. While this dreadful doubt was still upon her, Anne of Jesus sent for her, "My child," she said, "What was it that distressed you just now, during your prayer?" The novice was unable to answer—being quite faint from the struggle she was going through. Then her venerable Mother laid her finger on her pulse. "I can hardly feel it," she said to the Infirmarian, who was present, and added "Get this Sister something to eat." While Sister Margaret was away the Prioress said very gently, "Since you cannot speak, nor tell me what is the matter, I will tell you myself what ails you. You want to go away and marry that heretic. And a fine match it would be! No, no! What God meant you to understand during your prayer is this: Had you married him the evil you foresaw would have come to pass, but since you have not done so, this gentleman will be converted. As for yourself you will stay here and become a very good religious. Distract yourself for a time, and go to recreation. You need have no fear." Sister Madeleine

---

[126] Sr. Madeleine Florence was among those religious who knew no Spanish, she says that though Anne of Jesus used that language, she perfectly understood what was said.

Florence was never troubled again on this subject.

Often a single word from the holy Prioress was enough to change a Sister's heart, even though accompanied by no exhortation. A novice, beset with temptation, had resolved to return home, and her parents were already awaiting her outside the door of the enclosure. Anne of Jesus came with the big key to let her out. Before actually unlocking the door she looked kindly at the novice, and asked: "Once more, my child, do you really wish to go?" With the words a light penetrated the young Sister's heart, and throwing herself on her knees, she acknowledged her fault, and begged to be allowed to remain. Anne of Jesus, of course, consented, and in due time the novice became a fervent Carmelite.

To another who asked to be received, as a choir-sister, the venerable Mother replied, "You would do better as a lay-sister, my child." Without any hesitation the young girl asked for the white veil, and never repented her decision.

Sister Margaret of the Mother of God belonged to a Flemish family, and her brother, who had left the Netherlands, had not been heard of for many years. This was a source of great grief to his Carmelite sister, and she fretted about it a good deal. One day Anne of Jesus consoled her by telling her that her brother was in Italy. "He has fallen into the hands of the magistrates," the Prioress continued "and has narrowly escaped being hanged." Such news was sufficiently shocking, but at least the long lost brother was alive. Not very long afterwards, he returned to Brussels, and went to see Sister Margaret, to whom he related his story which agreed perfectly with what Anne of Jesus had said.

Nothing was too small to enlist the sympathy of the Servant of God. One day Sister Jeanne de Jesus broke an eye-tooth by biting some wire. The crown fell to pieces, but the root caused her much pain. At last a surgeon was called in, but he declared himself unable to extract the tooth. When Sister Jeanne went to give an account of the surgeon's visit,

Anne of Jesus called her to her side. "Come here," she said "and show me the tooth which is hurting you so much. Is it this one?" and she put her little finger on the broken stump. "Ah!" cried Sister Jeanne "may God reward your Reverence for the pain has gone." Nor did that tooth ever ache again.[127]

Many other instances of the holy Prioress's gift of healing could be given but the recital would become wearisome. The invalid Sister Jeanne du St. Esprit often declared that in the many sufferings she endured for more than eight years, the only relief she experienced came to her through Anne of Jesus. Now and again the sisters would urge Sister Jeanne to have recourse to this or that saint, but she always refused, because a persistent interior voice would simultaneously suggest the thought "If Our Lord wills to cure me through one of His saints, our Prioress is saint enough to do it." The sequel shows that this was really an inspiration from heaven.

As Anne of Jesus consoled others, she was in her turn comforted either by Our Lord Himself, or through His Saints. Time and again, the nuns on entering her cell perceived a most heavenly odour. Sometimes they ventured a question. "Dear Mother what is this heavenly perfume?" 'What perfume are you talking about?" "Oh, I cannot describe it, but it is very pleasant and delightful."

"Go outside and see where it comes from." But outside there was no perfume of any kind. Then the sister knew. Returning to the Prioress she said. "Mother, the perfume is only in here. Confess that our holy Mother Teresa has been to see your Reverence." At this Anne of Jesus smiled, but answered nothing; for St. Teresa often visited her, leaving after each visit what her Carmelite daughters call "the perfume of our holy Mother."

---

[127] Venerable Anne of Jesus is specially invoked in cases of toothache.

The following story belongs to her early days in the Netherlands. A well-known priest, who lived as a hermit, called one day at the Royal Convent, and asked to see the Prioress. Hardly was the venerable Mother seated at the grate, when, instead of inquiring the reason of his visit, she exclaimed: "Father, what are you carrying on your breast?" "Nothing" was the reply. But as Anne of Jesus insisted, he pulled from his bosom a small silver box, and showing it to her, said: "It is a reliquary which I value highly." "No, it is not a reliquary," answered the Servant of God. "It is much more than that. Tell me the truth, for I know that you are carrying something much greater than any relic." Overcome and confused the priest confessed that the silver box was in reality a pyx which contained several consecrated particles, which he was in the habit of carrying about with him, in order to be able to give Holy Viaticum secretly to those who lived among heretics.

A Jesuit Father,[128] who heard this story and who knew Anne of Jesus well, asked her about it. At the conclusion of her account, he inquired how she knew that the priest had the Blessed Sacrament with him. The holy Mother replied: "Whenever I am in the presence of the Blessed Sacrament I feel something interiorly, which tells me that Our Lord Jesus Christ is truly there."

---

[128] Fr. Roland van Overstraeten, S. J.

CHAPTER XXIII

LAST WORKS AND FINAL PURIFICATION

1610-1621

THE contemplative soul is the apostolic soul spiritual writers tell us, and this was certainly verified in the case of Anne of Jesus. In spite of the many calls made upon her in the Netherlands she always kept up a close correspondence with the Carmelites of France and Spain. To her dear friend Mother Juana del Espirito Santo at Salamanca, she wrote as early as 1612:

"The mere thought of seeing myself in your house comforts me, but it seems as if God does not wish me to be consoled in this world."

In the September of 1615:

"It is three years since I made the Sign of the Cross, nevertheless I am not without hope of seeing you again. God is powerful enough to give life to these dry bones."

Her interest in the spread of the Reform never slackened. In a letter dated 1617, she says:—

"Our Father General [i.e. the General of the Congregation of Spain] has done me the favour of setting about the foundation of Toro, concerning which I have been corresponding with him for several years, ever since I was at Madrid."

To the same correspondent, the Bishop in whose diocese Toro was situated, she writes a little later:—

"Do not pay any attention to the difficulties that crop up. All that your Lordship needs is some nuns to begin the foundation. If we were not so far off, we would send some from here, for I have some very good Spanish Sisters, ladies and others from the Infanta's household, and they would be quite willing to go. It is my advice that you should found at once, in the best way you can."

In another letter, probably to the same Bishop,[129] the thoughts of the venerable Religious turned to the home of her girlhood and she writes:

"I am longing for a foundation at Plasencia. May He undertake it Who has the power. It could easily be begun with the inheritance left by my family free of duty."

And again:

"I am not sending the relics. It seems to me that if your Lordship saw them, you would prefer their being kept for our foundation at Plasencia. I hope, if it is God's will, that your Lordship will yourself make this foundation, using for it the house formerly owned by my ancestors."

This wish was realised two or three years after the holy death of the Servant of God. When the convent in Talavera was opened in 1618, Anne of Jesus was equally full of interest and solicitude. She writes:

"I want to know the name of the founder [temporal] of Talavera. When an opportunity occurs I will write to him and send him some relics."

The Bishop of Badajos wrote[130] to Anne of Jesus complaining that the Carmelite friars would neither give him any nuns nor allow any foundation to be made giving obedience to the Ordinary. The prioress answered:

---

[129] Most of these extracts are taken from Manriquez, who gives no names or addresses and rarely any date.

[130] If this letter was written between January 1615 and October 1618, the Bishop was her cousin, Christopher de Lobera. See note p. 302.

"Do not leave off your acts of friendship towards our friars, my Lord, for though the General is at present uncompromising, he will not always be so. Do not give up hope, either, for many things come to those who wait. Nevertheless, your Lordship should certainly make a foundation if an opportunity presents itself, even if the nuns have to be subject to the Ordinary, but always on the condition that, if the friars consent, they should be governed by them."

To another correspondent, however, Anne of Jesus laments that the Father General is inexorable in the matter of granting either friars or nuns for Badajos, and urges that no effort should be spared, even to soliciting the influence of the Duke of Lerma, and that of the King of Spain. Until this authorisation is obtained, she says, the foundation will not be established. The attitude of the Servant of God is worth noting. If possible, she wants all Carmelite convents to be under the jurisdiction of the Order, but, if delays are pressed too far, she advises that convents should be founded under the direction of the Ordinaries, though with the option secured to the nuns of placing themselves under the government of the friars, should circumstances render it advisable. Another letter written by the holy prioress at this time is very explicit on that point:

"For some years considerable endowments have been made for a Convent of our Sisters at Jerez and elsewhere: but God has reserved this work for your Lordship. Let the foundation be made under the conditions mentioned: namely, that whenever our fathers wish to take over the government of the nuns, the bishop, whoever he may be at the time, shall resign his authority over them: and this, because those who make profession of the same life, can best help us to observe it, and we ought to pay attention to that which is most essential."

Nor was it only about new foundations that Anne of

Jesus interested herself. Letters of hers were in the hands of her first biographer, showing that she was consulted by the nuns in Spain concerning those received into the Order, about the maladies of the religious, and even about minor domestic details. Of the money received as alms at Brussels, large sums found their way to the struggling Carmels beyond the Pyrenees. Now and again Anne of Jesus specified what was to be purchased with the money sent. Thus, in a letter to her own convent of St. Joseph, Salamanca, she desired the prioress to provide each of the community with a new tunic, petticoat and mantle, as well as other necessary garments, and requests that she may be informed of the exact expenditure of her alms, in order that she may give a satisfactory account to their benefactor.

Sister Margaret of St. Francis, Philippine Batson, who had entered at Mons, but accompanied Anne of Jesus back to Brussels in 1608, where she was professed the following year, has left an interesting testimony to the esteem in which the venerable Mother was held. Writing in 1634, she says:—

> "When I used to ask her [Anne of Jesus], according to our custom, for permission to do some mortification, she would answer: 'Do all you can for poor sinners while you are young, for when you get old, you will have nothing to offer for them but your good will.' I had a great reverence for her, and before I went into Brittany, I cut a little piece off her habit, which I have kept ever since as a precious relic."

The narrative goes on to relate several cures worked through the "stolen" relic. More than once Our Lord gave Anne of Jesus light concerning the undertakings of the friars. Father Thomas of Jesus, while still Provincial of the Netherlands, had been asked to found a monastery of friars at Cologne. Many difficulties supervened, and the project was on the point of being abandoned, when, on the feast of the Presentation of Our Lady, November 21st, Anne of Jesus was assured by Our Lord during her thanksgiving after Holy Communion, that the foundation would succeed, and that He would be faithfully served there.

It is of special interest that, as early as 1607 the Servant of God was helping and encouraging English Benedictine Fathers, who had come to the Netherlands in the hope of founding a house at Douai,[131] whence priests could be sent as missionaries to England. For this the consent of the Holy See and the Archdukes was necessary, and so great was the opposition raised by already existing English colleges in Douai, that the Benedictines very nearly had to relinquish their project. Their Superior, Father Augustine of St. John (Bradshaw), with Father Leander of St. Martin (Jones), had recourse to prayer, and called upon the Prioress of the Royal Convent in order to secure prayers from the Carmelites. Anne of Jesus was always eager to help England, and she listened sympathetically to Father Augustine's plans. The next time they called at the Convent, she told them they need have no fear concerning the ultimate success of their enterprise. "Although His Highness seems opposed to you just now," she said, "he will shortly do you the favour of granting your request. Your project of preparing for missions will succeed perfectly, although the difficulties which always accompany the work of God will not be wanting." Her words came true. Archduke Albert shortly after made the grant of a site in Douai to the English

---

[131] These Benedictines were Englishmen who, after the dissolution and destruction of the monasteries in England, had joined the Spanish Congregation of St. Benedict. Downside Abbey is the direct descendant of the College at Douai referred to in the text. The Douai Abbey now at Woolhampton represents the post-revolution Douai, viz. St. Edmund's, founded at Paris 1615, revived at Douai 1818, and transferred to Woolhampton, 1903.

Benedictines, and letters were, almost at the same time, received from Cardinal de Givry authorising the foundation. This happy event was gratefully attributed by the sons of St. Benedict to the prayers of Anne of Jesus and her community. In return they granted to the Carmelite nuns in Flanders, then and for the future, a participation in the prayers and good works of the Benedictine order. This "Letter of Filiation"[132] bears the date 1610, the year in which the pact was ratified by the General chapter of the Spanish Congregation of Benedictines. For England and the English, Anne of Jesus had a warm and tender love. During her earlier years of suffering, shortly after her refusal to go to Poland, she wrote:

> "If the doors were open to us to go to England, I would go even if I had to crawl there. It is true I can no longer get about, but with the Sisters to help me, I should attempt it."

One of the venerable Mother's last undertakings was the foundation of a second Carmel at Antwerp, solely for English subjects. This was made possible in 1619 by the generosity of the widowed Lady Lovell, daughter of Baron Teynham, the first Prioress being Mother Anne of the Ascension (Worsley).

Between May, 1619, and the beginning of 1621, when the Flemish Carmels shared a common anxiety, Anne of Jesus wrote:

> "It is well to be on our guard, as are the English. Their Convent is already founded, and those who enter are such good Catholics that there is nothing to fear. God wills us to depend solely on Him."

---

[132] A copy of this document, duly attested, is kept at Lapherne. See Appendix

LAST WORKS AND FINAL PURIFICATION 315

From the English Carmel many religious went forth to found convents in other countries of Europe, and even across the Atlantic, to plant the Reform in the New World. Ladies came from America to enter with the English Carmelites, and in 1790 a Carmel was founded at Port Tobacco, Maryland. In 1831 the community removed to Baltimore.[133] On August 15th, 1931 seven nuns from Darlington (Lierre) went to found a Carmel in Johannesburg, the first in British South Africa.

It was in 1619 that the fourth triennium of Anne of Jesus expired, and she again begged to be released from all responsibility. Her letters show clearly what she felt.

> "Is it possible that Holy Church has pity on me, and sets me free from every tie,[134] and that Religion will not exempt me from this trial?"

she writes, though the letter ends on a note of submission to God's will:

> "May Thy holy will be done in me. I have no other desire than to do whatever is pleasing to Thee until the moment of my death."

To her bishop-cousin she expresses herself more freely:

> "I am vexed beyond measure with this secretary of mine [Mother Beatrix of the Conception], and I do not wish her to say anything of herself, for all that she is so

---

[133] All the Carmels in the U.S.A. (1930), except two communities exiled from Mexico, had for their first prioresses nuns trained at Baltimore, with the exception of two offshoots from St. Louis, Mo.

[134] The reference is to Canon Law, which prescribes that in general Religious Superiors may not be immediately re-elected in the same house after a term of six years.

devoted to your Lordship.[135] She is delighted because quite recently the Superiors in Rome and those here, have insisted on my retaining this wearisome office of Prioress. Their Highnesses and everyone else have fallen into this madness (for madness it most surely is) of having a shadow to govern them, for—without any doubt—such I am, in every way."

And in another letter to the same:

"I could never have believed that bodily sufferings could be so terrible; yet even so, what I feel most is my difficulty in speaking. Every word costs me an immense effort. I can no longer accuse myself in confession, but this is not sufficient to get me excused from retaining my office. If God in His mercy did not Himself look after the nuns, I do not know what would become of our Order."

What distressed the venerable religious most was the report that the Archdukes insisted on her remaining Prioress, and she wrote:

"Even the Princes, notwithstanding their great talents, have been foolish about this. They do not know me for what I am, though they have had many opportunities of learning."

Except when it touched her to the quick like this, Anne of Jesus made gentle fun of the regard in which she was held. The Bishop of Osma wrote asking her to send him her religious habit, promising that he would treasure it as a relic, and assuring her that another holy person of his acquaintance had sent him hers. Her reply was characteristic:

"The giving of the habit gave me a good laugh, but for all that I shall not send you mine. I hope to be buried in

---

[135] Anne of Jesus was dictating to Mother Beatrix.

it, as a reward for the service it has rendered me for forty-eight years. If I live to see the feast of St. Peter's Chains, I shall enter my fiftieth. Your Lordship must pray God to deliver me from this body of mine before that."

Similarly, when Margaret, Queen of Philip III of Spain, sent to ask the Servant of God for her portrait the holy Prioress replied:

> "It would be very difficult for anyone to take my likeness, because my head is always shaking. But I hope that with that God will satisfy and protect your Majesty."[136]

At the same time the venerable Mother strictly forbade her daughters ever to have her portrait painted, or to write her life. Both these undertakings were carried out by the Infanta Isabella.

On account of her many sufferings the limbs of the Servant of God became contracted. She speaks of this quite simply:

> "I have just exchanged sleeves with the writer of this letter [Mother Beatrix of the Conception], because hers are not so long, and I am becoming quite small. It is the great pain that has done this."

About five years before her death, Our Lord appeared to her, His Sacred Body covered with wounds. He gave her to understand that she would become like to Him in this, as well as in her dereliction of spirit. A few days later, three big sores formed on her knees and thigh, caused, it was supposed, by the friction of the bones due to her constant trembling. Later on, two more formed, one on the palm of each hand, while her feet were racked with gout. Thus was

---

[136] The Queen was about to become a mother. Anne of Jesus is still invoked in such cases.

Anne of Jesus favoured with a likeness to her crucified Spouse, as He hung wounded on the cross.[137] These fresh sufferings made it almost impossible for her to sit up, and the swelling in her throat made it dangerous for her to lie down. Every few minutes she had to be helped to change her posture. "If God would but give you a couple of hours' rest," one of the nuns exclaimed while lifting her. "A couple, my child," answered the holy Mother, "I should be content with half an hour. But may God's will be done, even if I should have to suffer till the day of Judgment."

No word of complaint ever passed her lips, though she would say to her Infirmarian: "My daughter, refresh my hands with yours for I feel as if they were being pierced with red-hot iron."

The Infanta Isabella was distressed that she could do nothing to alleviate the sufferings of her life-long friend. "I am hoping to solace the many pains you are enduring," she wrote at this time, "although I know that you yourself do not wish it." The court physician attended the invalid, but could do little for her. "Nothing remains to be done," wrote the Princess again, "except to obtain peace of mind for you. As for that of the body, I know well that you no longer wish for it in this life. Our Lord knows how necessary you are here, therefore, I hope, that on this point, He will hear, not your prayers, but ours."

By February, 1621, the venerable Mother was unable to take any solid food, and her breathing became very laboured. Nevertheless she went to Mass and Holy Communion every morning, and as often as she could, had herself carried to the Community exercises. On returning

---

[137] It is generally held that Anne of Jesus had the Stigmata, but her biographer gives no attestation of the fact; the wounds on her knees and feet were open sores, those on her hands inflamed purple swellings not unlike large nail-heads in appearance. She also shed tears of blood.

she would ask to have the Passion read to her, or the, Office of the day. She very often had the Profession of Faith made aloud for her, or the Recommendation of a Departing Soul. On Ash Wednesday, which fell that year on February 24th, the feast of St. Matthias, a day of holy memories for her, Anne of Jesus felt much worse than usual, and while she was at Mass, a voice said to her: "My child, go to the infirmary. There thou wilt be cured of thy ills." She related this, radiant with joy, to her daughters, and had herself carried to the infirmary without delay. Once there she set about her immediate preparation for death. Father Hilary of St. Augustine was sent for, and she made a general confession of her whole life. He afterwards declared that she had never lost her Baptismal innocence, and had never during her whole life, told a lie, even in jest. Nor does she seem ever to have been troubled with vain glory, or self complacency, for when Mother Teresa of Jesus said to her one day, "Is it possible, dear Mother, that in all the great works your Reverence has had part in, you have not sometimes gloried a little?" the answer came immediately: "Indeed no, my child, for there was no reason why I should. On the contrary, I found so many mistakes in all I did, that they furnished me with plenty of motives for humility." In the infirmary the venerable Mother either sat painfully in her chair, or lay stretched on a small straw mattress placed on the ground. This may have been necessary on account of her great weight, which made it difficult for the nuns to lift her. February 25th and 26th passed, and on the 27th a slight improvement took place, which raised the hopes of the sorrowing community, but it was quickly followed by a relapse. The Servant of God begged to receive the last Sacraments, but as she had no fever, and was still able to go to Mass and Holy Communion, the doctors said there was no immediate danger, and promised to warn her of the end in good time. Tuesday March 2nd saw her as usual at the grate for Mass and Holy Communion, but on again reaching the Infirmary, she felt so ill that she herself gave orders that all should be prepared for the administration of the Last Sacraments, and that Father Hilary of St. Augustine should come to her at once.

Her last confession over, the community entered the Infirmary for the ceremony of Extreme Unction. Looking at them each in turn, she managed to say: "Forgive me, my dearest children, all the faults I have committed while leading you to God, and ask His Divine Majesty to pardon me." Amid the tears and sobs of all around Father Hilary proceeded at once to the anointing. At the moment when the Sign of the Cross was traced with the holy oil upon her feet, Sister Margaret of the Mother of God saw them brilliantly white, and shining like the sun; while a beautiful arc of light—blue, red, and gold—played above them. Manriquez, with his quaint symbolism, says of this marvel, "Her Divine Spouse seemed to say '*Quam pulchri sunt gressus tui in calceamentis*,' How beautiful are the steps thou hast made in planting the Reform in Spain, France and Flanders." The next day, Wednesday, Anne of Jesus was unable to receive Holy Viaticum, though she asked for, and was given, the water from the ablutions. She had great difficulty in swallowing anything, and took nothing that day but a few spoonfuls of jelly mixed with cordial, which had been sent by the Infanta. Each hour seemed to increase the agony of the dying Mother, especially her almost intolerable thirst. In spite of their grief, the nuns experienced a supernatural joy while waiting upon her, and she promised that, as soon as she got to Heaven, she would ask God to reward them for all their care of her.

At four o'clock on the morning of Thursday, March 4th, the venerable Mother was suffering so acutely that those watching her thought her last hour had come. When the bell rang summoning the Community to the choir, they paid no heed, as they expected every minute to be her last. But Anne of Jesus reassured them, and sent them away. A like scene was repeated three hours later, when the dying Prioress dismissed those who were in her room to Mass and Holy Communion. The nuns hastened back as soon as they could, and, when she saw them all gathered round her, she asked to be lifted into her chair. Then one by one, each came to her for a last word and blessing. When the invalid, Sister Jeanne du St. Esprit, was wheeled beside her, Anne of Jesus said very tenderly: "Do not grieve, my child, for I shall come back to see about you." Those standing near heard what was said, and immediately asked: "And me, dear Mother, will you not come back for me too?" for they thought she spoke of Sister Jeanne's death. The dying Prioress smiled at them, but gave no answer.

Then rousing herself for a last effort, she spoke to them all together, and Mother Beatrix asked her to bless her absent daughters also, especially those of Salamanca, where she and Anne of Jesus had made their Profession. She gave a sign of assent, and at that same moment she was seen by Mother Mary of the Trinity (Hannivel), Prioress of the Paris Carmel. This Mother was at prayer, and saw the venerable Mother sick and suffering as she actually was at Brussels. An interior command urged her, at the same moment, to pray for her happy death.

She asked the community to offer their Communion for Anne of Jesus, and afterwards had the consolation of knowing that she had passed away just at the hour of the conventual Mass in Paris.

Father Hilary of St. Augustine had been asked to come earlier than usual, in case the invalid was able to receive Holy Viaticum. For many hours the poor sufferer had had her teeth clenched, and was unable to open them, even to take a little water to assuage her burning thirst. But when Mother Beatrix told her Father Hilary had come, she opened her mouth, painfully and with great difficulty, in order to show that she was able to receive her Lord. The Blessed Sacrament was brought at once, and her face, as she received Holy Viaticum was radiant with joy, as Father Hilary himself remarked. "Reverend Mother," he said, "Our Lord has come to fetch you. He is saying to you what he said to the penitent thief: 'This day thou shalt be with me in Paradise.'" When relating the scene, he added, "She gave me a beautiful smile, and bowed her head as if in assent." Then the nuns accompanied the Blessed Sacrament back to the Choir, and Jesus and Anne of Jesus were alone together for the last time on earth.

According to their Mother's wish, the community dispersed, each going to her allotted task, while, in the infirmary, the last purification of her beautiful soul took place. Consumed with thirst, Anne of Jesus begged for a little water. There was none at hand, and the Infirmarian durst not leave the dying Prioress to fetch some. Our Lord arranged that to the last His faithful servant should keep the promise she had made to Him in the bright days of her youth, never to satisfy herself in anything. After some minutes she asked to be laid on the floor, where she wished to die. To her great surprise Sister Margaret found her Mother light, and easy to lift. Very tenderly she laid her upon the poor straw mattress, and there the nuns found her a little before nine o'clock, each one impelled by an interior voice to leave her work, and hasten to her dying Mother's cell. They all noticed the heavenly joy upon her face and Mother Beatrix of the Conception, guessing the reason, asked if their holy Mother had been with her, coming, according to her promise, to assist her beloved daughter in her hour of direst need. Anne of Jesus could no longer speak, but she pressed the sub-prioress's hand in token of assent, a sign pre-arranged between them.

Just as the last member of the community entered her

cell their Mother opened her eyes, smiled gently and sweetly on her assembled daughters, and then looking up to Heaven, with a gentle sigh or two of supreme content, gave up her soul to her Creator. She was seventy-five years old, and had spent fifty-one in religion.

That same day, her former Confessor at Madrid, the Licentiate Barcena, saw Anne of Jesus going up to Heaven accompanied by St. Teresa. Thus was the latter's promise, made at Vas, fulfilled.[138] This apparition is exceptionally well authenticated. Barcena at once related his experience to Dom Diego de Corral, knight of the Order of St. James, who held many important posts under the King of Spain. He, in his turn, told it on oath, to Manriquez who relates the incident as follows:

> "I had here in Madrid a priest—a great friend of mine, and of my country, Assessor of the Holy Office [i.e. of the Inquisition], a great servant of God of mature age, who had been intimate with the Holy Mother [Anne of Jesus] and her Confessor. One day when I was ill, he came to see me, and said to me in confidence, 'Sir, I must inform you that Anne of Jesus is dead. Being in prayer I had a remarkable vision, and saw her going into Heaven, led thither by the Holy Mother Teresa of Jesus, who was holding her hand. I noticed their white mantles were shorter than those worn here.' About two months later news of her death reached Spain, and it had taken place exactly at the time the priest had told me he had seen her."

Father Hilary of St. Augustine also saw his illustrious penitent entering Heaven clothed in glittering white, and embracing the feet of her Divine Spouse. To many others, also, God vouchsafed this consoling vision. In Paris Mother

---

[138] See p. 52, Fr. Berthold says Toledo, but that was where St. Teresa promised to assist Anne of Jesus on her death bed.

Mary of the Trinity (Hannivel) saw her in glory, and at Antwerp she was seen by the Prioress and several religious.

Mother Anne of St. Bartholomew wrote on May 2nd, 1621, to Mother Mary of the Incarnation, at the Carmel of Consuegra, Spain:—

> "I thank God for the arrival of your Reverence's letter. I should have liked to have received it sooner, because I wanted to tell you that God has called to Himself Mother Anne of Jesus, and given her the grace of being saved from a long Purgatory to be transported into Heaven, for soon after her death, several religious saw her in glory. . . She has ended her life well, and great is now her happiness. As I cannot write at length on this subject I am asking Don Francisco de Torres-Gutierrez to send you the letter which I wrote to him, in order that you may know all the details of this happy death. Ask Our Lord to grant me, in His mercy, the grace of a like end, although I do not deserve it as does this good Mother. Indeed I envy her, and I am praying to her to help me, since she is where she is able to do this."

CHAPTER XXIV

"THE HUMBLE SHALL BE EXALTED"

AFTER her death the body of Anne of Jesus remained fresh and supple. All her limbs, shrunken and bent by suffering, resumed their normal appearance, and exhaled a sweet fragrance, unlike any perfume known on earth. The nuns, eager to possess her garments as relics, took off the habit which she had worn for so many years, and clothed her afresh. Then they laid her on a bier, strewn with flowers and carried her to the choir. Sister Jeanne du St. Esprit had remained in the Prioress's cell while her body was being prepared for burial. She greatly desired to kiss her feet, hoping thereby to be cured, but everyone was too busy to notice her. Great was her grief at seeing the remains of her venerable Mother carried out of the room, and when the Infirmarian returned, she could contain. herself no longer, "I implore you, Sister," she said, "to roll my carriage as far as the steps leading to the choir. Some one is sure to be there, who will help you to carry me into the choir, so that I may kiss the feet of our holy Prioress." Sister Margaret could not refuse so pathetic a request. Once beside the flower-decked bier, Sister Jeanne, lifted in the arms of her sisters, covered her beloved Mother with kisses—her face, her hands, her feet. While her lips were still pressed against these last, a violent trembling shook her whole body, and the sisters hastily laid her back in her carriage. But Sister Jeanne threw aside the covering they were throwing over her, and springing up, declared herself cured. Her astonished Sisters at once intoned the Te Deum, Sister Jeanne kneeling upright the whole time. Then she walked firmly and quickly to the refectory, where Mother Beatrix of the Conception, who had been unable to be present at the community meal, was taking her dinner. "See what our Holy Prioress has done for me," Sister Jeanne cried, and the Mother Sub-prioress could hardly believe her eyes. That evening the Court physician, Doctor Paz, was called in to verify the cure, and also Father Thomas of Jesus.

Manriquez, writing ten years later, says: "From that day to this her malady never returned. She was always able to follow the Community exercises without any exception." A juridical enquiry was held later, and the miracle was declared authentic by Mgr. Bagni, papal Nuncio at Brussels, on December 2nd, 1621.

Meanwhile the people at Brussels, hearing the passing-bell of the Royal Carmel said to one another: "They are tolling for a saint!" One lady who had an invalid son, on whom all that money could procure had been lavished in vain, said to herself: "This nun was a really holy person. My boy must recover his health through her."

Strong in this hope, she took him to assist at Vespers at the Carmelite church, and, animating him with her own lively faith, bade him say his Paternosters,[139] and ask the venerable Mother to cure him. No change in the boy's state took place, but both mother and son returned home with undiminished faith and hope. That night the boy slept well, and he woke the next morning perfectly cured. Another visit was made to the Carmelite church, this time for thanksgiving. All day long the body of the Servant of God lay before the grate, and was visited by a constant stream of people, who came to show their veneration, or to ask for favours. A heavenly light radiated from the features of the deceased Mother, and from hour to hour, the nuns were kept

---

[139] When all Europe was Catholic it was the custom among the laity to assist regularly at the daily office of the Church. Those who could not read or recite the Psalms in Latin used to say a Psalter of 150 Paternosters.

Cure of Sr. Jeanne du St. Espirit

busy laying rosaries and medals on her sacred remains. Contrary to custom, but in concession to the clamours of the people thronging the church, the grate of the choir was opened from early morning till late at night. The next morning Saturday, March 7th, everything was prepared for the funeral. The great doors of the church were opened earlier than usual, and an immense concord of people poured in. At ten o'clock the Archdukes arrived, Duke Albert being carried in a chair, for though ill in bed with gout, he had insisted on getting up in order to be present. The Infanta with her ladies-in-waiting went to the nuns' choir, thus leaving more room for the court officials and the general public. Father Hilary of St. Augustine celebrated the solemn Requiem Mass, and the court musicians rendered the choral parts and chanted the "Libera." After the sermon, preached by Father Thomas of Jesus, in which he publicly announced the miraculous cure of Sister Jeanne du St. Esprit, who was present among the community, the bier was placed close to the grate, and the Archdukes approached to pay their last tribute of respect to Anne of Jesus. The Infanta kissed her feet, an example followed by all the ladies of her train. Then thirty-six Carmelite Friars, headed by Father Hilary of St. Augustine, entered the enclosure to carry the body to its last resting place beneath the Chapter room.

It happened that the double coffin ordered for the burial had not been delivered, so after the last Rites had been solemnly performed, the body remained in the Chapter Room all through the Sunday. The limbs retained their suppleness, and the face of the venerable Mother showed its natural colouring, while her whole body exhaled a heavenly perfume. On March 8th, the coffin arrived and the body was then lowered into the vault, a plain slab of stone being placed over it. Opposite this was hung a picture painted by order of the Infanta Isabella, representing the cure of Sister Jeanne du St. Esprit. The royal lady begged for the flowers which had covered the bier, to send to her cousin Queen Margaret.[140]

Mother Beatrix of the Conception gave her as well the crucifix which the venerable Mother had held when dying, and also her scapular. Isabella sent the crucifix to her half-brother, the King of Spain,[141] the scapular to her niece the Queen of France.

Henceforth whenever the Infanta visited the Royal Convent, she always went first to the Chapter-Room, and remained a long time kneeling in prayer beside the tomb of her former friend and counsellor, to whom she still recommended all her affairs.[142]

The miraculous answers to prayer obtained through the intercession of Anne of Jesus would fill a volume, but only a few can be narrated here. The venerable Mother's faithful and devoted Infirmarian was one of the first to experience her help. A sister who found great difficulty in speaking openly to Mother Beatrix, who had been elected Prioress, betook herself to the tomb of her venerated Mother, and there poured out her heart in prayer. Almost at once St. Teresa, accompanied by Anne of Jesus, appeared to her; and the latter, placing her hand on her head, said: "My child, henceforth you will have great liberty of spirit, so that you will easily be able to make yourself known, and your soul

---

[140] The same who had begged for a portrait of Anne of Jesus.

[141] The king was already dead but the news had not then reached Brussels.

[142] So faithful was the Royal House of Spain in its admiration for Mother Anne of Jesus, that, just two centuries later, her name was given to the youngest daughter of King John VI of Portugal who had married a Bourbon princess, sister of King Ferdinand VII of Spain. The Infanta Aña de Jesus married the Marquis de Louie, and during her residence in France became well known in Parisian Society.

will enjoy great peace." From that moment, all difficulty left her, as well as a great fear of death, from which she had formerly suffered. Later on the same religious again saw her venerable Mother clothed in glory, and heard her say, "See, my child, how our labours are rewarded in Heaven."

It will be remembered how the Servant of God helped Sister Madeleine Florence of the Cross. When her beloved Mother was laid in the tomb, this Sister became a prey to overwhelming grief, which grew more poignant from day to day. About ten o'clock on the ninth day after her death, Sister Madeleine Florence went to the holy Prioress's empty cell, and there abandoned herself to her sorrow. However, as she was a thoroughly good nun, her conscience soon began to reproach her, and she heard a voice saying: "Take care! these thoughts are contrary to the will and good pleasure of God." Perhaps she did not at once control her thoughts, for the next instant, she heard her name called, with the warning, "Understand that all this is against God." Terrified she threw herself on her knees, ejaculating "Jesus! Mary! My God, have mercy on me!" Then she heard a noise as of some one walking towards her, though she knew the cell was empty except for herself. Lifting her head, for she had bent down almost to the ground in her fear, she saw Anne of Jesus approach. The venerable Mother very gently took Sister Madeleine's head in her own two hands,[143] and said "Have confidence, my child." These words were an allusion to something that had passed between Mother and daughter on a former occasion, when Sister Madeleine had spoken of her many temptations. Anne of Jesus had replied: "God wishes to test you in many ways, dear child," and as Sister Madeleine was still unconsoled, she had added, "Do you not

---

[143] This was a characteristic gesture with Anne of Jesus. It was in this way that she greeted St. Teresa of the Child Jesus.

"THE HUMBLE SHALL BE EXALTED"

trust me, my child?" "Yes, Mother, I trust you entirely." "Very well then, believe that I shall not fail to assist you in all this." The promise faithfully kept during the holy Mother's life, was continued after her death, and her devoted daughter often felt her presence sensibly. On the first anniversary of the holy death of Anne of Jesus, Father Master Francis de Vivero, Preacher to the Archdukes, publicly mentioned the help received by this Religious in his sermon at the Royal Convent.

> "Every time Anne of Jesus appears she is resplendent with light, and gives this daughter of hers to understand how great is the glory she is enjoying in recompense for the labours and trouble she endured on earth, and how pleasing to God it is when people trust in her intercession. She assured her that because she had trusted her she would help her in her temptations. This promise she has abundantly fulfilled, for the Religious affirms that whenever Satan attacks her she feels Anne of Jesus near. The venerable Mother gives her a little tap on the side, close to her heart, and encourages her so much, that she becomes eager to endure more for the love of God."

Another Sister relates the following experience:

> "The Sunday after her happy death I was in great grief; for before she was buried I felt solace in my sadness by kneeling near her body. Now it seemed as if I had no more consolation left on earth. I went to Mass and received Holy Communion, with the words '*Deus meus et omnia*,' (My God and my All) upon my lips. As I received Our Lord I understood, I do not know how, for it was from no spoken word and yet with very great truth, that our Mother Anne of Jesus was in God Himself, as indeed are all the Blessed. But I saw no one in Him except our Mother Anne of Jesus. I had a particular sensible realisation of the presence of God, and of her presence in Him, together with great consolation of soul. She told me in the same instant that I might be quite happy about all

I had done up to that time, as my state of consolation would prove."

Yet another of her daughters was shown the fruit of the venerable Mother's intense devotion to the Passion.

"In the same year that our venerable Mother died," she writes, "I saw a lofty throne, on which was the Blessed Trinity in great glory. On their knees before the Godhead were our holy Mother Teresa of Jesus with our Mother Anne of Jesus. They were so close that the Blessed Trinity could touch them. Our holy Mother presented the soul of venerable Mother Anne of Jesus to Our Lord Jesus Christ, Who, in His turn, offered it to His Eternal Father, saying, 'Behold the fruit of my Passion!' The Blessed Trinity inclined forward and embraced our Mother Anne, showing special pleasure in the beauty of her soul."

When praying beside the tomb of the Servant of God, another Sister saw the stone slab covering her body resplendent with light, which continued to issue from it for a considerable space of time. Nor was it only to the nuns of her own community that Anne of Jesus was allowed to communicate these favours. God glorified His humble servant in all the countries where her name was known. Mother Beatrix wrote to tell the Prior of the Discalced Carmelites at Paris of the venerable Mother's death, and received the following letter in reply.

"To the Reverend Mother Beatrix of the Conception Prioress of the Royal Convent of Discalced Carmelites at Brussels.

"When I received your Reverence's letter with an account of the happy death of Mother Anne of Jesus, I already knew about it, as also about the miracle God worked through her, and I have already sent the notice about it to the Convents of the Province.[144]

"I praise God and offer Him immense thanksgiving for the graces He bestowed upon this chosen soul, and particularly for those which helped her to so holy a death. For the consolation of your Reverence, but primarily for the glory of God and for the honour of the deceased, I will say that this holy soul has appeared since her death to a person[145] to whom His Divine Majesty has given graces more than ordinary.

"This person was saying Mass, for he is a priest, when she appeared to Him in great glory, and (if I remember aright), she rejoiced in the sufferings she had undergone, which were the cause of her happiness. She promised to assist several people in a difficult affair in which they are engaged. Praised be Our Lord for all.

"Father Bernard of St. Joseph."

As soon as news of the death of Anne of Jesus reached the Convent of the Incarnation, Paris, Mother Mary of the Trinity had the Office of the Dead solemnly chanted.

During it she saw, in the midst of a white-robed choir of virgins, the venerable Mother, whom Our Lord was caressing with special favour, conversing with her and showing her many things, which the French Prioress could not interpret. Later on during the same day, when Mother Mary of the Trinity was at prayer, Our Lord told her that what she had seen denoted the great glory Anne of Jesus had received in reward of her sufferings, particularly for having borne patiently her complete inability to help herself, a great trial to one of so active a temperament. This together with her great interior desolation had won for her a special

---

[144] The "Convents" were really Priories of Friars. The Carmelite nuns in France were not governed by the Order.

[145] This person was himself as appears from other evidence.

glory.

In Spain, as in France, Anne of Jesus visibly consoled and helped her Sisters, especially those of Veas and Consuegra. At Veas, a Sister to whom the venerable Mother had given the habit was one day in prayer, when she heard her name called. Recognising her former Prioress's voice, the Sister looked up, saw Anne of Jesus radiant in glory and exclaimed, 'What is this, dear Mother?" "God through the merits of His Divine Son," was the answer, "has given me the glory you behold," and immediately the vision disappeared.

Another sister of the same convent was thinking affectionately of her former Mother, and asked God to allow her, too, to see something of her glory. Her Heavenly Father granted her prayer, and showed Our Lord seated on a throne of great splendor, and Anne of Jesus on her knees before Him. The holy Mother was clothed in a mantle of glittering gold so long and ample that it enveloped what seemed to be two kingdoms of distinct language and government. The religious was given to understand that these kingdoms were France and the Netherlands, where the Servant of God had established the Carmelite Reform.

On one occasion she appeared at Consuegra at two o'clock in the morning to a nun who was praying in her cell. A host of demons were in the passage into which the nuns' cells opened, and the Sister saw the devils trying to force open the doors, while angels struggled with them to prevent it, and finally chased the devils away. Immediately a great light shone in the corridor, and Our Lady, borne on a splendid throne and accompanied by a multitude of angels, appeared there. With her was St. Teresa, while Anne of Jesus and Mother Isabel of St. Dominic,[146] who had then

---

[146] The Mother who had been named for France but was crippled by a fall.

lately died in the odour of sanctity, walked on either side of the Blessed Virgin. These two opened the door of each cell as they came to it, and Mary blessed its occupant, smiling sweetly upon her at the same time. When all the community had been thus visited, the vision disappeared.

Many cures were also wrought by Anne of Jesus after her death. At Cologne a Franciscan nun was cured of a malady from which she had been suffering for thirty years, by applying a piece of the venerable Mother's tunic. At Mechlin the Servant of God healed a Carmelite who was attacked by the plague, appearing at the same time to the prioress to tell her that no one else should contract the disease.

At Brussels a Bernardine nun, who had been suffering for three years from inability to retain any food, invoked Anne of Jesus, who appeared to her and promised to help her, telling her at the same time to resign herself to God's will. For the next eight days the Sister suffered from almost continual sickness. On the ninth day she went to the refectory, where she received the same portion as the others—Lenten fare, which was not suited to her state. Anne of Jesus appeared to her there a second time, bidding her take what was put before her. The Sister, strong in faith, obeyed, and from that hour experienced no further inconvenience.

Not was it only religious whom the Servant of God helped: a madman at Bordeaux was soothed in the midst of a terrible outburst of frenzy by the application of a small portion of the habit worn by the Servant of God, while similar relics used elsewhere were instrumental in curing persons suffering from consumption and other diseases.

Miracles continued to be wrought by the intercession of Anne of Jesus for many years after her death. One in particular is of special interest, as it shows the affectionate remembrance in which the holy Mother was held by the

Carmelites of France. When Mother Beatrix of the Conception was returning to Spain in 1630, she stayed for a night or two at the Carmel of St. Denis, then recently founded. The prioress there, Mere Angelique de Jesus, was very ill, and Mother Beatrix, who had with her some portions of the white mantle worn by Anne of Jesus, gave one to her, telling her to recommend herself to the venerable Mother's intercession. No sooner was the relic placed on the sick prioress than she felt herself perfectly cured. She and her community were so grateful for this favour that they made a vow to observe 4th March henceforth as a holy day, having a Mass of the Blessed Trinity said, as Anne of Jesus had had a particular devotion to that sublime Mystery. In addition to this the nuns built a hermitage in the enclosure garden in honour of the Servant of God, made a novena of Communions in thanksgiving for the miracle, and said from July (the time of the cure) till the following 4th March the collect "Of the Saints" after Compline. An inquiry into the miracle was set on foot by Jean Francois de Gondi, Archbishop of Paris, and it was solemnly declared authentic. The deed was signed by Denis le Blanc on behalf of the archbishop, and countersigned by Charles Baudouyn, Notary Apostolic. Not content with what she and her community could do to honour their venerable Mother, the Prioress of St. Denis wrote as follows:

> "To the Reverend Mother Prioress of the Royal Convent of Discalced Carmelites at Brussels.
>
> "Dear Reverend Mother, we beg that your Reverence will visit the tomb of our blessed Mother Anne of Jesus, and there render her thanks for the perfect cure she worked in me, which continues without relapse.
>
> "We have practically none of her relics, and each

"THE HUMBLE SHALL BE EXALTED" 337

sister keeps asking for one.[147] I beseech your Reverence to send us some, together with her portrait, as soon as possible. Our Community have a great devotion to her, and with every reason, since it is owing to her that they are Carmelites. She is our Mother, and we acknowledge her as such. As long as I live I shall honour her as a saint.

"She has cured the Prioress of the Annonciades in this town, who had been suffering from a diseased stomach for four months, and was very near death. No sooner had she made use of a small piece of our blessed Mother's mantle than she was instantly cured. She continues to keep well, and can take milk and fruit, which she could not retain during her illness. We are all overflowing with consolation that God has thus made known and glorified our blessed Mother. I implore Him to continue to do more for her glorification, and that He will preserve your Reverence. Amen.

"From St. Denis, July 24th, 1630."

Long before this date Anne of Jesus had worked many similar cures in Spain and elsewhere. In September of 1621 her cousin, the Bishop of Osma,[148] was a confirmed invalid with some internal malady which kept him bent double, wholly unable to do anything for himself. Having received

---

[147] When the Carmel of St. Deals was dispersed at the time of the French Revolution one of the nuns joined the English Carmelites at Hoogstraet. Thus the latter, now at Chichester, possess all the relics given to Mme Louise de France, Mere Therese de St. Augustin, on her Profession, as well as other precious souvenirs of the saintly princess.

[148] Christopher de Lobera y Torres was consecrated Bishop of Badajos in January 1615. He was translated to the see of Osma 20th October 1618 and held it until September 1622. From 24th May 1623 to 31st August 1625 he was Bishop of Pampeluna. From February 1626 to 2nd December 1630 Archbishop of Cordova. From December 1630 till his death, October 1632, Bishop (or probably Archbishop) of Plasencia. He had already been nominated to the see of Santiago de Compostella but died before the translation could take place.

a relic of his saintly relative from Mother Beatrix of the Conception, he wore it on his person hoping for a speedy relief. But no improvement took place: then, knowing how Anne of Jesus had turned aside all homage paid to her sanctity during life, and afraid lest he might be doing something contrary to her wishes, he addressed her thus: "Dear Cousin, I do not ask for a miracle, but only that you ask Almighty God to take away the pain I am suffering, in the manner which accords best with the good pleasure of His Divine Majesty." The words were hardly out of his mouth when all his pain disappeared. He was able to get up and dress, and afterwards went about as if he had never been ill. The following year he attested his cure on oath before the public Notary of Ucero, 18th April, 1622, as well as that of a parish priest of the same town, whom Anne of Jesus had cured of a violent and persistent toothache, through the bishop's relic which he had lent to him.

Writing eighteen years after the holy death of the Servant of God, Manriquez declares that accounts of fresh miracles attributed to her intercession reached him almost daily. Maria Bermeja, aged sixty-seven, lady-in-waiting to the Infanta Isabella, was instantly cured of a grievous illness through using a relic of Anne of Jesus. It was sent to her by Isabella de la Camara, who had a great devotion to the Servant of God, having often been helped by her during her lifetime. At Rouen, on the other hand, a Carmelite nun was only gradually cured of a disease in the knee. She made a novena to Anne of Jesus, visiting each day a hermitage where some of her relics were kept. The improvement begun on the first day increased steadily, until on the ninth day the cure was complete. The Archbishop of Rouen, after careful inquiry, declared the miracle authentic on 27th December, 1615.

While these wonders were being worked, the nuns of the Royal Convent also experienced the help of their venerable

Mother, and her tomb was rarely without a suppliant.

The Queen of France, and Margaret of Lorraine, Duchess of Orleans, often prayed there, where they both perceived a celestial perfume. Indeed, Mother Anne's veil and anything she had used, or which had touched her body after death, exhaled this heavenly odour. Some portions of her flesh had been severed from the body as relics, and those also remained fresh and fragrant, so much so, that, about six years after the venerable Mother's death, permission was given, on the strength of their preservation, for the tomb to be opened, and the state of her body reported upon. It was found intact. The flesh was still supple, white and fresh, and gave forth a most delicious perfume, though it had been buried without being embalmed, and wrapped only in a winding sheet placed over the religious habit. From one of the arms where incisions had been made to obtain the above-mentioned relics fresh blood flowed. All this was attested in due form, but the ecclesiastical superiors, who presided at the exhumation, decided, much to the distress of the nuns, to place quick-lime over the body when it was re-interred. All objections were met with the irrefragable argument that, if the remains of the venerable Mother were miraculously incorrupt, they would not be affected by the quick-lime, since God is omnipotent.

Eight years later God vouchsafed to glorify His faithful servant by the manifestation of this very miracle. In 1635 the tomb of Anne of Jesus was opened for the second time, in the presence of the ecclesiastical authorities and of four famous doctors, sent by the King of Spain, Philip IV. The body was found in exactly the same state as at the previous exhumation. The quick-lime had made the skin of the hands and face a little brown, but that was all. The relics kept by the sisters were also incorrupt, though they had been exposed to the air all those years.

The four doctors unanimously declared that the

preservation of the body was altogether contrary to, or rather, above nature. This they attested in a document signed and sealed by each of them. Further, they laid their report, six months later, before an assembly of doctors held expressly to receive them at the University of Louvain. Their verdict was accepted as genuine and irrefutable, and countersigned by professors delegated to examine their report.

So many and so great prodigies worked through the intercession of a humble religious could not fail to emphasize the thought that God was indeed witnessing to the heroic virtues of His servant. Seven weeks after her death,[149] 24th April, 1621, her great friend, Father Diego de Guevara, wrote to Mother Beatrix of the Conception:

> "...The sufferings of this holy woman are over, and her end has been glorious, as the circumstances of her death prove, and also the great miracle which God has worked through her.[150] This is but the beginning of greater things... It has been God's will that France and Flanders should both enjoy this treasure and, as Spain possesses the holy Virgin Teresa of Jesus, so Flanders should have the privilege of possessing the precious remains of Mother Anne. Before the very eyes of obstinate heretics, God is working miracles through this *great saint.*
>
> "Now that she is no longer with us, we must get her life printed, distribute pictures of her, and work to obtain her beatification and canonisation.
>
> "Dear Mother, this is God's cause, and it is your Reverence's duty to make use of the favour you enjoy with regard to the Archdukes, to set this deserving cause on foot...."

---

[149] That is by return of post after he had received the news.

[150] The cure of Sr. Jeanne du St. Esprit.

"I beg your Reverence to send me her likeness, and some of her relics, for I recommend myself to her as to a saint."

A year later Father Diego wrote again, an even more pressing appeal, telling Mother Beatrix how to proceed with regard to the documents she was collecting, and insisting on their being well authenticated.

"Hurry is not so important as substantial documents, thoroughly well drawn up and attested. These help the cause most. We must work together in this great task. . .

"Since your Reverence has such influence with her Serene Highness, the Infanta, you must urge her to get the Ordinary to set up a Tribunal of Inquiry.

"When your Reverence next visits the tomb of the Holy Mother be so good as to place this letter upon it, and to recommend me to her. I should like to keep a lamp burning there, fed with the blood from my veins."

Mother Beatrix evidently sent some of the documents referred to by Father Diego to the Infanta, who returned them with the following affectionate note:

"To Mother Beatrix of the Conception, Prioress of the Discalced Carmelites of Brussels. "Having examined these papers, I am entirely satisfied with them, and I return them to you, in order that you may keep them as the greatest treasure of this house,[151] and that all who are there may try to imitate so holy a Mother, and be honoured by so doing. I trust that she will not forget us, nor any of those who formerly knew her and conversed with her, particularly those who, like myself, have so much need of her intercession with Our Lord. May He preserve you, as I ask Him to do.
                                                                "A. Isabella."

---

[151] The Royal Convent.

In 1630 matters were sufficiently advanced for the Infanta to write to Cardinal Barberini at Rome,[152] begging him to obtain permission from His Holiness, Urban VIII, to set up a court of inquiry to make the preliminary juridical process required before the Cause of Beatification is formally introduced. This was accorded, and in 1632 the Archduchess was called as a witness. Her deposition was given in Spanish, and signed with her own hand.

Letters of sympathy and support poured in from all parts, and the highest in the land vied with one another in their eagerness to see the humble Anne of Jesus raised to the altars of the Church. Her cause was recommended to the patronage of the King of Spain, Philip IV, by his brother the Cardinal Infant, while Philip's sister, Maria, Queen of Hungary, wrote to the Prioress of Brussels, saying that she would willingly use her influence to promote the cause of the venerable Mother's Beatification. Louis XIII of France and his Queen, Anne of Austria, also instructed their Ambassador, Count de Noailles, to present letters to Cardinal Barberini begging the Pope to advance the Cause. Cardinal Gymnasio, formerly Nuncio in the Netherlands, wrote from Rome in 1635 to the prioress at Brussels, assuring her that he was happy to use his influence to attain the same great end.

Meanwhile a Discalced Carmelite friar, Father Elias of St. Teresa, had been appointed Postulator of the Cause. Up to the year 1636, seventeen well-authenticated miracles were worked in the diocese of Mechlin alone. The documents resulting from the diocesan inquiry were forwarded to Rome that same year, with the following letter from the Cardinal

---

[152] There were three Cardinals Barberini in Rome at that time, one brother, a Capuchin, and two nephews of Urban VIII. It is not clear which is referred to here as no Christian name is given in the books consulted.

Infant.[153]

"Most Holy Father,

"The venerable Mother Anne of Jesus, the Companion and Assistant of the Holy Mother Teresa of Jesus, in the course of founding Convents of her Order, was called to Flanders by His Serene Highness, Archduke Albert, and Her Serene Highness, Isabella-Clara-Eugenia, my Aunt of glorious memory, and founded there some Convents of her Order, as she had formerly done in France and Spain. She signalised herself by her numerous and excellent virtues, and by the great miracles she worked both during her life, and after her death. Among these not the least remarkable at the present moment, is the integrity of her body, preserved without corruption for a space of fifteen years, as has been declared, after due examination by the Physicians of the King, my brother, and the doctors of the Medical Faculty of the University of Louvain.

"In view of such remarkable signs of the sanctity of the venerable Mother it has seemed advisable for me to write a covering letter in forwarding the documents of the Process. which attest that all formalities have been complied with by the Ordinaries of the different localities, concerning the life, virtues and miracles of the said venerable Mother. In this letter I beg your Holiness, by the affection I bear to the present good of Holy Church, and to the saints already reigning in Heaven, to be good enough to dispatch the Remissorial Letters for her Beatification and Canonisation. This will be held by me as a very great favour, on account of the particular affection I profess for this Order.

"May God preserve Your Holiness for many long and

---

[153] He succeeded the Infanta as Sovereign of the Netherlands in 1633.

happy years, for the good of the whole Christian World.

"From Cambrai, August 29th, 1636.
"Most Holy Father, I kiss the feet of your Beatitude,
Your most humble son,
"Ferdinand, Cardinal Infant."

Letters similar to this, from crowned heads or notabilities throughout Western Europe, continued to reach Rome from time to time until 1771. In that year the Empress Maria Teresa,[154] whom the English supported during the War of Austrian Succession, wrote to the then Prioress of the Carmel of Brussels:

"It will always be a pleasure to me to second your praiseworthy purpose [the Beatification of Anne of Jesus] as far as circumstances permit, and you may always count upon me."

Her son, who succeeded her in 1780, banished many religious from the Austrian Netherlands, among them the Carmelites. On 10th June, 1783, the community of the Royal Convent of Brussels set out for Paris, where the Carmel of St. Denis offered them a refuge, through the saintly Mere Therese de St. Augustin, Mme. Louise de France, aunt to Louis XVI. They took with them the bones of Anne of Jesus, and of Anne of St. Bartholomew, with the official identification, the ceremony of exhumation having been presided over by the Archbishop of Mechlin. A heavenly perfume was distinctly perceived by those who exhumed the relics of Anne of Jesus in order to transfer them to a new

---

[154] Maria Teresa was the daughter of Charles VI of Austria and Empress in her own right. Her husband, Francis of Lorraine, was only recognised as Emperor in 1745. After his death in 1768 his son Joseph II was joint-Sovereign with his mother. It was only after the death of the Empress that Joseph II carried out his disastrous reforms.

casket.

The nuns were treated at once as members of the French community, taking their place in choir, etc., according to the date of their profession.

In 1790, when the upheaval of the French Revolution caused all religious communities in France to be dispersed, the Flemish Carmelites found themselves able to return to Brussels.[155] Their Royal Convent had been destroyed, as Anne of Jesus had predicted, but they hired a temporary lodging, and on 25th June the nuns in several coaches were met three-quarters of a mile from the city by a detachment of volunteers, as well as by the magistrates and representatives of the State. "Cannon were fired," says the Carmelite Chronicle, "and the bells rung and fine music. Thus they were conducted to the Church of St. Gudule, where the Blessed Sacrament of Miracles was exposed. An abbot intoned the *Te Deum*. The Benediction and the *Te Deum* was in fine music. After this they were conducted to their refuge after a banishment of seven years."

The nuns carried with them the relics of Anne of Jesus, and the very day of their return the preliminaries for the Cause of her Beatification were resumed, and a fresh record opened of offerings received towards it. Donations were frequently entered until 21st November, 1796. On that day the victorious French Republic confiscated the revenues of all religious communities living within the sphere of its control.

Nearly fifty years passed before anything further could be done for the glorification of God in His faithful Servant. On 17th September, 1844, the General of the Carmelite

---

[155] Joseph II died in February 1790 while the Netherlands were in revolt against him. His brother Leopold soon occupied Brussels and by promising to cancel the distasteful measures enforced by Joseph succeeded in securing peace.

Congregation of Italy held a meeting to consider the question of renewing the appeal to Rome. Cardinal Sterchx, then Archbishop of Mechlin, presided, and it was unanimously resolved that the Cause should be re-opened. In August, 1852, the relics of Anne of Jesus were again canonically examined, declared authentic, and transferred, on 29th December of the same year, to a fresh casket. On a silver plate attached to the lid is the following inscription:

CORPUS VENERABILIS SERVAE DEI
ANNAE A JESU
SOCIAE S. MATRIS THERESIAE:
SANCTE OBIIT
BRUXELLIS IV MARTII ANNI MDCXXI

"THE BODY OF THE VENERABLE SERVANT OF GOD, ANNE OF JESUS COMPANION OF THE HOLY MOTHER TERESA: WHO DIED IN THE ODOUR OF SANCTITY AT BRUSSELS, 4TH MARCH OF THE YEAR, 1621."[156]

In 1872 the reports concerning the Beatification were declared favourable, and Anne of Jesus was officially declared "Venerable" in 1878. On the 17th of December, 1885, Pope Leo XIII signed the decree sanctioning the formal introduction of the Cause of her Beatification. May it soon be brought to a happy conclusion!

Laus Deo Semper

---

[156] The Casket is in the possession of the present Carmel of Brussels (83 rue de la Source), where it is kept in a cell set apart for that purpose. (1930).

PRAYER IN HONOUR OF VENERABLE ANNE OF JESUS

P. P. Rubens, pinx: E. J. Arenezen, sc.

PRAYER

which may be said during a Novena made to obtain some grace through the intercession of Venerable Mother Anne of Jesus.

O Most Holy and Adorable Trinity, we give Thee thanks for all the graces Thou didst bestow upon Thy Servant, Venerable Mother Anne of Jesus, and we beg of Thee to grant us, through her intercession, the favour we ask in this Novena. Amen.

We grant a Pardon of two hundred days, to be gained once a day, to all who shall recite devoutly the above prayer.

FRANCIS CARDINAL BOURNE,
Archbishop of Westminster.

25th January 1931.[157]

---

[157] This indulgence is subject to the revision of the book of Indulgences issued by Pope Paul VI, whereby Indulgences are understood only as partial or plenary. -Editor.

OTHER TITLES FROM MEDIATRIX PRESS

St. Thérèse and the Faithful
by Benedict Williamson

The Life of St. Philip Neri
by Mrs. Anne Hope

The Life of St. Francis
Rev. Candide Chalippe, OFM

On the Marks of the Church
by St. Robert Bellarmine, S.J.

A Small Catechism for Catholics
by St. Peter Canisius, S.J.

The Spiritual Life of Cardinal Merry del Val
Jerome dal Gal

Sermons of the Cure d'Ars
St. John Marie Vianney

The Autobiography of St. Robert Bellarmine
St. Robert Bellarmine

Visit us at www.mediatrixpress.com

www.ingramcontent.com/pod-product-compliance
Lightning Source LLC
Chambersburg PA
CBHW070604170426
43200CB00012B/2588